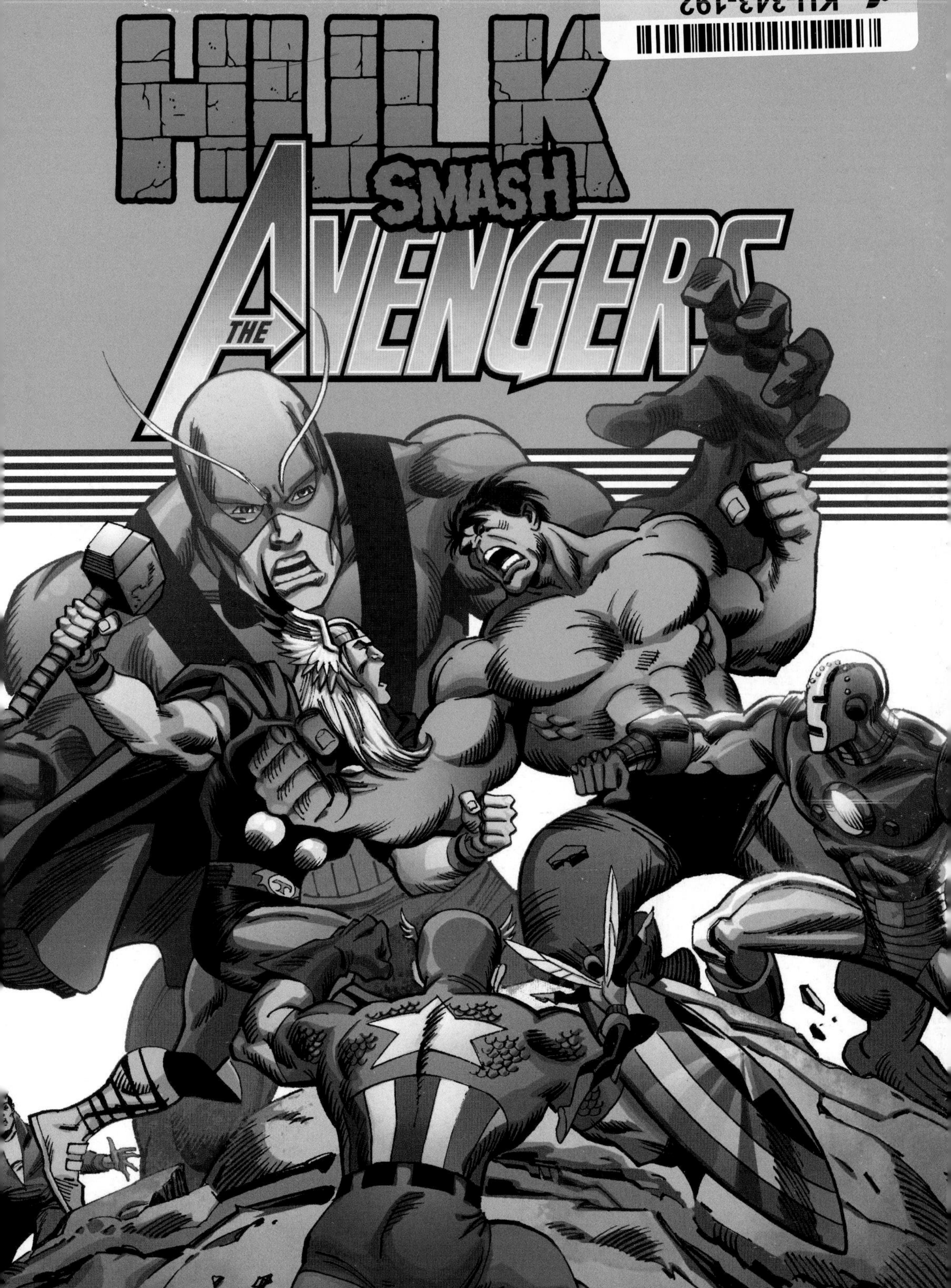
HULK
SMASH
THE
AVENGERS

ULK SMASH AVENGERS. Contains material originally published in magazine form as HULK SMASH AVENGERS #1-5. First printing 2012. ISBN# 978-0-7851-6305-3. Published by MARVEL WORLDWIDE, INC., subsidiary of MARVEL ENTERTAINMENT, LLC. OFFICE OF PUBLICATION: 135 West 50th Street, New York, NY 10020. $14.99 per copy in the U.S. nd $16.99 in Canada (GST #R127032852); Canadian Agreement #40668537. **Printed in the U.S.A.** ALAN FINE, EVP - Office of the President, Marvel Worldwide, Inc. and EVP & CMO Marvel Characters B.V.; DAN BUCKLEY, Publisher & President - Print, nimation & Digital Divisions; JOE QUESADA, Chief Creative Officer; TOM BREVOORT, SVP of Publishing; DAVID BOGART, SVP of Operations & Procurement, Publishing; RUWAN JAYATILLEKE, SVP & Associate ublisher, Publishing; C.B. CEBULSKI, SVP of Cre … CIULLO, SVP of Brand Planning & Communications; JIM O'KEEFE, P of Operations & Logistics; DAN CARR, Exe … ORALES, Publishing Operations Manager; STAN LEE, Chairman meritus. For information regarding advertising … t ndisla@marvel.com. For Marvel subscription inquiries, please all 800-217-9158. **Manufactured between 7** …

0987654321

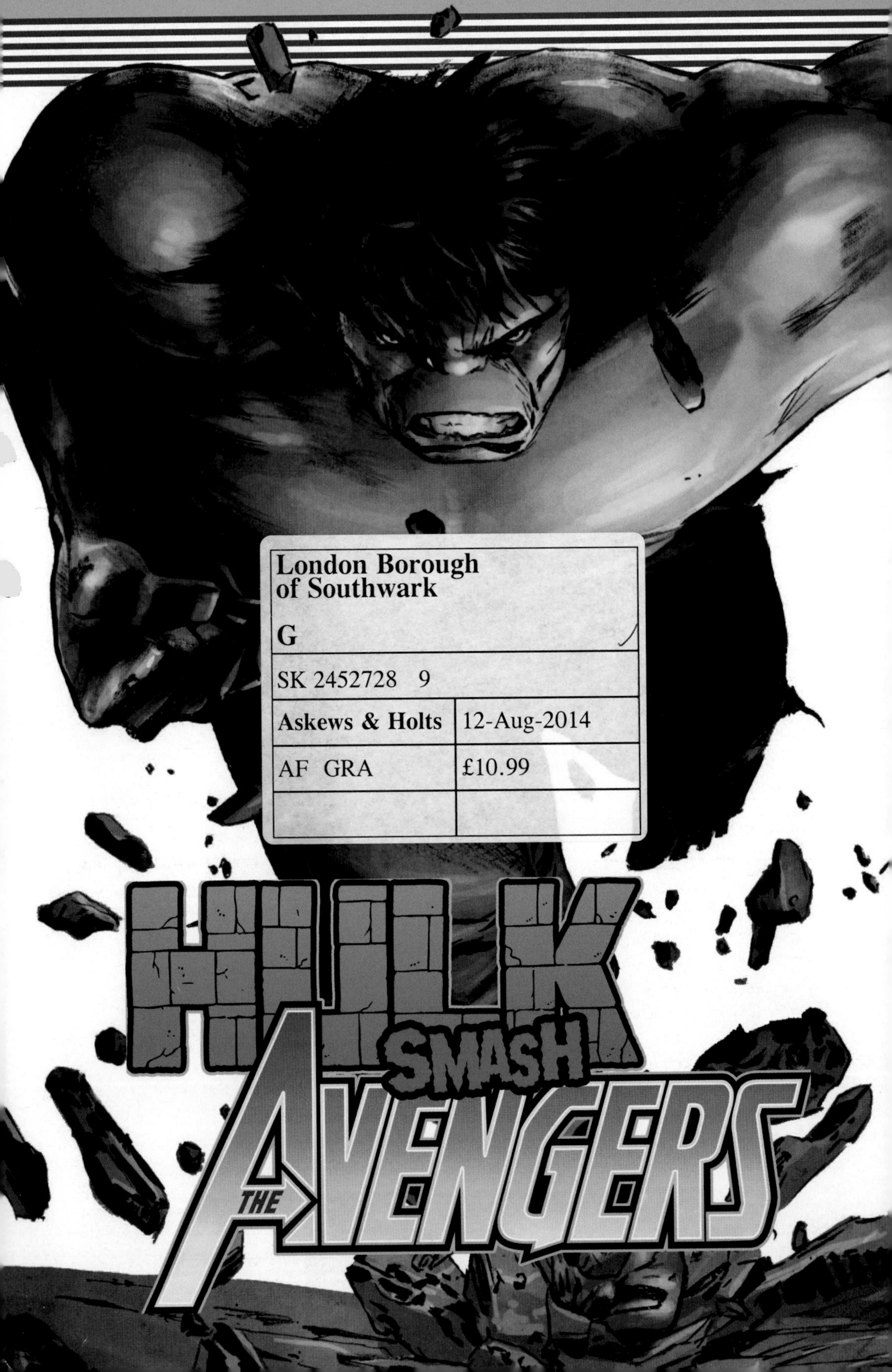
HULK
SMASH
THE AVENGERS

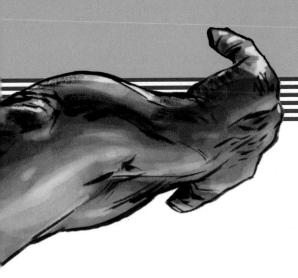

"BY BANNER BETRAYED!"
WRITER TOM DeFALCO
PENCILER RON FRENZ
FINISHED ART SAL BUSCEMA
COLORIST NICK FILARDI

"THE FILTH AND THE FURY"
WRITER JOE CASEY
ARTIST MAX FIUMARA
COLORIST JEAN-FRANCOIS BEAULIEU

"ONCE AN AVENGER..."
WRITER ROGER STERN
PENCILER KARL MOLINE
INKER JAY LEISTEN
COLORIST JEAN-FRANCOIS BEAULIEU

"WHAT SMASHES IN VEGAS"
WRITER JIM McCANN
PENCILER AGUSTIN PADILLA
INKER JAIME MENDOZA
COLORIST JAVIER TARTAGLIA

"THE CONVERSATION"
WRITER FRED VAN LENTE
ARTIST MICHAEL AVON OEMING
COLORIST FELIX SERRANO

LETTERER CHRIS ELIOPOULOS
COVER ARTISTS LEE WEEKS & ANDY TROY
ASSISTANT EDITOR JAKE THOMAS
EDITOR BILL ROSEMANN
SPECIAL THANKS TO TOM BRENNAN
& TOM BREVOORT

COLLECTION EDITOR & DESIGN CORY LEVINE
ASSISTANT EDITORS ALEX STARBUCK & NELSON RIBEIRO
EDITORS, SPECIAL PROJECTS JENNIFER GRÜNWALD & MARK D. BEAZLEY
SENIOR EDITOR, SPECIAL PROJECTS JEFF YOUNGQUIST
SENIOR VICE PRESIDENT OF SALES DAVID GABRIEL
SVP OF BRAND PLANNING & COMMUNICATIONS MICHAEL PASCIULLO

EDITOR IN CHIEF AXEL ALONSO
CHIEF CREATIVE OFFICER JOE QUESADA
PUBLISHER DAN BUCKLEY
EXECUTIVE PRODUCER ALAN FINE

#1

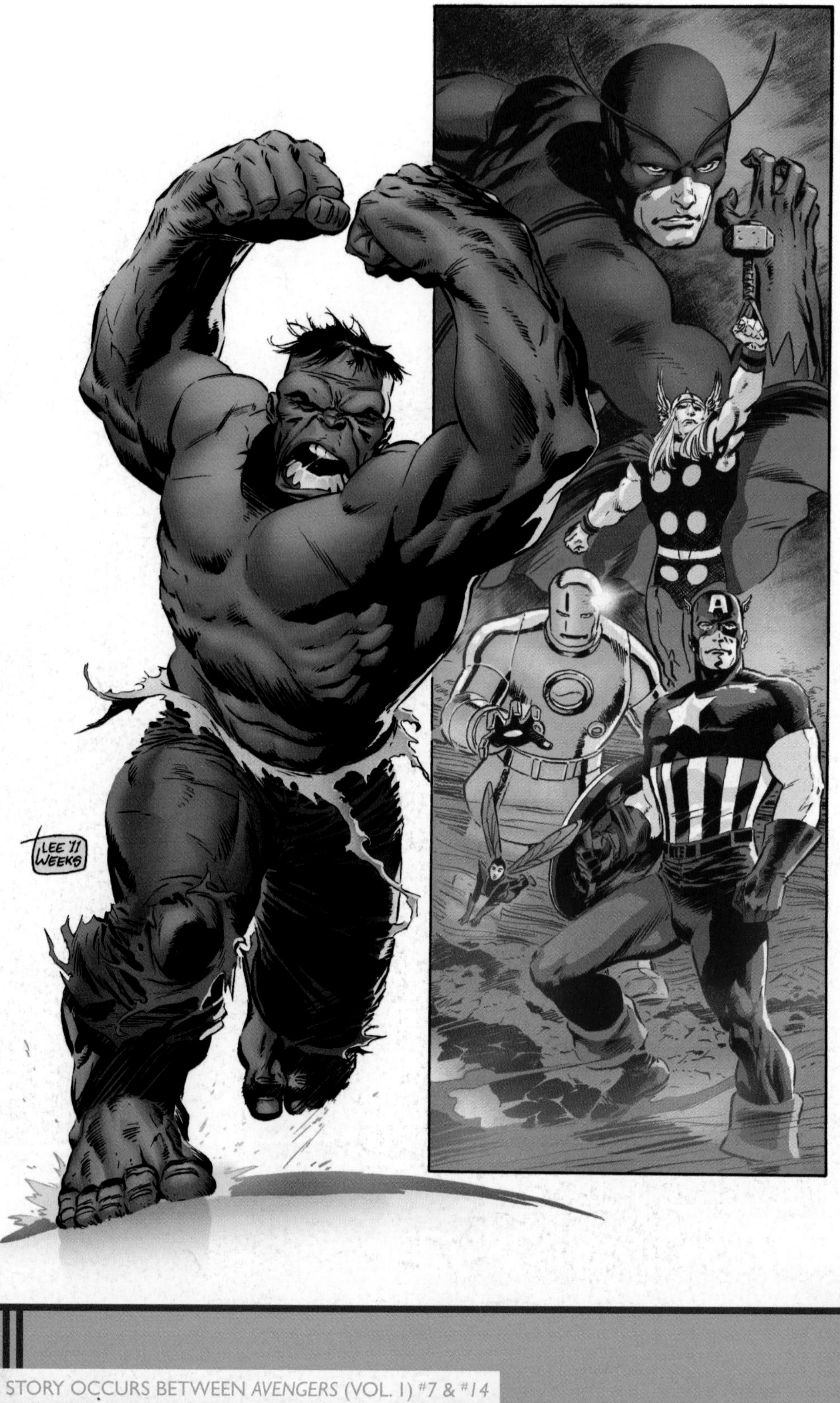
LEE '11
WEEKS

THIS STORY OCCURS BETWEEN *AVENGERS* (VOL. 1) #7 & #14

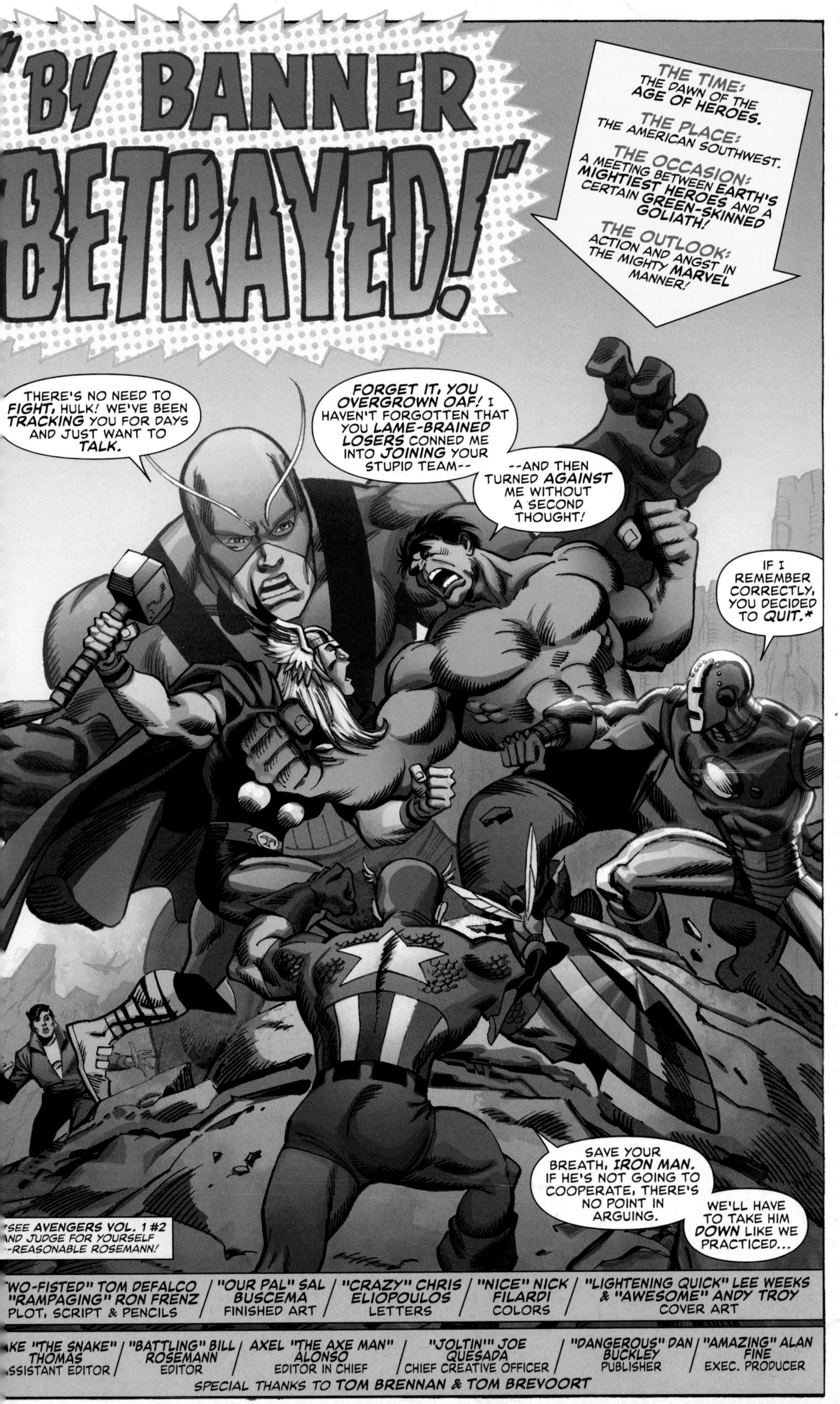
"BY BANNER BETRAYED!"
THE TIME: THE DAWN OF THE AGE OF HEROES. THE PLACE: THE AMERICAN SOUTHWEST. THE OCCASION: A MEETING BETWEEN EARTH'S MIGHTIEST HEROES AND A CERTAIN GREEN-SKINNED GOLIATH! THE OUTLOOK: ACTION AND ANGST IN THE MIGHTY MARVEL MANNER!
THERE'S NO NEED TO FIGHT, HULK! WE'VE BEEN TRACKING YOU FOR DAYS AND JUST WANT TO TALK.
FORGET IT, YOU OVERGROWN OAF! I HAVEN'T FORGOTTEN THAT YOU LAME-BRAINED LOSERS CONNED ME INTO JOINING YOUR STUPID TEAM--
--AND THEN TURNED AGAINST ME WITHOUT A SECOND THOUGHT!
IF I REMEMBER CORRECTLY, YOU DECIDED TO QUIT.*
SAVE YOUR BREATH, IRON MAN. IF HE'S NOT GOING TO COOPERATE, THERE'S NO POINT IN ARGUING.
WE'LL HAVE TO TAKE HIM DOWN LIKE WE PRACTICED...
*SEE AVENGERS VOL. 1 #2 AND JUDGE FOR YOURSELF --REASONABLE ROSEMANN!
"TWO-FISTED" TOM DEFALCO "RAMPAGING" RON FRENZ PLOT, SCRIPT & PENCILS
"OUR PAL" SAL BUSCEMA FINISHED ART
"CRAZY" CHRIS ELIOPOULOS LETTERS
"NICE" NICK FILARDI COLORS
"LIGHTENING QUICK" LEE WEEKS & "AWESOME" ANDY TROY COVER ART
JAKE "THE SNAKE" THOMAS ASSISTANT EDITOR
"BATTLING" BILL ROSEMANN EDITOR
AXEL "THE AXE MAN" ALONSO EDITOR IN CHIEF
"JOLTIN'" JOE QUESADA CHIEF CREATIVE OFFICER
"DANGEROUS" DAN BUCKLEY PUBLISHER
"AMAZING" ALAN FINE EXEC. PRODUCER
SPECIAL THANKS TO TOM BRENNAN & TOM BREVOORT

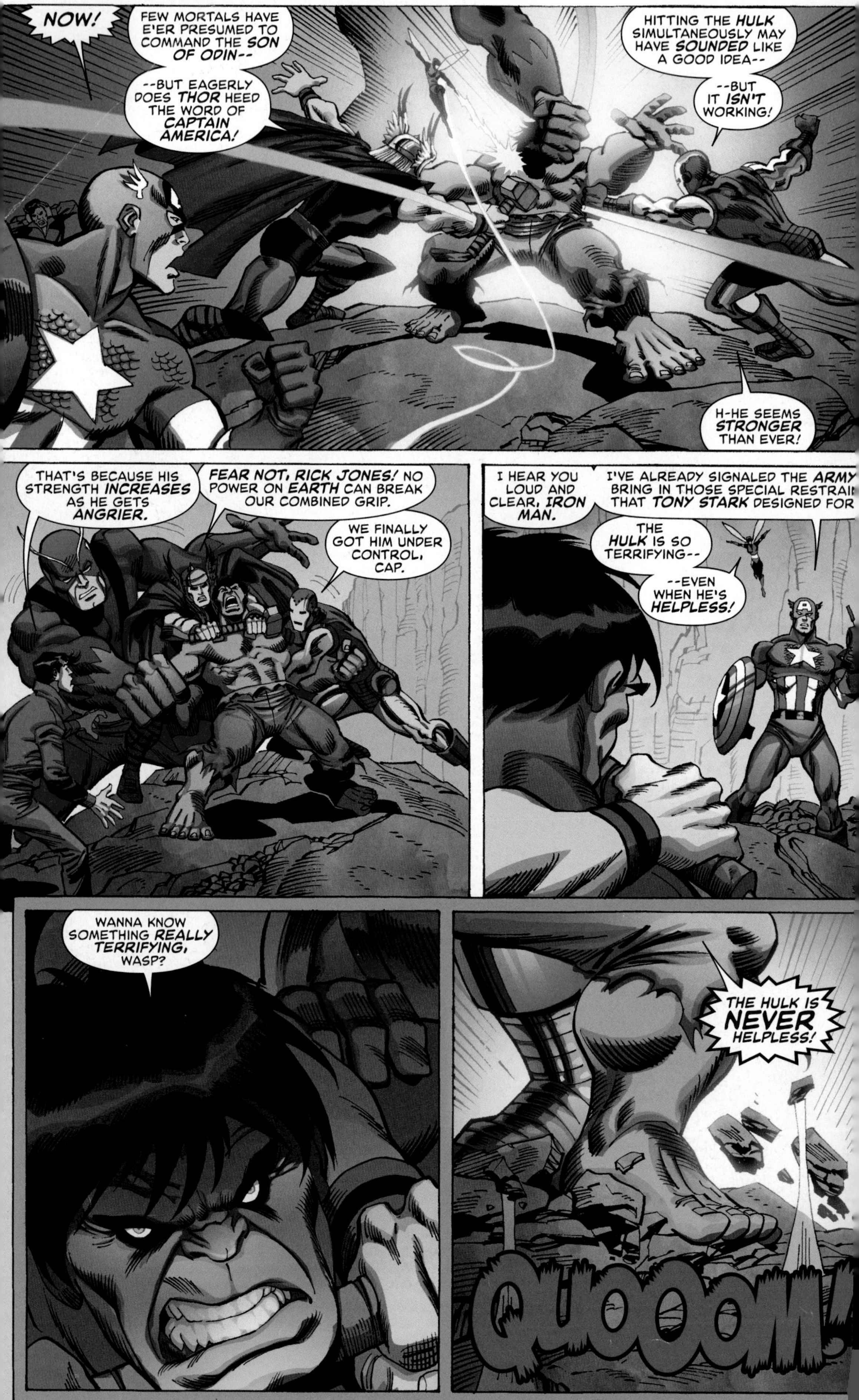
NOW!
FEW MORTALS HAVE E'ER PRESUMED TO COMMAND THE SON OF ODIN--
--BUT EAGERLY DOES THOR HEED THE WORD OF CAPTAIN AMERICA!
HITTING THE HULK SIMULTANEOUSLY MAY HAVE SOUNDED LIKE A GOOD IDEA--
--BUT IT ISN'T WORKING!
H-HE SEEMS STRONGER THAN EVER!
THAT'S BECAUSE HIS STRENGTH INCREASES AS HE GETS ANGRIER.
FEAR NOT, RICK JONES! NO POWER ON EARTH CAN BREAK OUR COMBINED GRIP.
WE FINALLY GOT HIM UNDER CONTROL, CAP.
I HEAR YOU LOUD AND CLEAR, IRON MAN.
I'VE ALREADY SIGNALED THE ARMY BRING IN THOSE SPECIAL RESTRAI THAT TONY STARK DESIGNED FOR
THE HULK IS SO TERRIFYING--
--EVEN WHEN HE'S HELPLESS!
WANNA KNOW SOMETHING REALLY TERRIFYING, WASP?
THE HULK IS NEVER HELPLESS!
QUOOOM!

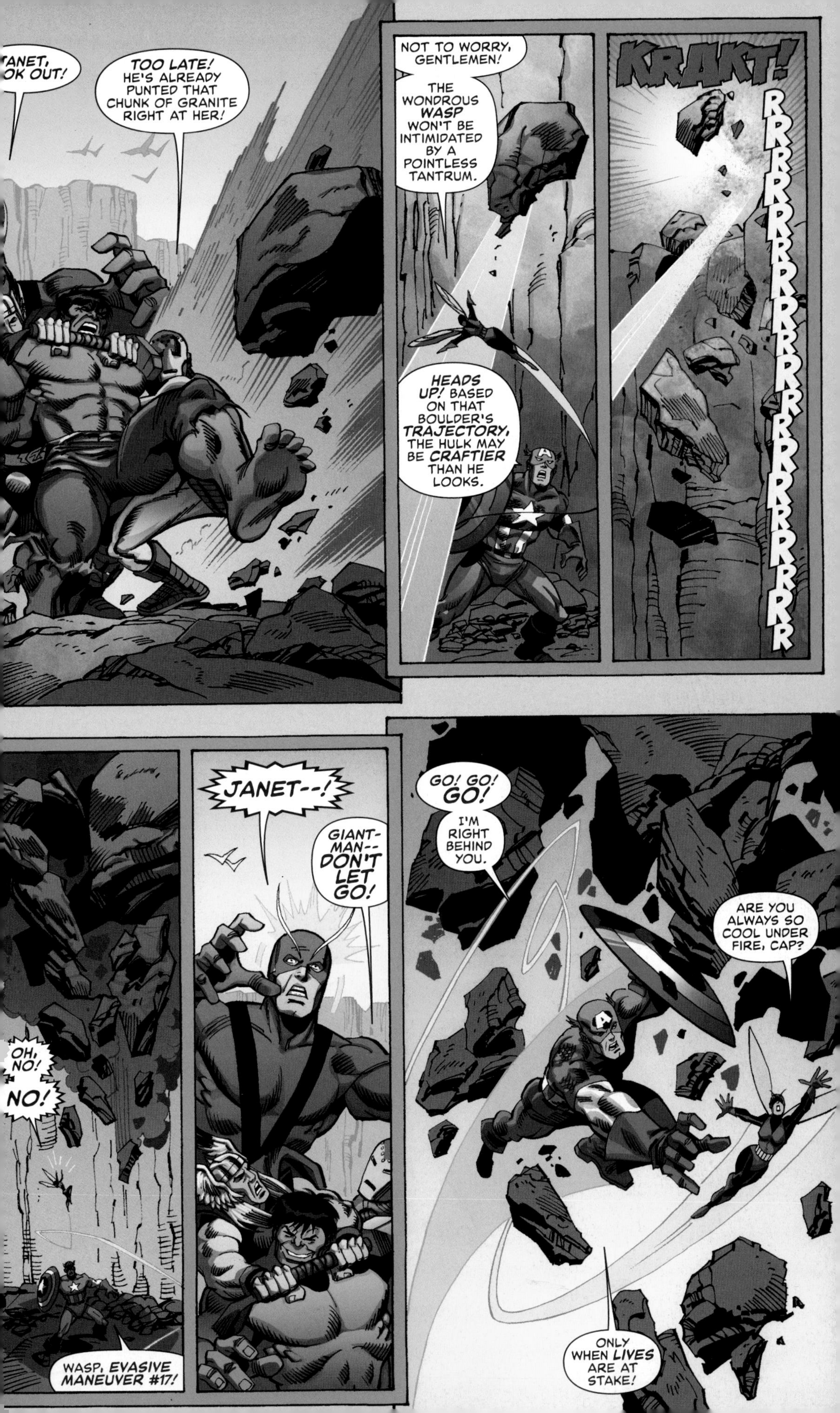

ANET, OK OUT!
TOO LATE! HE'S ALREADY PUNTED THAT CHUNK OF GRANITE RIGHT AT HER!
NOT TO WORRY, GENTLEMEN!
THE WONDROUS WASP WON'T BE INTIMIDATED BY A POINTLESS TANTRUM.
HEADS UP! BASED ON THAT BOULDER'S TRAJECTORY, THE HULK MAY BE CRAFTIER THAN HE LOOKS.
KRAKT!
RRRRRRRRRRRRRRRRRR
OH, NO! NO!
WASP, EVASIVE MANEUVER #17!
JANET--!
GIANT-MAN--DON'T LET GO!
GO! GO! GO!
I'M RIGHT BEHIND YOU.
ARE YOU ALWAYS SO COOL UNDER FIRE, CAP?
ONLY WHEN LIVES ARE AT STAKE!

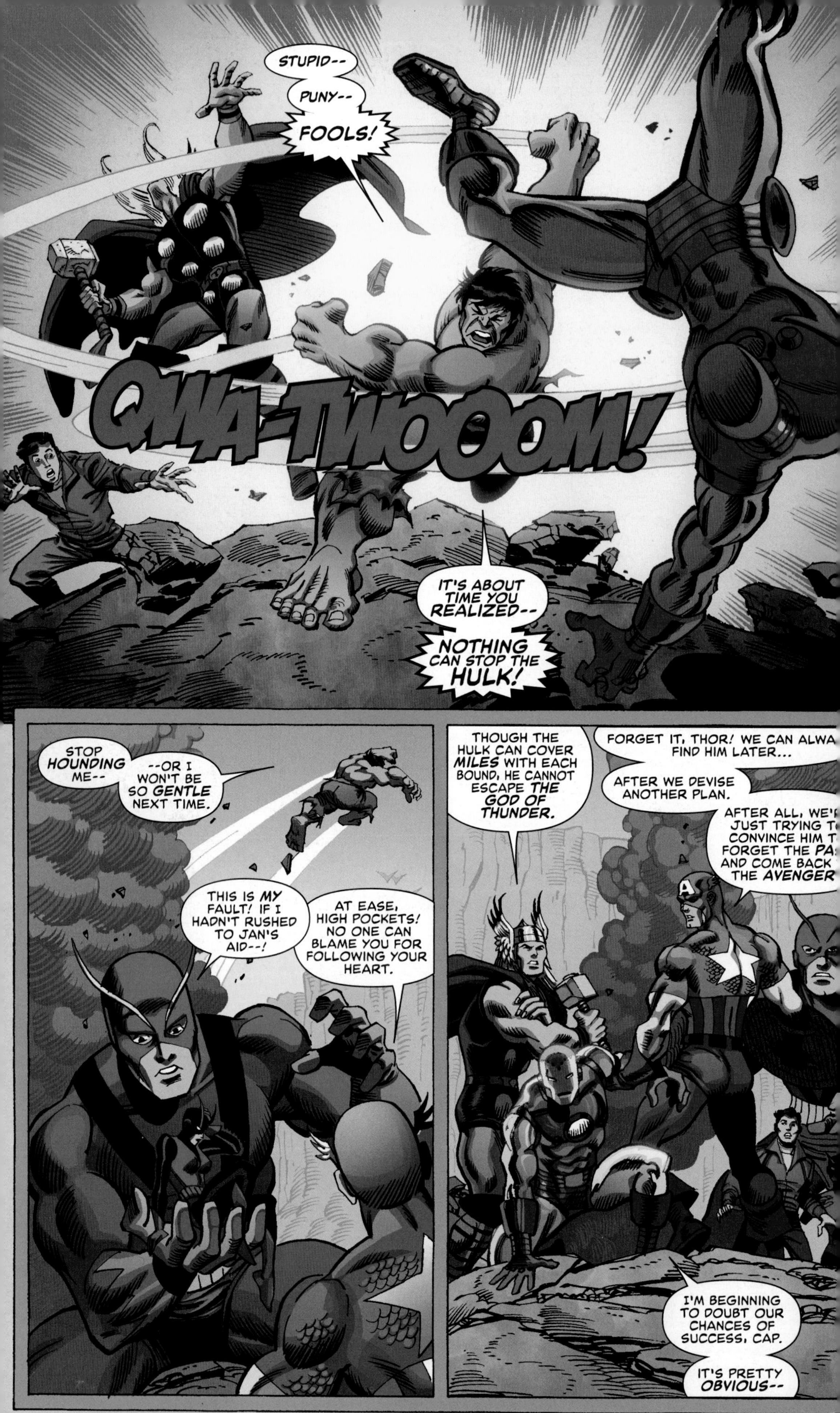

STUPID--
PUNY--
FOOLS!
QWA-TWOOOM!
IT'S ABOUT TIME YOU REALIZED--
NOTHING CAN STOP THE HULK!
STOP HOUNDING ME--
--OR I WON'T BE SO GENTLE NEXT TIME.
THIS IS MY FAULT! IF I HADN'T RUSHED TO JAN'S AID--!
AT EASE, HIGH POCKETS! NO ONE CAN BLAME YOU FOR FOLLOWING YOUR HEART.
THOUGH THE HULK CAN COVER MILES WITH EACH BOUND, HE CANNOT ESCAPE THE GOD OF THUNDER.
FORGET IT, THOR! WE CAN ALWA FIND HIM LATER...
AFTER WE DEVISE ANOTHER PLAN.
AFTER ALL, WE' JUST TRYING T CONVINCE HIM T FORGET THE PA AND COME BACK THE AVENGER
I'M BEGINNING TO DOUBT OUR CHANCES OF SUCCESS, CAP.
IT'S PRETTY OBVIOUS--

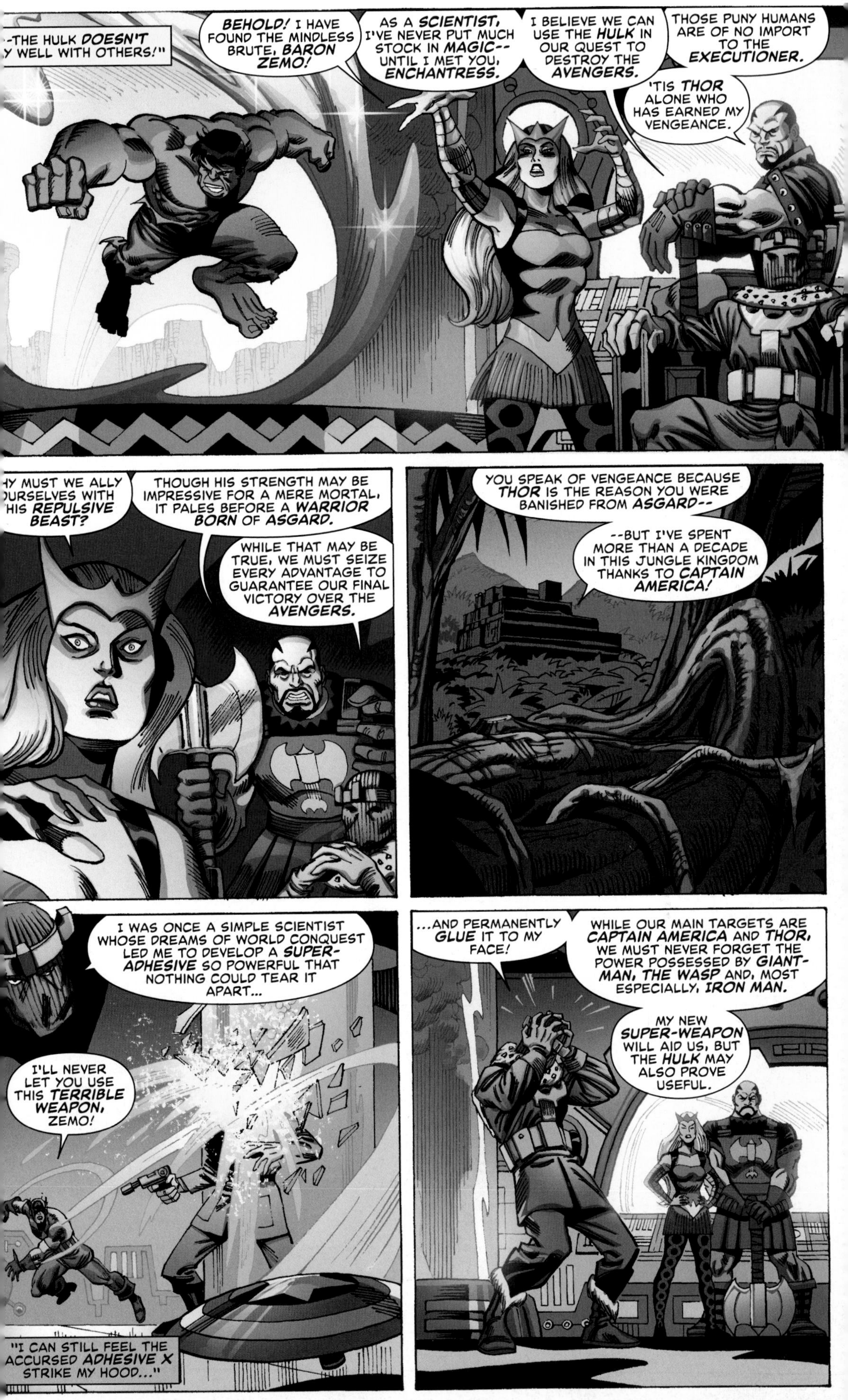

-THE HULK *DOESN'T*
Y WELL WITH OTHERS!"
BEHOLD! I HAVE FOUND THE MINDLESS BRUTE, *BARON ZEMO!*
AS A *SCIENTIST,* I'VE NEVER PUT MUCH STOCK IN *MAGIC--* UNTIL I MET YOU, *ENCHANTRESS.*
I BELIEVE WE CAN USE THE *HULK* IN OUR QUEST TO DESTROY THE *AVENGERS.*
THOSE PUNY HUMANS ARE OF NO IMPORT TO THE *EXECUTIONER.*
'TIS *THOR* ALONE WHO HAS EARNED MY VENGEANCE.
HY MUST WE ALLY OURSELVES WITH THIS *REPULSIVE BEAST?*
THOUGH HIS STRENGTH MAY BE IMPRESSIVE FOR A MERE MORTAL, IT PALES BEFORE A *WARRIOR BORN* OF *ASGARD.*
WHILE THAT MAY BE TRUE, WE MUST SEIZE EVERY ADVANTAGE TO GUARANTEE OUR FINAL VICTORY OVER THE *AVENGERS.*
YOU SPEAK OF VENGEANCE BECAUSE *THOR* IS THE REASON YOU WERE BANISHED FROM *ASGARD--*
--BUT I'VE SPENT MORE THAN A DECADE IN THIS JUNGLE KINGDOM THANKS TO *CAPTAIN AMERICA!*
I WAS ONCE A SIMPLE SCIENTIST WHOSE DREAMS OF WORLD CONQUEST LED ME TO DEVELOP A *SUPER-ADHESIVE* SO POWERFUL THAT NOTHING COULD TEAR IT APART...
I'LL NEVER LET YOU USE THIS *TERRIBLE WEAPON,* ZEMO!
"I CAN STILL FEEL THE ACCURSED *ADHESIVE X* STRIKE MY HOOD..."
...AND PERMANENTLY *GLUE* IT TO MY FACE!
WHILE OUR MAIN TARGETS ARE *CAPTAIN AMERICA* AND *THOR,* WE MUST NEVER FORGET THE POWER POSSESSED BY *GIANT-MAN, THE WASP* AND, MOST ESPECIALLY, *IRON MAN.*
MY NEW *SUPER-WEAPON* WILL AID US, BUT THE *HULK* MAY ALSO PROVE USEFUL.

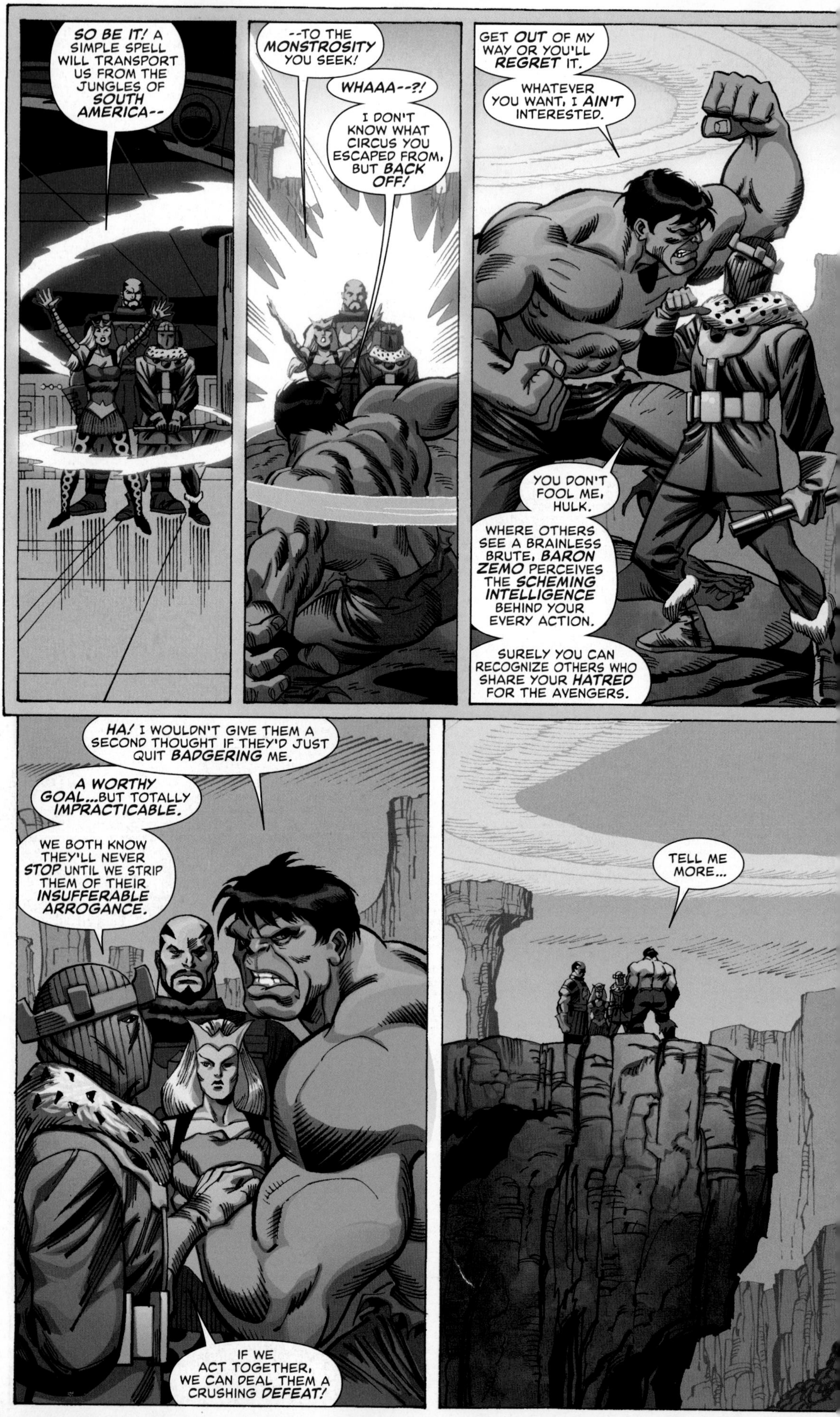
SO BE IT! A SIMPLE SPELL WILL TRANSPORT US FROM THE JUNGLES OF SOUTH AMERICA--
--TO THE MONSTROSITY YOU SEEK!
WHAAA--?!
I DON'T KNOW WHAT CIRCUS YOU ESCAPED FROM, BUT BACK OFF!
GET OUT OF MY WAY OR YOU'LL REGRET IT.
WHATEVER YOU WANT, I AIN'T INTERESTED.
YOU DON'T FOOL ME, HULK.
WHERE OTHERS SEE A BRAINLESS BRUTE, BARON ZEMO PERCEIVES THE SCHEMING INTELLIGENCE BEHIND YOUR EVERY ACTION.
SURELY YOU CAN RECOGNIZE OTHERS WHO SHARE YOUR HATRED FOR THE AVENGERS.
HA! I WOULDN'T GIVE THEM A SECOND THOUGHT IF THEY'D JUST QUIT BADGERING ME.
A WORTHY GOAL...BUT TOTALLY IMPRACTICABLE.
WE BOTH KNOW THEY'LL NEVER STOP UNTIL WE STRIP THEM OF THEIR INSUFFERABLE ARROGANCE.
IF WE ACT TOGETHER, WE CAN DEAL THEM A CRUSHING DEFEAT!
TELL ME MORE...

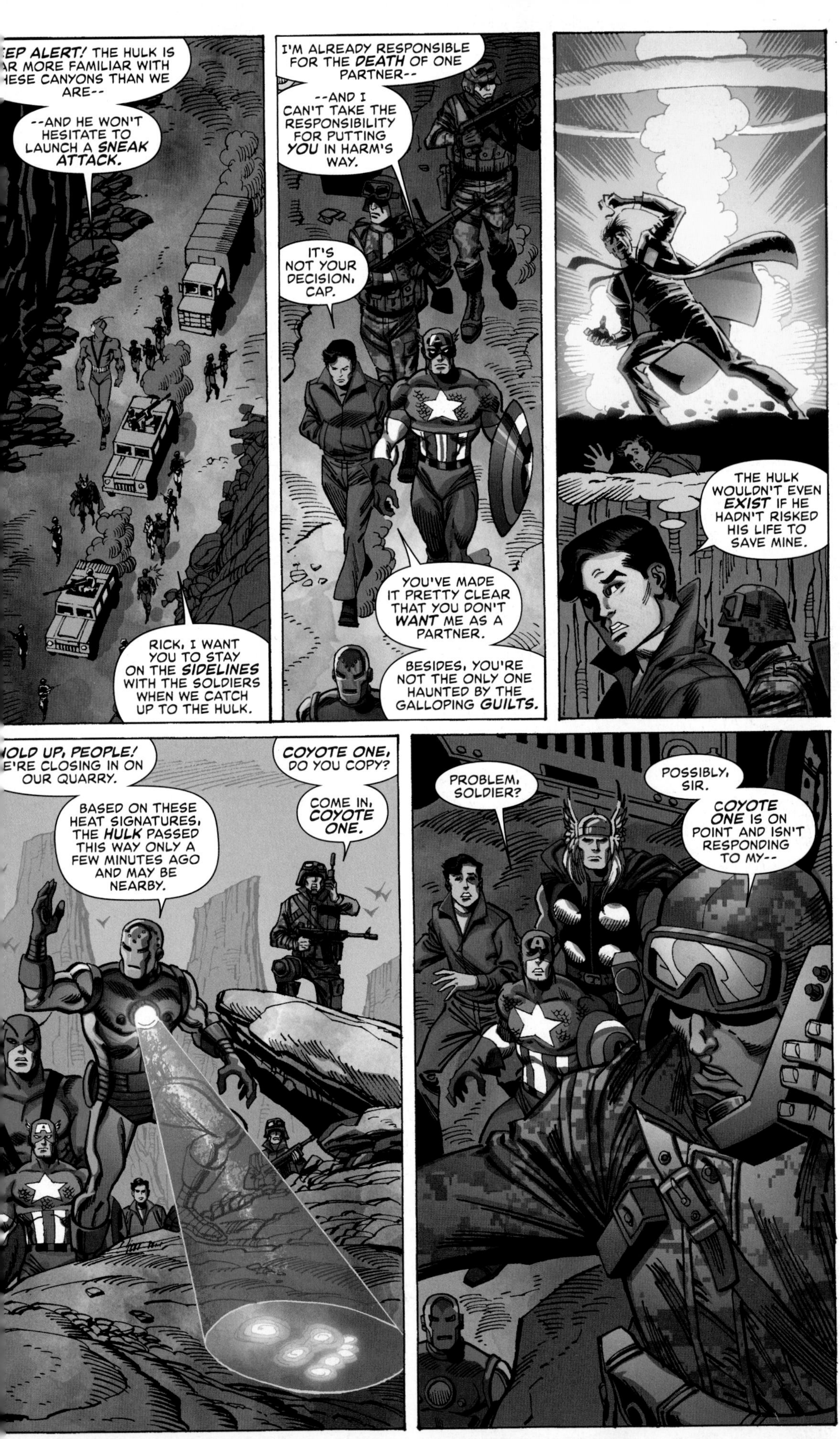

EP ALERT! THE HULK IS AR MORE FAMILIAR WITH HESE CANYONS THAN WE ARE--
--AND HE WON'T HESITATE TO LAUNCH A SNEAK ATTACK.
RICK, I WANT YOU TO STAY ON THE SIDELINES WITH THE SOLDIERS WHEN WE CATCH UP TO THE HULK.
I'M ALREADY RESPONSIBLE FOR THE DEATH OF ONE PARTNER--
--AND I CAN'T TAKE THE RESPONSIBILITY FOR PUTTING YOU IN HARM'S WAY.
IT'S NOT YOUR DECISION, CAP.
YOU'VE MADE IT PRETTY CLEAR THAT YOU DON'T WANT ME AS A PARTNER.
BESIDES, YOU'RE NOT THE ONLY ONE HAUNTED BY THE GALLOPING GUILTS.
THE HULK WOULDN'T EVEN EXIST IF HE HADN'T RISKED HIS LIFE TO SAVE MINE.
OLD UP, PEOPLE! E'RE CLOSING IN ON OUR QUARRY.
BASED ON THESE HEAT SIGNATURES, THE HULK PASSED THIS WAY ONLY A FEW MINUTES AGO AND MAY BE NEARBY.
COYOTE ONE, DO YOU COPY?
COME IN, COYOTE ONE.
PROBLEM, SOLDIER?
POSSIBLY, SIR.
COYOTE ONE IS ON POINT AND ISN'T RESPONDING TO MY--

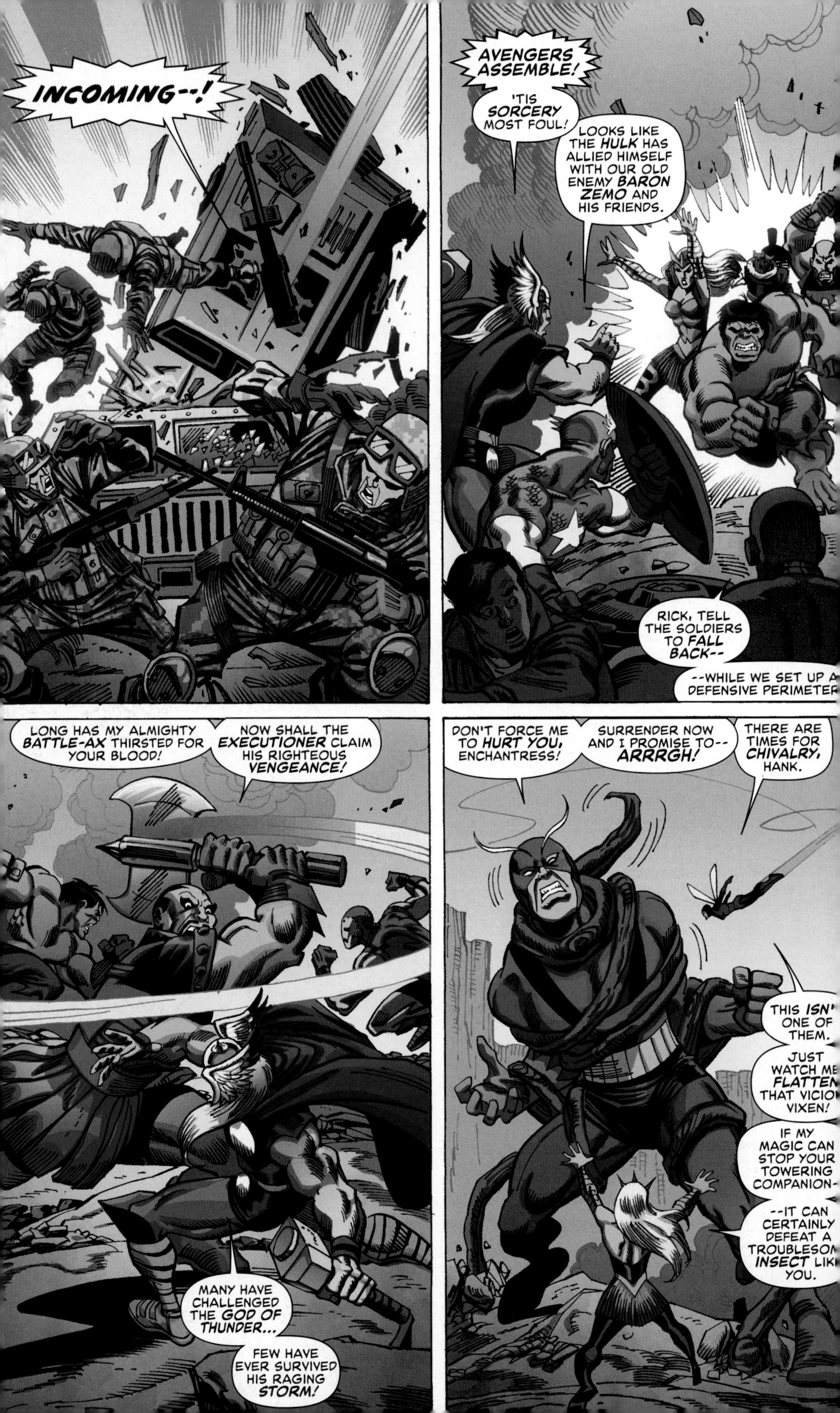
INCOMING--!
AVENGERS ASSEMBLE!
'TIS SORCERY MOST FOUL!
LOOKS LIKE THE HULK HAS ALLIED HIMSELF WITH OUR OLD ENEMY BARON ZEMO AND HIS FRIENDS.
RICK, TELL THE SOLDIERS TO FALL BACK--
--WHILE WE SET UP A DEFENSIVE PERIMETE
LONG HAS MY ALMIGHTY BATTLE-AX THIRSTED FOR YOUR BLOOD!
NOW SHALL THE EXECUTIONER CLAIM HIS RIGHTEOUS VENGEANCE!
MANY HAVE CHALLENGED THE GOD OF THUNDER...
FEW HAVE EVER SURVIVED HIS RAGING STORM!
DON'T FORCE ME TO HURT YOU, ENCHANTRESS!
SURRENDER NOW AND I PROMISE TO-- ARRRGH!
THERE ARE TIMES FOR CHIVALRY, HANK.
THIS ISN' ONE OF THEM.
JUST WATCH ME FLATTEN THAT VICIO VIXEN!
IF MY MAGIC CAN STOP YOUR TOWERING COMPANION-
--IT CAN CERTAINLY DEFEAT A TROUBLESOM INSECT LIK YOU.

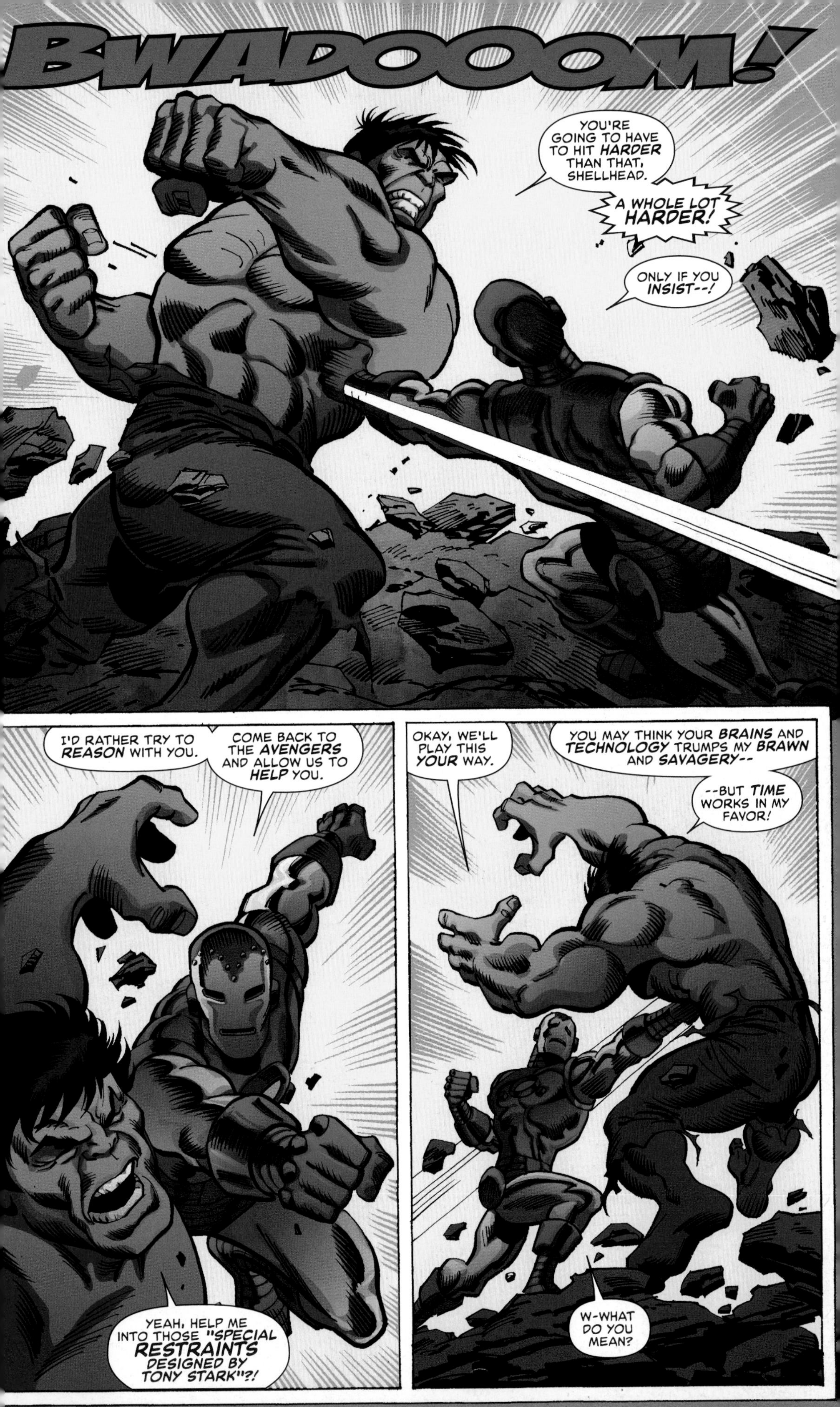
BWADOOOM!
YOU'RE GOING TO HAVE TO HIT HARDER THAN THAT, SHELLHEAD.
A WHOLE LOT HARDER!
ONLY IF YOU INSIST--!
I'D RATHER TRY TO REASON WITH YOU.
COME BACK TO THE AVENGERS AND ALLOW US TO HELP YOU.
YEAH, HELP ME INTO THOSE "SPECIAL RESTRAINTS DESIGNED BY TONY STARK"?!
OKAY, WE'LL PLAY THIS YOUR WAY.
YOU MAY THINK YOUR BRAINS AND TECHNOLOGY TRUMPS MY BRAWN AND SAVAGERY--
--BUT TIME WORKS IN MY FAVOR!
W-WHAT DO YOU MEAN?

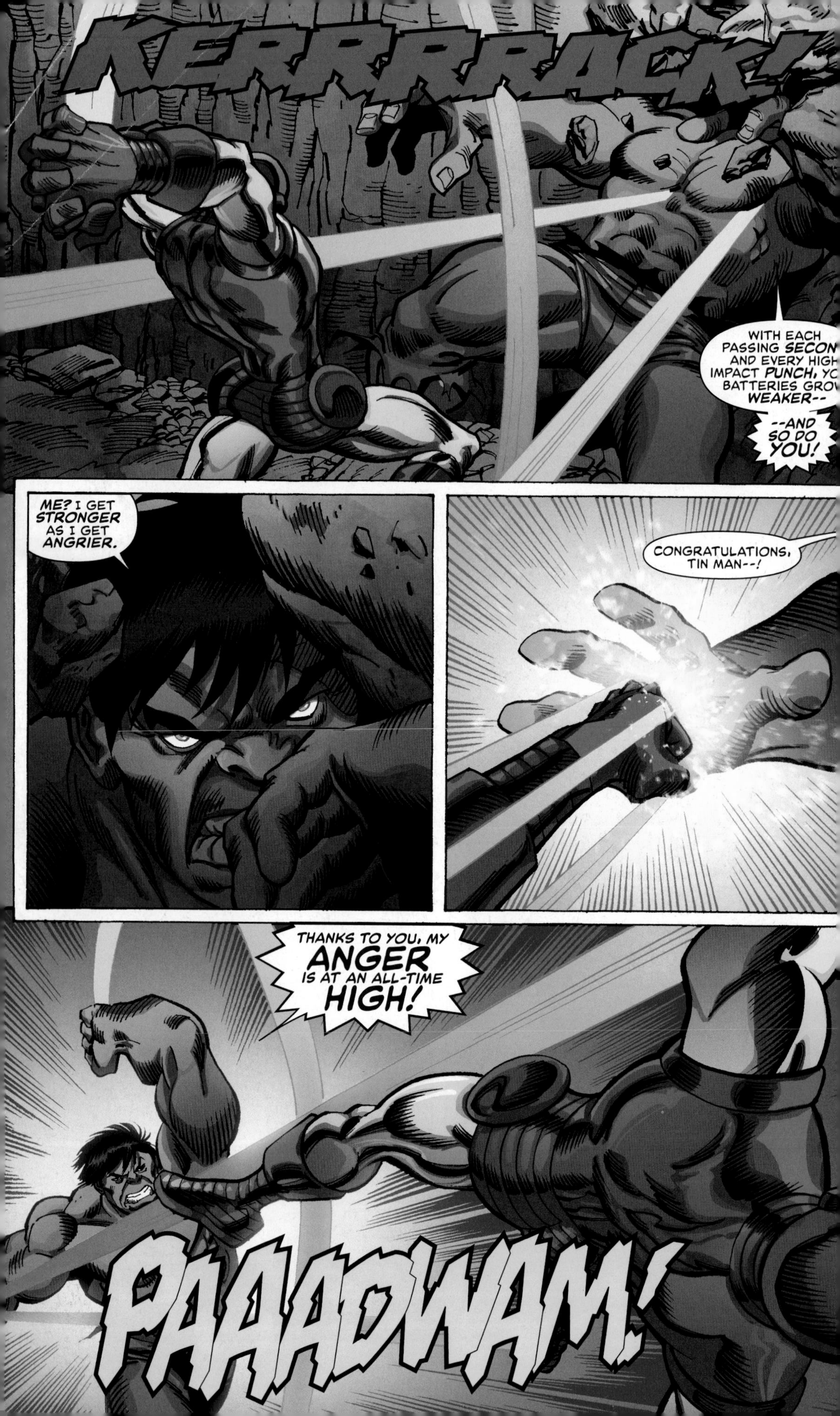
KERRRRACK!
WITH EACH PASSING SECON AND EVERY HIGH IMPACT PUNCH, YO BATTERIES GROW WEAKER--
--AND SO DO YOU!
ME? I GET STRONGER AS I GET ANGRIER.
CONGRATULATIONS, TIN MAN--!
THANKS TO YOU, MY ANGER IS AT AN ALL-TIME HIGH!
PAAADWAM!

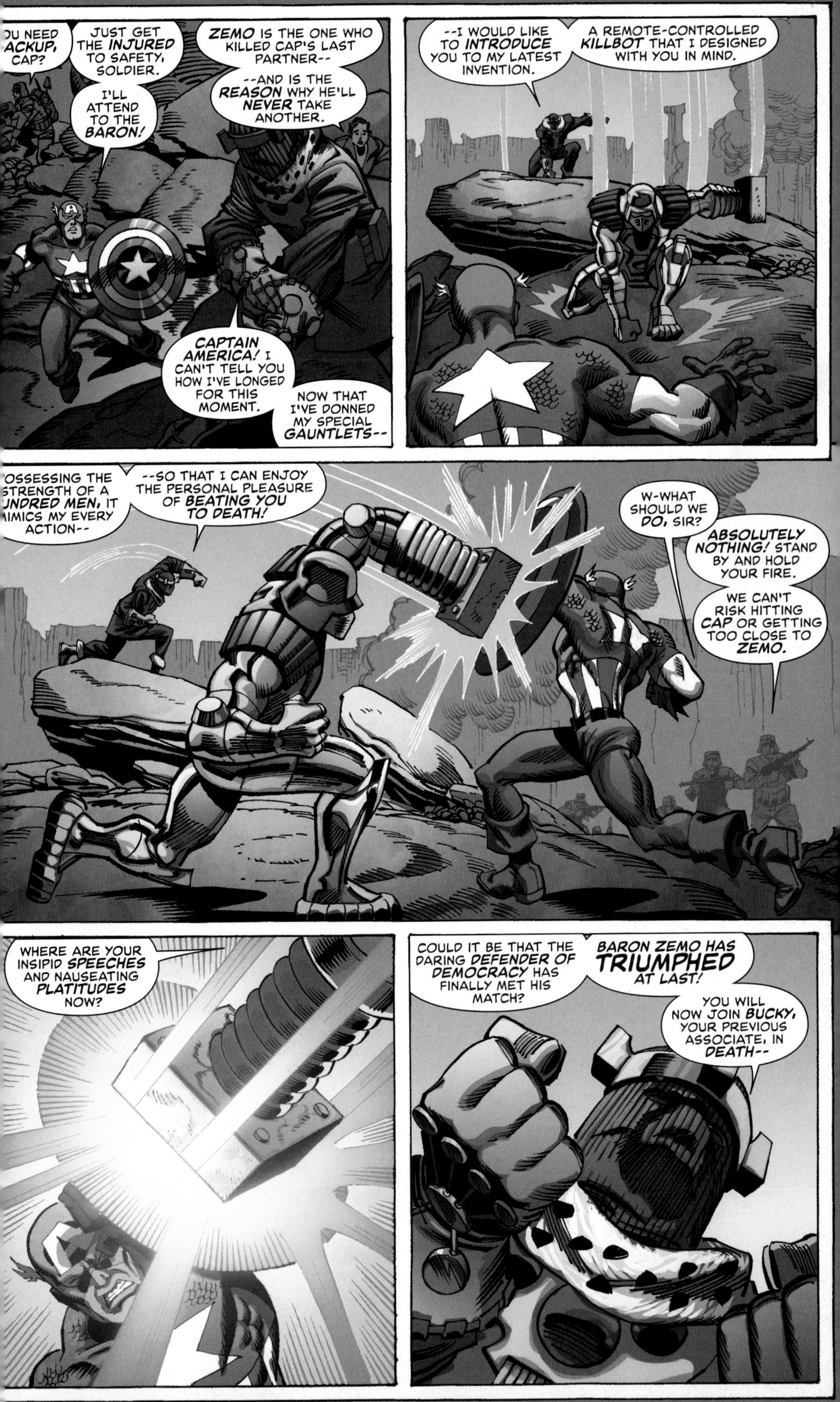
OU NEED
ACKUP,
CAP?
JUST GET THE INJURED TO SAFETY, SOLDIER.
I'LL ATTEND TO THE BARON!
ZEMO IS THE ONE WHO KILLED CAP'S LAST PARTNER--
--AND IS THE REASON WHY HE'LL NEVER TAKE ANOTHER.
CAPTAIN AMERICA! I CAN'T TELL YOU HOW I'VE LONGED FOR THIS MOMENT.
NOW THAT I'VE DONNED MY SPECIAL GAUNTLETS--
--I WOULD LIKE TO INTRODUCE YOU TO MY LATEST INVENTION.
A REMOTE-CONTROLLED KILLBOT THAT I DESIGNED WITH YOU IN MIND.
OSSESSING THE STRENGTH OF A UNDRED MEN, IT IMICS MY EVERY ACTION--
--SO THAT I CAN ENJOY THE PERSONAL PLEASURE OF BEATING YOU TO DEATH!
W-WHAT SHOULD WE DO, SIR?
ABSOLUTELY NOTHING! STAND BY AND HOLD YOUR FIRE.
WE CAN'T RISK HITTING CAP OR GETTING TOO CLOSE TO ZEMO.
WHERE ARE YOUR INSIPID SPEECHES AND NAUSEATING PLATITUDES NOW?
COULD IT BE THAT THE DARING DEFENDER OF DEMOCRACY HAS FINALLY MET HIS MATCH?
BARON ZEMO HAS TRIUMPHED AT LAST!
YOU WILL NOW JOIN BUCKY, YOUR PREVIOUS ASSOCIATE, IN DEATH--

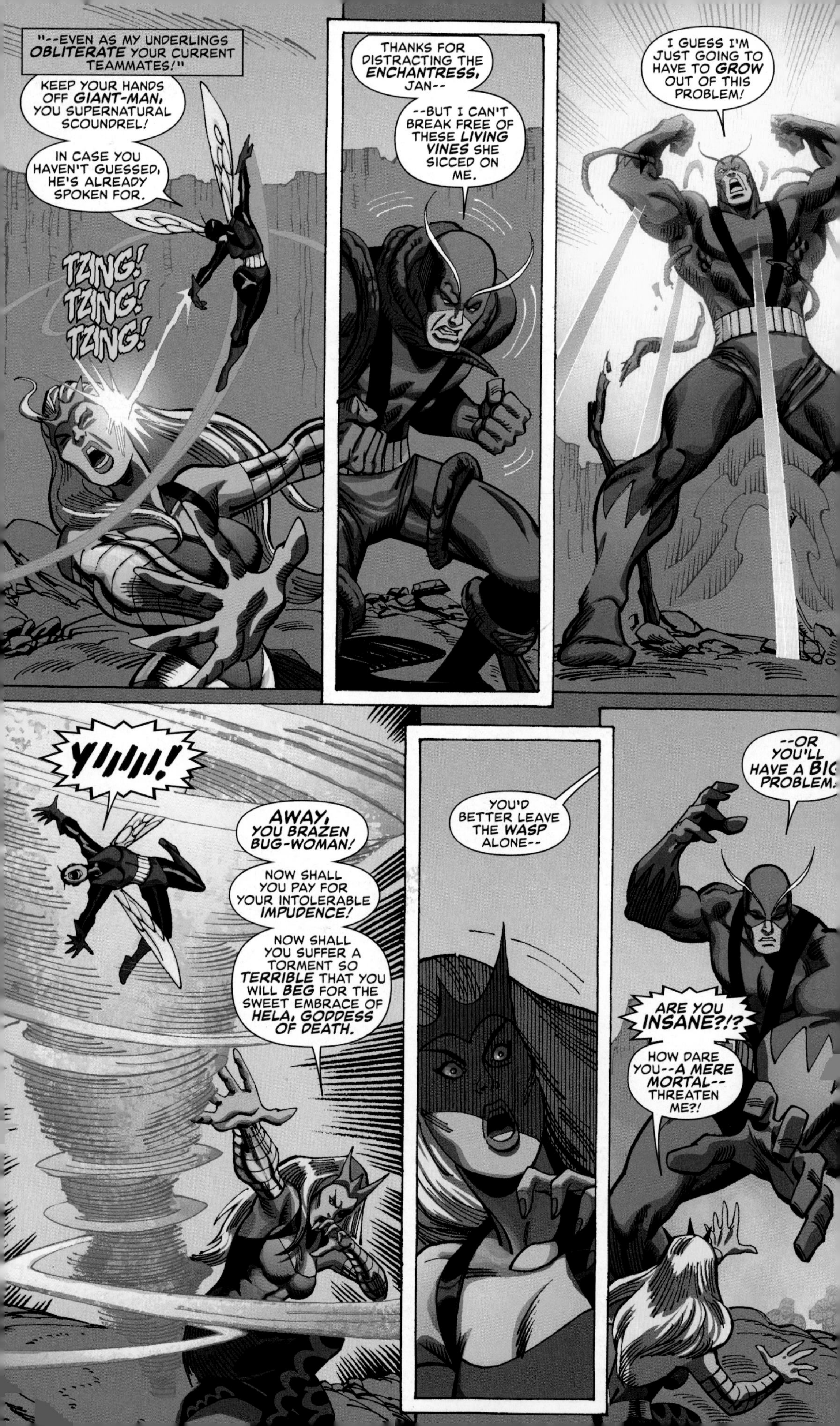
"--EVEN AS MY UNDERLINGS OBLITERATE YOUR CURRENT TEAMMATES!"
KEEP YOUR HANDS OFF GIANT-MAN, YOU SUPERNATURAL SCOUNDREL!
IN CASE YOU HAVEN'T GUESSED, HE'S ALREADY SPOKEN FOR.
TZING! TZING! TZING!
THANKS FOR DISTRACTING THE ENCHANTRESS, JAN--
--BUT I CAN'T BREAK FREE OF THESE LIVING VINES SHE SICCED ON ME.
I GUESS I'M JUST GOING TO HAVE TO GROW OUT OF THIS PROBLEM!
YIIIII!
AWAY, YOU BRAZEN BUG-WOMAN!
NOW SHALL YOU PAY FOR YOUR INTOLERABLE IMPUDENCE!
NOW SHALL YOU SUFFER A TORMENT SO TERRIBLE THAT YOU WILL BEG FOR THE SWEET EMBRACE OF HELA, GODDESS OF DEATH.
YOU'D BETTER LEAVE THE WASP ALONE--
--OR YOU'LL HAVE A BIG PROBLEM.
ARE YOU INSANE?!?
HOW DARE YOU--A MERE MORTAL--THREATEN ME?!

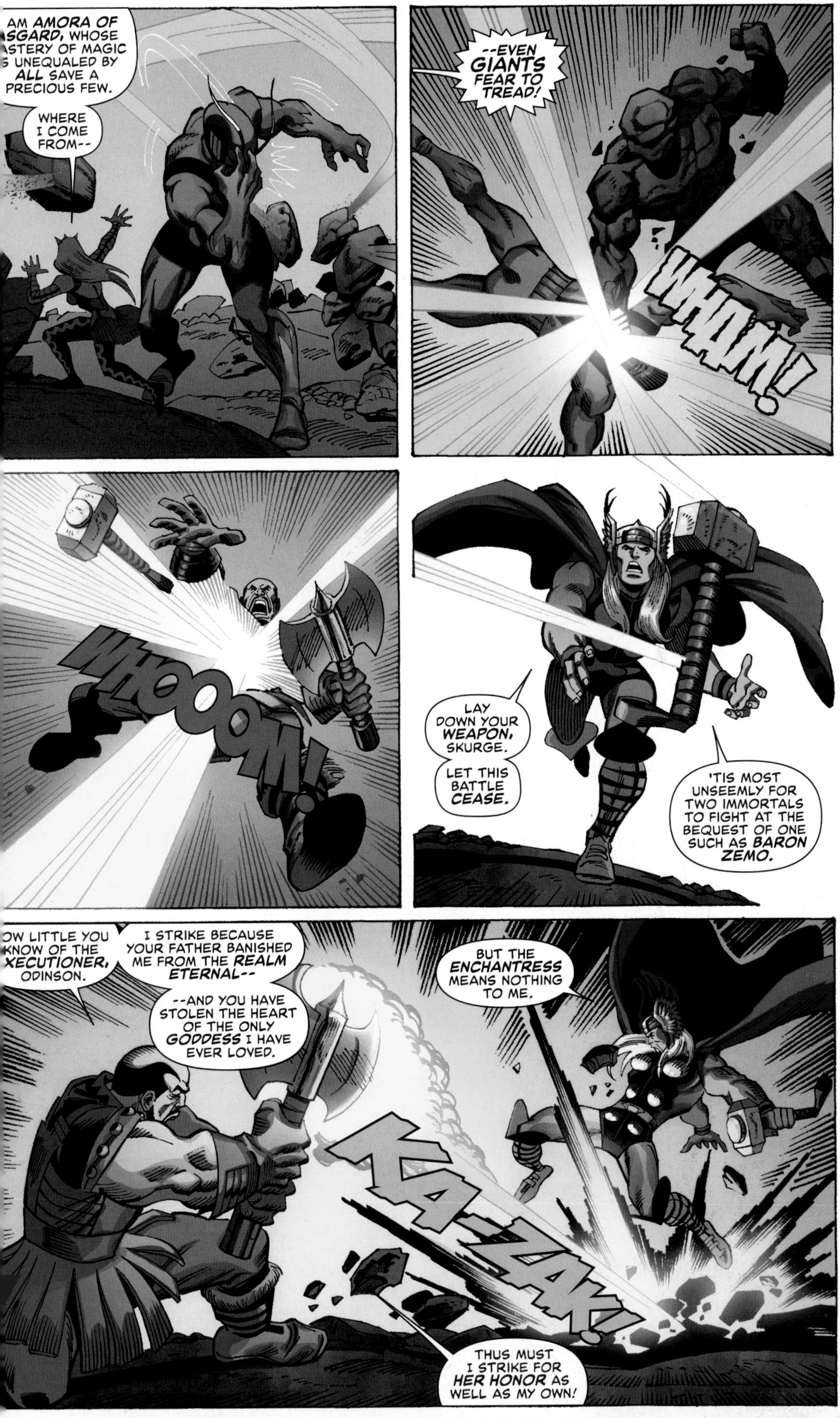
AM AMORA OF
SGARD, WHOSE
ASTERY OF MAGIC
S UNEQUALED BY
ALL SAVE A
PRECIOUS FEW.
WHERE I COME FROM--
--EVEN GIANTS FEAR TO TREAD!
WHAM!
WHOOOM!
LAY DOWN YOUR WEAPON, SKURGE.
LET THIS BATTLE CEASE.
'TIS MOST UNSEEMLY FOR TWO IMMORTALS TO FIGHT AT THE BEQUEST OF ONE SUCH AS BARON ZEMO.
OW LITTLE YOU KNOW OF THE XECUTIONER, ODINSON.
I STRIKE BECAUSE YOUR FATHER BANISHED ME FROM THE REALM ETERNAL--
--AND YOU HAVE STOLEN THE HEART OF THE ONLY GODDESS I HAVE EVER LOVED.
BUT THE ENCHANTRESS MEANS NOTHING TO ME.
KA-ZAK!
THUS MUST I STRIKE FOR HER HONOR AS WELL AS MY OWN!

SO BE IT!

WHEN *REASON* FAILS, *STRENGTH* MUST SUFFICE.

--STILL DOES ITS POWER PALE BEFORE *MJOLNIR*, THE ALMIGHTY HAMMER OF *THOR!*

THOUGH YOUR FABLED *BATTLE-AX* CAN CLEAVE THROUGH ALMOST ANY OBJECT--

HURLED AM I TOWARD THE JAGGED ROCKS BELOW--!

IF THIS IS FATED TO BE MY FINAL BATTLE, CONTENT AM I TO DIE IN THE SERVICE OF MY BELOVED *AMORA.*

A GREATER *FOOL* I HAVE NE'ER KNOWN!

NONE SHAL DIE WHEN *THOR* CA ACT.

WHERE THERE IS *LIFE*, THERE IS *HOPE!*

THERE COULD STILL COME A DAY WHEN MY ALL-POWERFUL FATHER WELCOMES YOU BACK TO *ASGARD.*

YOU SHOULD HAVE LET ME *DIE*, THUNDER GOD.

WHILE THE *EXECUTIONER* BREATHES--

"--THE *AVENGERS* HAVE CAUSE TO *FEAR!*"

PWW-TINGGG!

P-POWER RUNNING LOW...

CAN'T TAK MUCH MOR PUNISHMEN

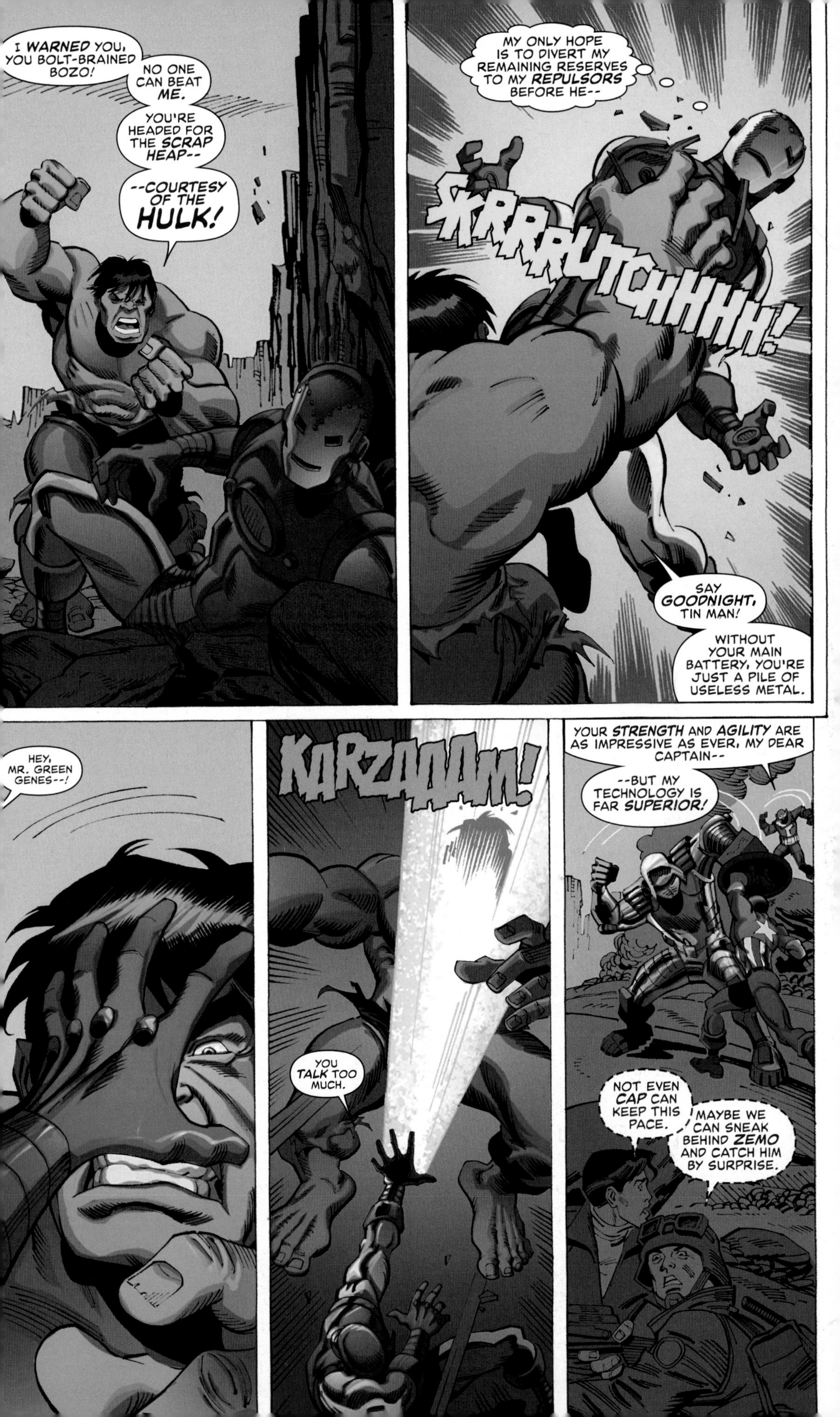
I WARNED YOU, YOU BOLT-BRAINED BOZO!
NO ONE CAN BEAT ME.
YOU'RE HEADED FOR THE SCRAP HEAP--
--COURTESY OF THE HULK!
MY ONLY HOPE IS TO DIVERT MY REMAINING RESERVES TO MY REPULSORS BEFORE HE--
SKRRRRUTCHHHHH!
SAY GOODNIGHT, TIN MAN!
WITHOUT YOUR MAIN BATTERY, YOU'RE JUST A PILE OF USELESS METAL.
HEY, MR. GREEN GENES--!
KARZAAAM!
YOU TALK TOO MUCH.
YOUR STRENGTH AND AGILITY ARE AS IMPRESSIVE AS EVER, MY DEAR CAPTAIN--
--BUT MY TECHNOLOGY IS FAR SUPERIOR!
NOT EVEN CAP CAN KEEP THIS PACE.
MAYBE WE CAN SNEAK BEHIND ZEMO AND CATCH HIM BY SURPRISE.

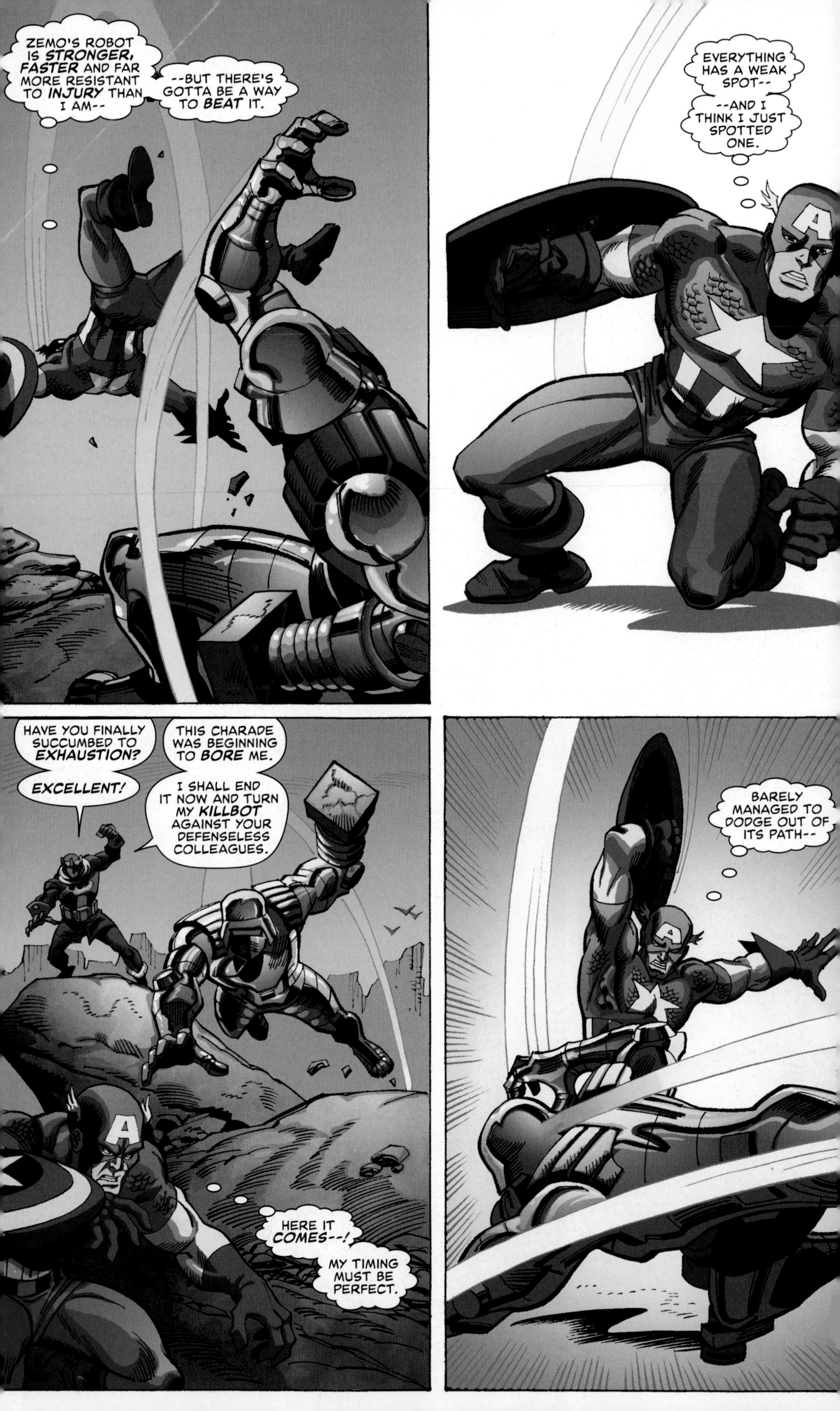
ZEMO'S ROBOT IS STRONGER, FASTER AND FAR MORE RESISTANT TO INJURY THAN I AM--
--BUT THERE'S GOTTA BE A WAY TO BEAT IT.
EVERYTHING HAS A WEAK SPOT--
--AND I THINK I JUST SPOTTED ONE.
HAVE YOU FINALLY SUCCUMBED TO EXHAUSTION?
EXCELLENT!
THIS CHARADE WAS BEGINNING TO BORE ME.
I SHALL END IT NOW AND TURN MY KILLBOT AGAINST YOUR DEFENSELESS COLLEAGUES.
HERE IT COMES--!
MY TIMING MUST BE PERFECT.
BARELY MANAGED TO DODGE OUT OF ITS PATH--

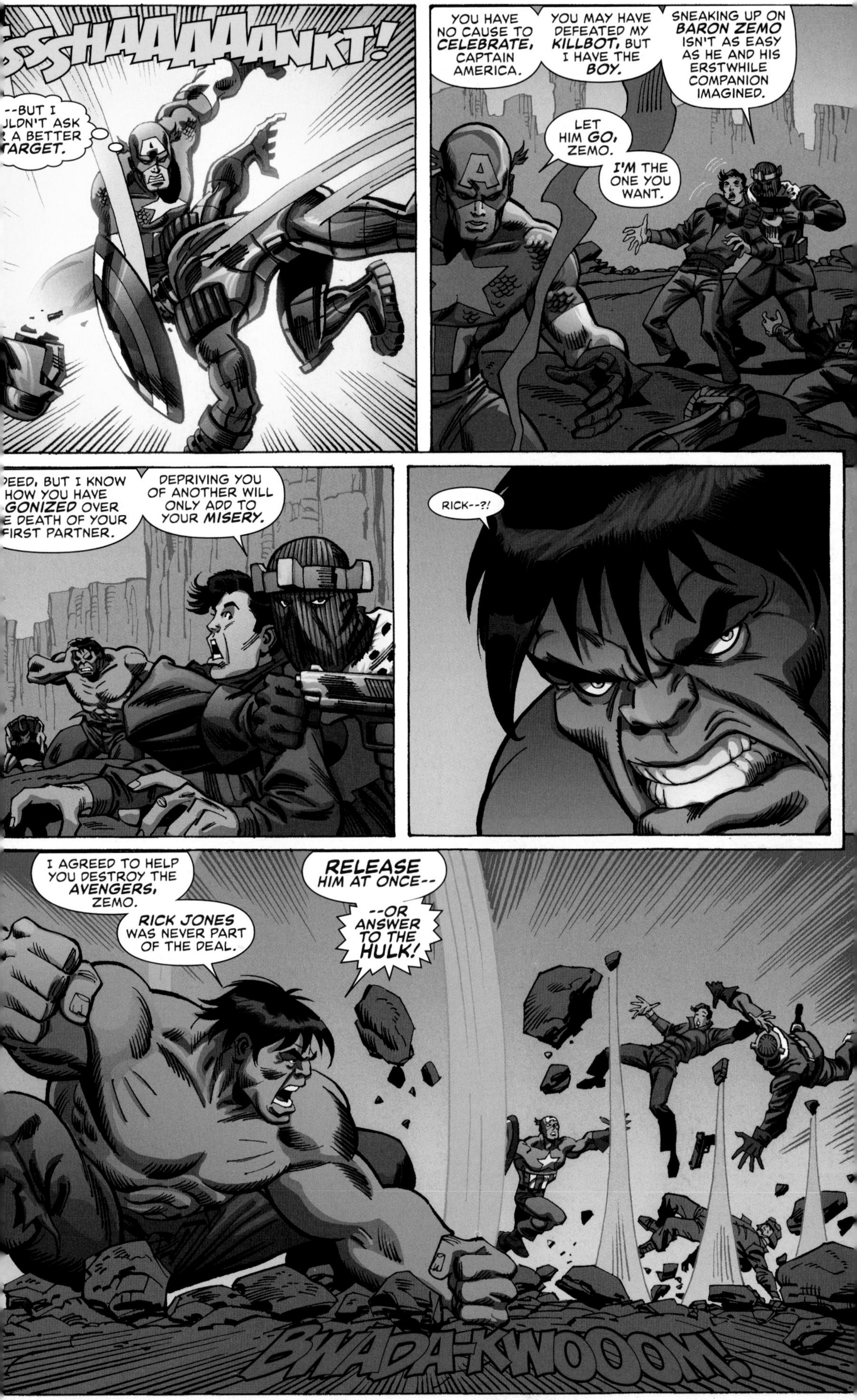

SSHAAAAAANKT!
--BUT I
ULDN'T ASK
R A BETTER
TARGET.
YOU HAVE NO CAUSE TO CELEBRATE, CAPTAIN AMERICA.
YOU MAY HAVE DEFEATED MY KILLBOT, BUT I HAVE THE BOY.
SNEAKING UP ON BARON ZEMO ISN'T AS EASY AS HE AND HIS ERSTWHILE COMPANION IMAGINED.
LET HIM GO, ZEMO.
I'M THE ONE YOU WANT.
DEED, BUT I KNOW HOW YOU HAVE GONIZED OVER E DEATH OF YOUR FIRST PARTNER.
DEPRIVING YOU OF ANOTHER WILL ONLY ADD TO YOUR MISERY.
RICK--?!
I AGREED TO HELP YOU DESTROY THE AVENGERS, ZEMO.
RICK JONES WAS NEVER PART OF THE DEAL.
RELEASE HIM AT ONCE--
--OR ANSWER TO THE HULK!
BWADA-KWOOOOM!

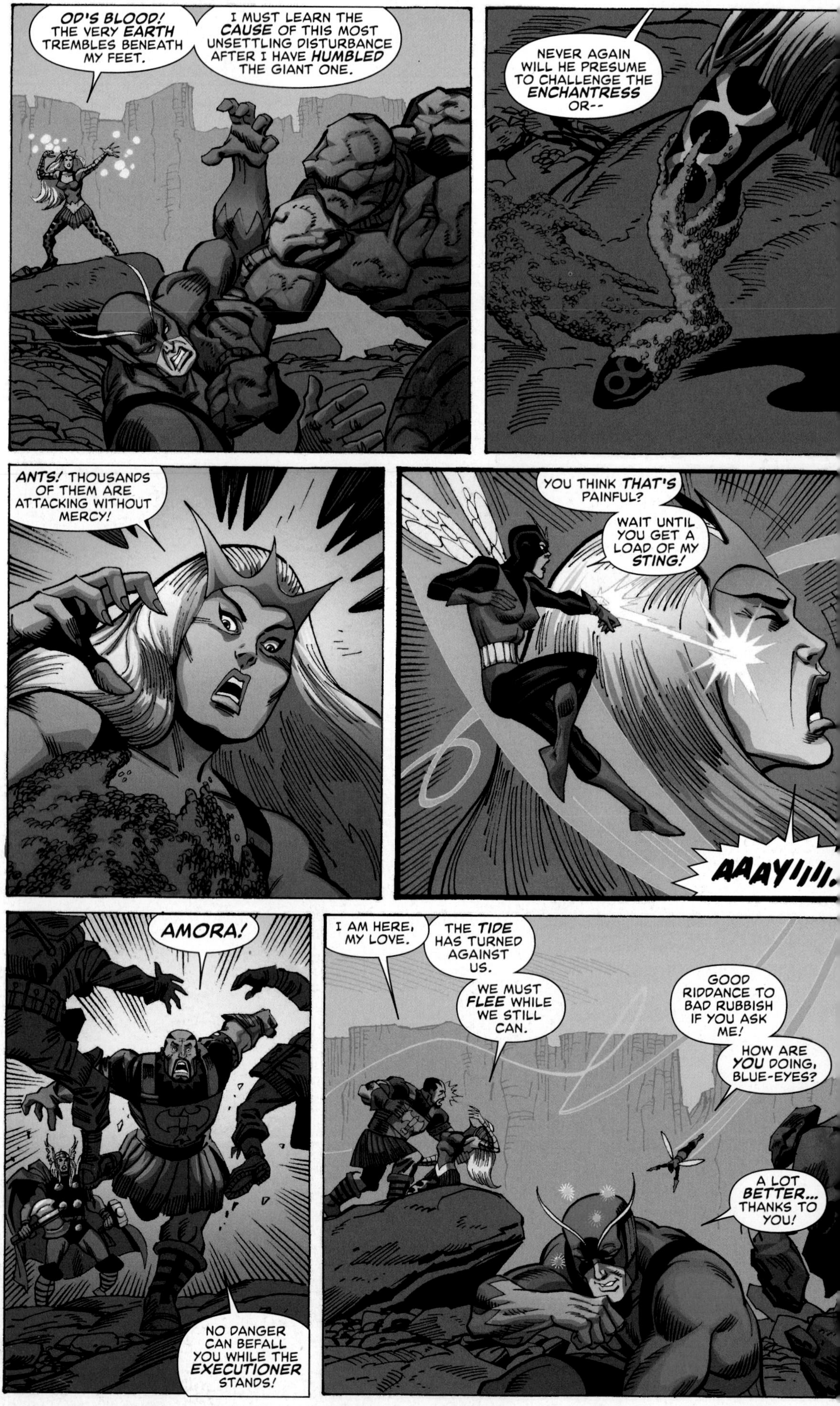
OD'S BLOOD! THE VERY EARTH TREMBLES BENEATH MY FEET.
I MUST LEARN THE CAUSE OF THIS MOST UNSETTLING DISTURBANCE AFTER I HAVE HUMBLED THE GIANT ONE.
NEVER AGAIN WILL HE PRESUME TO CHALLENGE THE ENCHANTRESS OR--
ANTS! THOUSANDS OF THEM ARE ATTACKING WITHOUT MERCY!
YOU THINK THAT'S PAINFUL?
WAIT UNTIL YOU GET A LOAD OF MY STING!
AAAYIIII.
AMORA!
NO DANGER CAN BEFALL YOU WHILE THE EXECUTIONER STANDS!
I AM HERE, MY LOVE.
THE TIDE HAS TURNED AGAINST US.
WE MUST FLEE WHILE WE STILL CAN.
GOOD RIDDANCE TO BAD RUBBISH IF YOU ASK ME!
HOW ARE YOU DOING, BLUE-EYES?
A LOT BETTER... THANKS TO YOU!

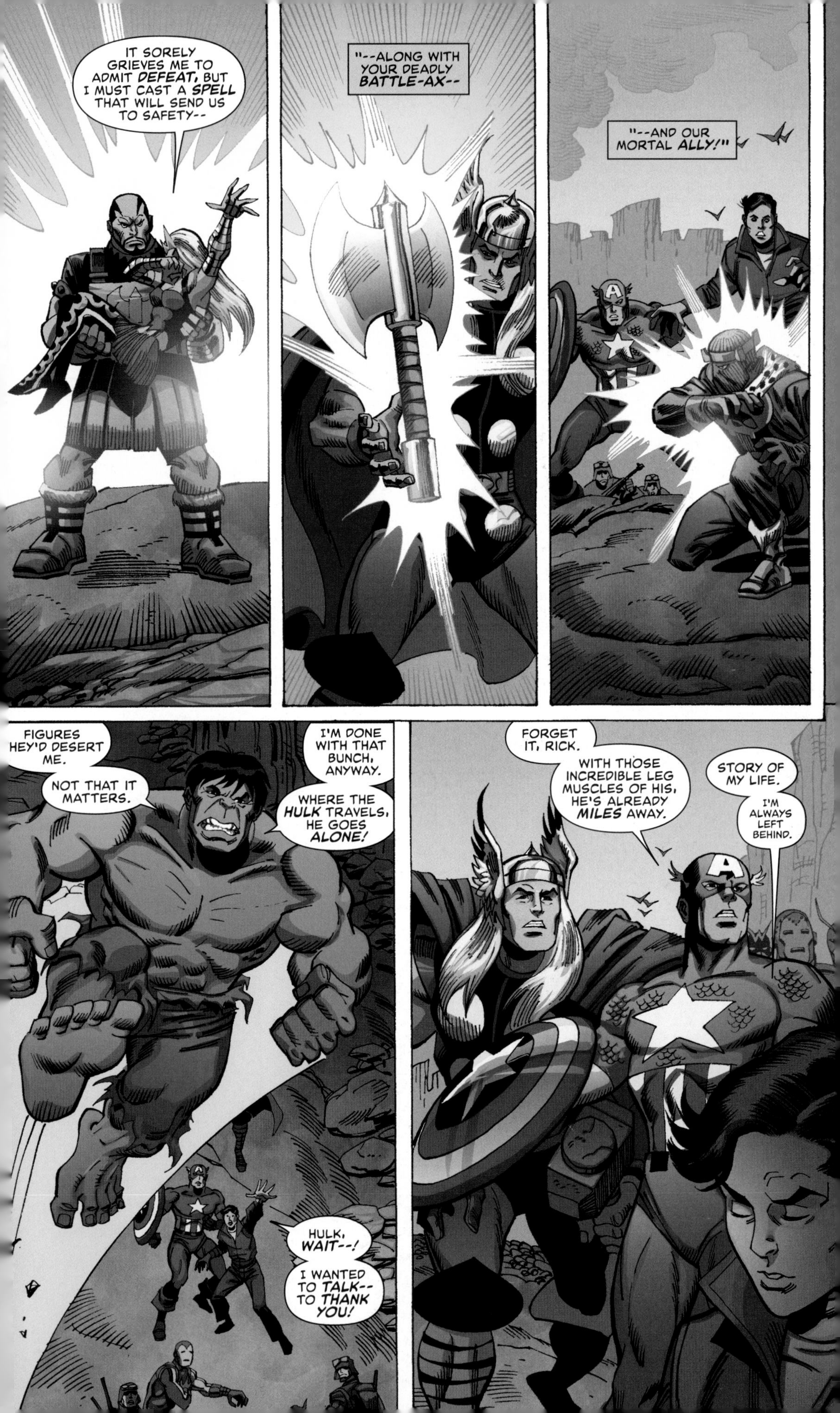
IT SORELY GRIEVES ME TO ADMIT DEFEAT, BUT I MUST CAST A SPELL THAT WILL SEND US TO SAFETY--
"--ALONG WITH YOUR DEADLY BATTLE-AX--
"--AND OUR MORTAL ALLY!"
FIGURES HEY'D DESERT ME.
NOT THAT IT MATTERS.
I'M DONE WITH THAT BUNCH, ANYWAY.
WHERE THE HULK TRAVELS, HE GOES ALONE!
HULK, WAIT--!
I WANTED TO TALK-- TO THANK YOU!
FORGET IT, RICK.
WITH THOSE INCREDIBLE LEG MUSCLES OF HIS, HE'S ALREADY MILES AWAY.
STORY OF MY LIFE.
I'M ALWAYS LEFT BEHIND.

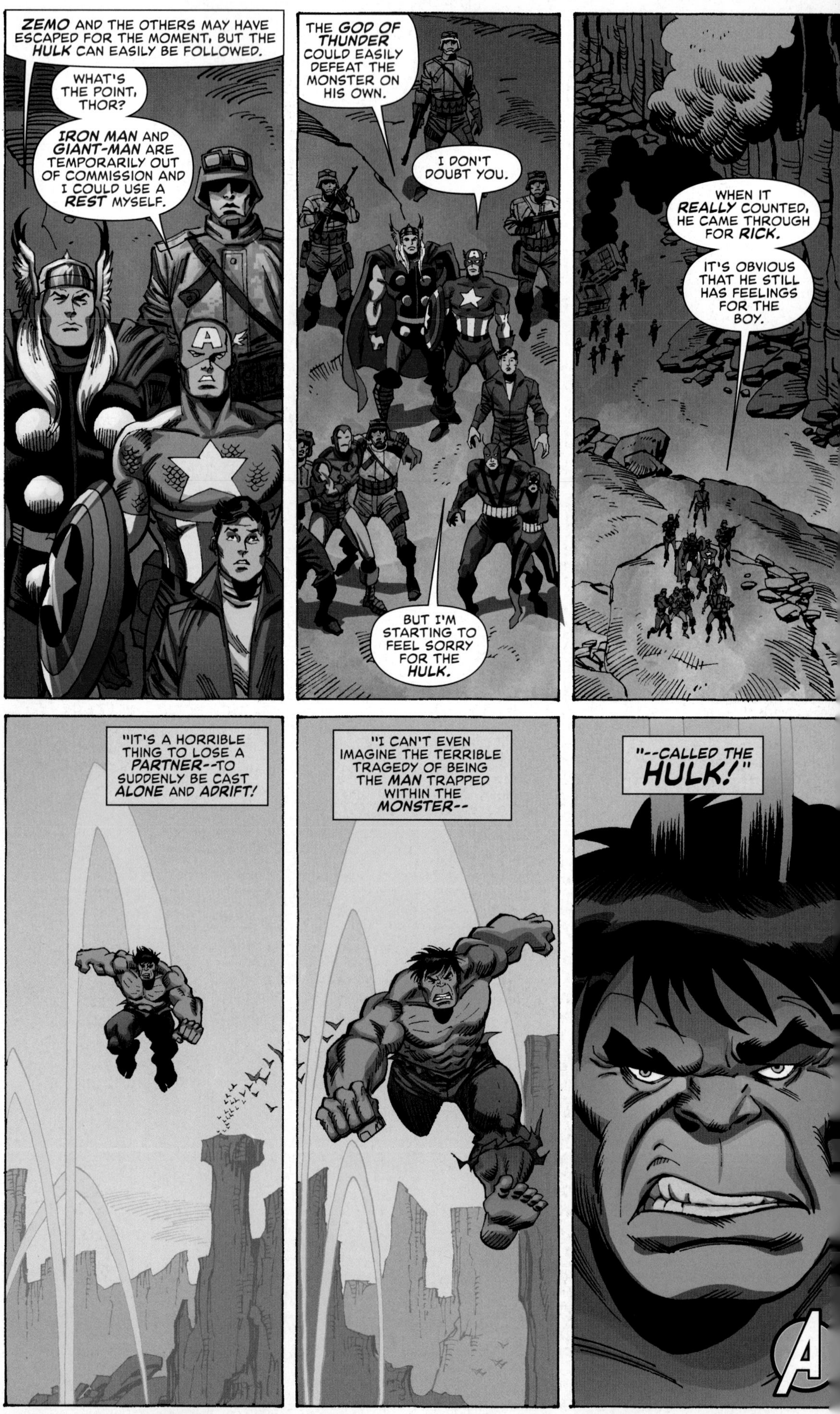
ZEMO AND THE OTHERS MAY HAVE ESCAPED FOR THE MOMENT, BUT THE HULK CAN EASILY BE FOLLOWED.
WHAT'S THE POINT, THOR?
IRON MAN AND GIANT-MAN ARE TEMPORARILY OUT OF COMMISSION AND I COULD USE A REST MYSELF.
THE GOD OF THUNDER COULD EASILY DEFEAT THE MONSTER ON HIS OWN.
I DON'T DOUBT YOU.
BUT I'M STARTING TO FEEL SORRY FOR THE HULK.
WHEN IT REALLY COUNTED, HE CAME THROUGH FOR RICK.
IT'S OBVIOUS THAT HE STILL HAS FEELINGS FOR THE BOY.
"IT'S A HORRIBLE THING TO LOSE A PARTNER--TO SUDDENLY BE CAST ALONE AND ADRIFT!
"I CAN'T EVEN IMAGINE THE TERRIBLE TRAGEDY OF BEING THE MAN TRAPPED WITHIN THE MONSTER--
"--CALLED THE HULK!"

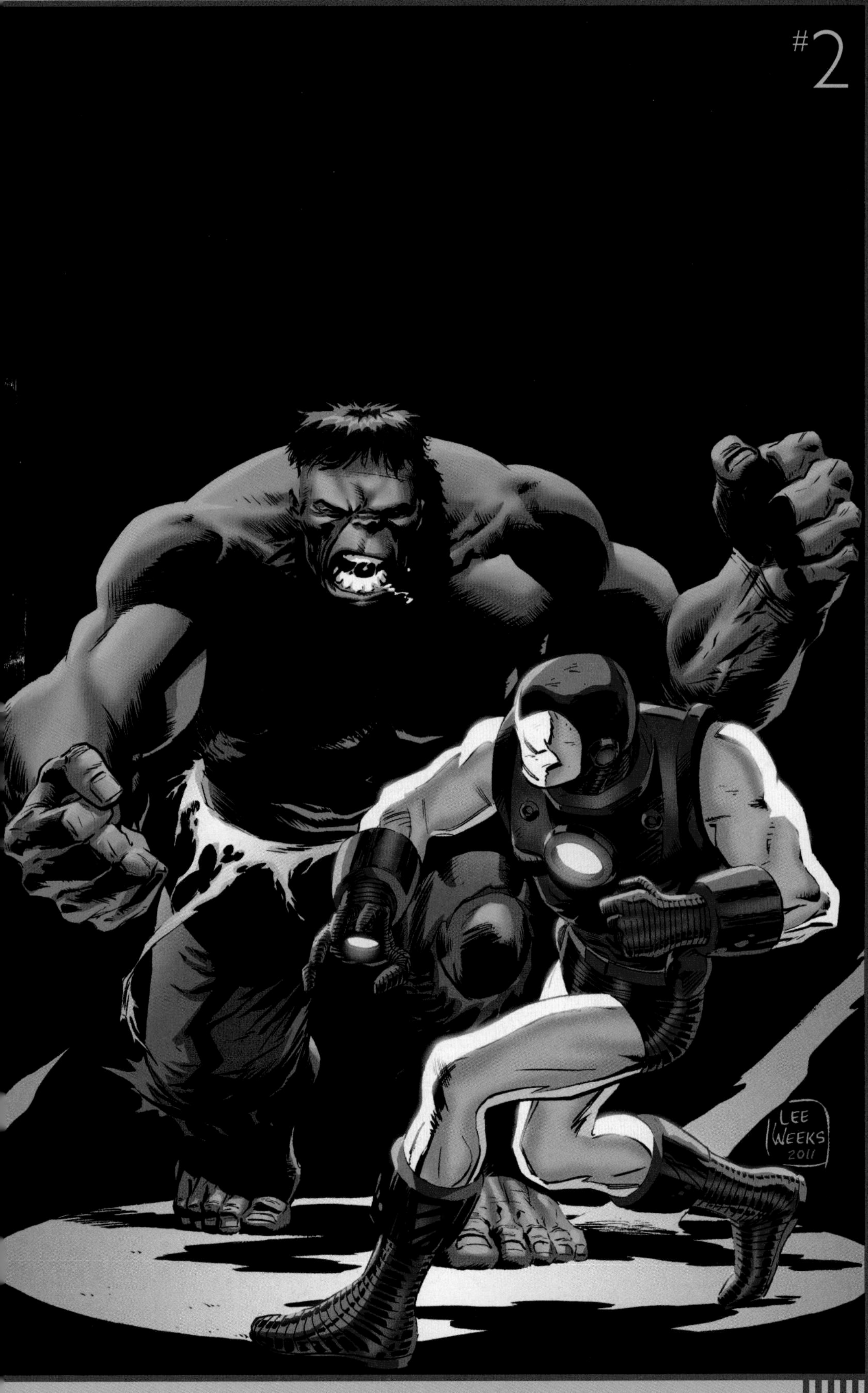
#2
LEE
WEEKS
2011

THIS STORY OCCURS IMMEDIATELY PRIOR TO THE EVENTS OF *AVENGERS* (VOL. 1) #*181*

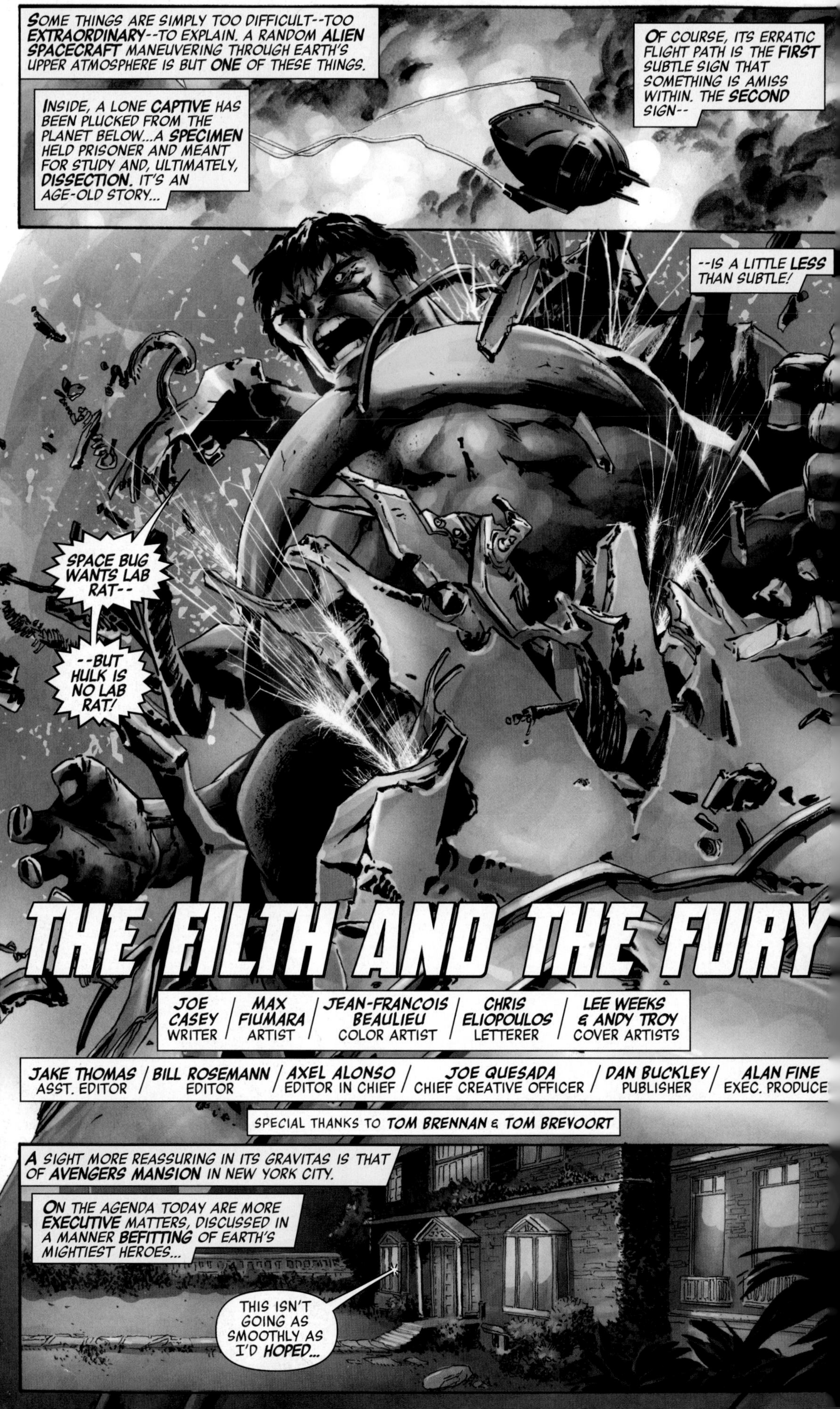
SOME THINGS ARE SIMPLY TOO DIFFICULT--TOO EXTRAORDINARY--TO EXPLAIN. A RANDOM ALIEN SPACECRAFT MANEUVERING THROUGH EARTH'S UPPER ATMOSPHERE IS BUT ONE OF THESE THINGS.
INSIDE, A LONE CAPTIVE HAS BEEN PLUCKED FROM THE PLANET BELOW...A SPECIMEN HELD PRISONER AND MEANT FOR STUDY AND, ULTIMATELY, DISSECTION. IT'S AN AGE-OLD STORY...
OF COURSE, ITS ERRATIC FLIGHT PATH IS THE FIRST SUBTLE SIGN THAT SOMETHING IS AMISS WITHIN. THE SECOND SIGN--
--IS A LITTLE LESS THAN SUBTLE!
SPACE BUG WANTS LAB RAT--
--BUT HULK IS NO LAB RAT!
THE FILTH AND THE FURY
JOE CASEY WRITER
MAX FIUMARA ARTIST
JEAN-FRANCOIS BEAULIEU COLOR ARTIST
CHRIS ELIOPOULOS LETTERER
LEE WEEKS & ANDY TROY COVER ARTISTS
JAKE THOMAS ASST. EDITOR
BILL ROSEMANN EDITOR
AXEL ALONSO EDITOR IN CHIEF
JOE QUESADA CHIEF CREATIVE OFFICER
DAN BUCKLEY PUBLISHER
ALAN FINE EXEC. PRODUCE
SPECIAL THANKS TO TOM BRENNAN & TOM BREVOORT
A SIGHT MORE REASSURING IN ITS GRAVITAS IS THAT OF AVENGERS MANSION IN NEW YORK CITY.
ON THE AGENDA TODAY ARE MORE EXECUTIVE MATTERS, DISCUSSED IN A MANNER BEFITTING OF EARTH'S MIGHTIEST HEROES...
THIS ISN'T GOING AS SMOOTHLY AS I'D HOPED...

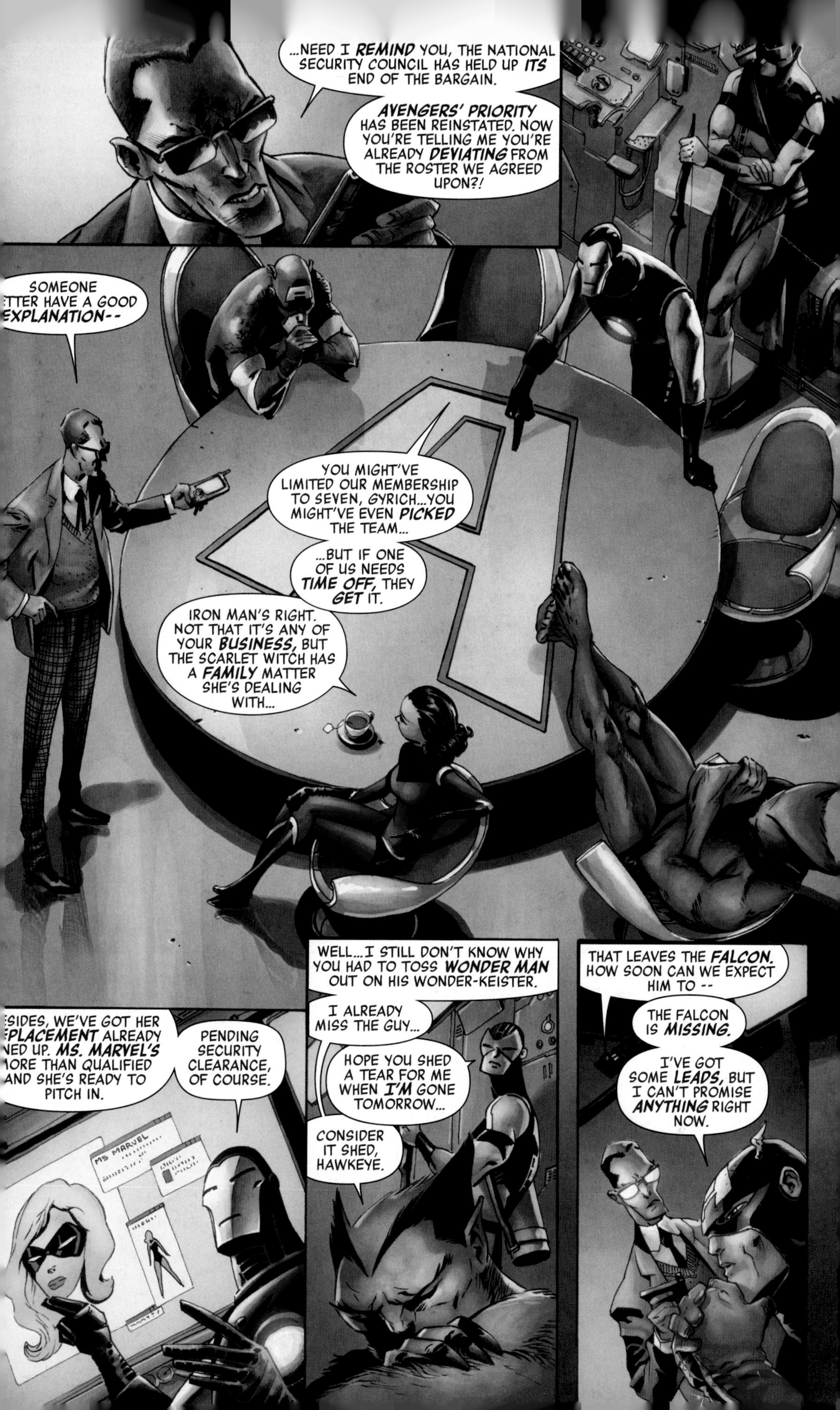
...NEED I REMIND YOU, THE NATIONAL SECURITY COUNCIL HAS HELD UP ITS END OF THE BARGAIN.
AVENGERS' PRIORITY HAS BEEN REINSTATED. NOW YOU'RE TELLING ME YOU'RE ALREADY DEVIATING FROM THE ROSTER WE AGREED UPON?!
SOMEONE ETTER HAVE A GOOD EXPLANATION--
YOU MIGHT'VE LIMITED OUR MEMBERSHIP TO SEVEN, GYRICH...YOU MIGHT'VE EVEN PICKED THE TEAM...
...BUT IF ONE OF US NEEDS TIME OFF, THEY GET IT.
IRON MAN'S RIGHT. NOT THAT IT'S ANY OF YOUR BUSINESS, BUT THE SCARLET WITCH HAS A FAMILY MATTER SHE'S DEALING WITH...
ESIDES, WE'VE GOT HER EPLACEMENT ALREADY NED UP. MS. MARVEL'S MORE THAN QUALIFIED AND SHE'S READY TO PITCH IN.
PENDING SECURITY CLEARANCE, OF COURSE.
MS MARVEL
WELL...I STILL DON'T KNOW WHY YOU HAD TO TOSS WONDER MAN OUT ON HIS WONDER-KEISTER.
I ALREADY MISS THE GUY...
HOPE YOU SHED A TEAR FOR ME WHEN I'M GONE TOMORROW...
CONSIDER IT SHED, HAWKEYE.
THAT LEAVES THE FALCON. HOW SOON CAN WE EXPECT HIM TO --
THE FALCON IS MISSING.
I'VE GOT SOME LEADS, BUT I CAN'T PROMISE ANYTHING RIGHT NOW.

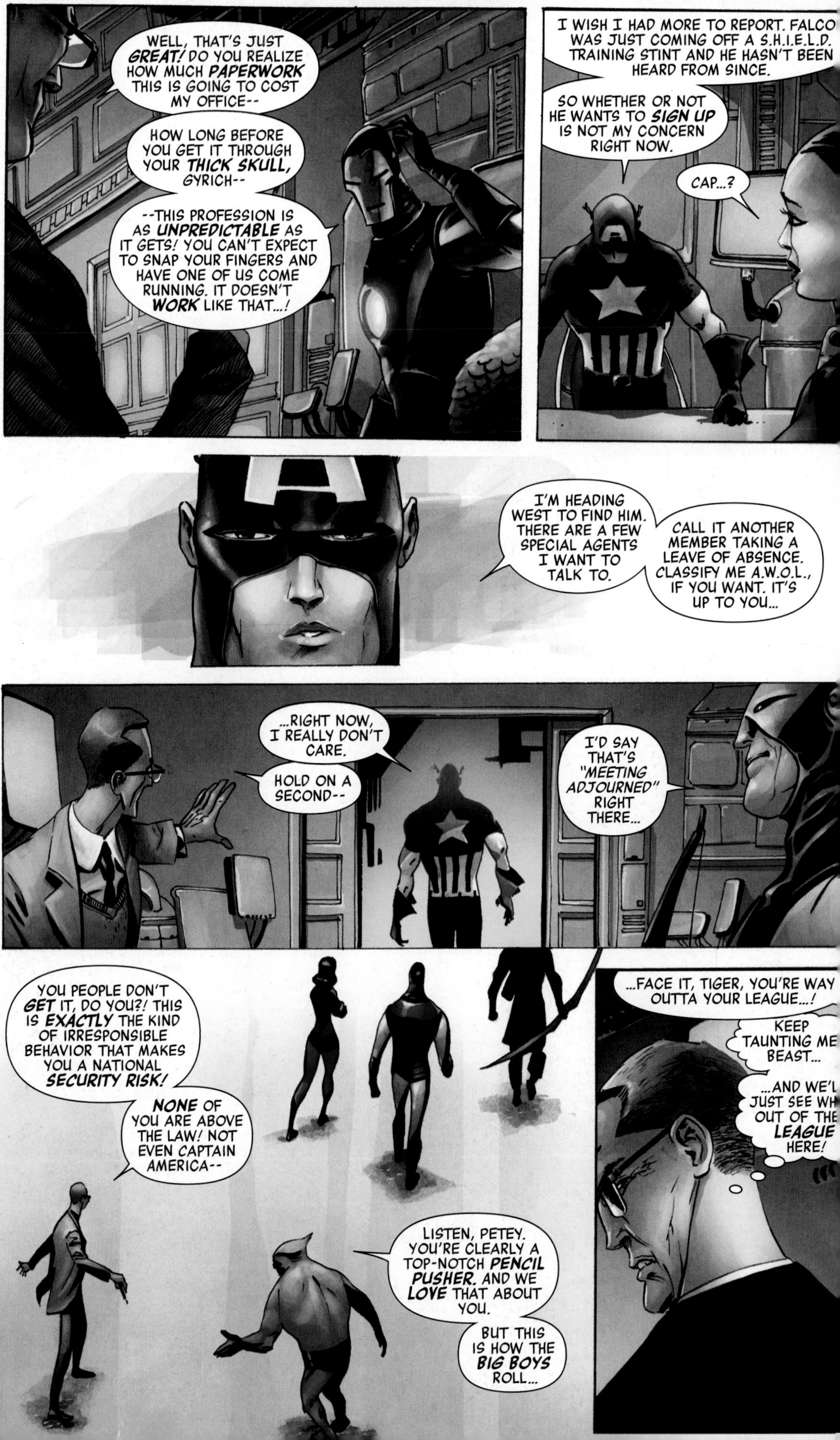
WELL, THAT'S JUST GREAT! DO YOU REALIZE HOW MUCH PAPERWORK THIS IS GOING TO COST MY OFFICE--
HOW LONG BEFORE YOU GET IT THROUGH YOUR THICK SKULL, GYRICH--
--THIS PROFESSION IS AS UNPREDICTABLE AS IT GETS! YOU CAN'T EXPECT TO SNAP YOUR FINGERS AND HAVE ONE OF US COME RUNNING. IT DOESN'T WORK LIKE THAT...!
I WISH I HAD MORE TO REPORT. FALCO WAS JUST COMING OFF A S.H.I.E.L.D. TRAINING STINT AND HE HASN'T BEEN HEARD FROM SINCE.
SO WHETHER OR NOT HE WANTS TO SIGN UP IS NOT MY CONCERN RIGHT NOW.
CAP...?
I'M HEADING WEST TO FIND HIM. THERE ARE A FEW SPECIAL AGENTS I WANT TO TALK TO.
CALL IT ANOTHER MEMBER TAKING A LEAVE OF ABSENCE. CLASSIFY ME A.W.O.L., IF YOU WANT. IT'S UP TO YOU...
...RIGHT NOW, I REALLY DON'T CARE.
HOLD ON A SECOND--
I'D SAY THAT'S "MEETING ADJOURNED" RIGHT THERE...
YOU PEOPLE DON'T GET IT, DO YOU?! THIS IS EXACTLY THE KIND OF IRRESPONSIBLE BEHAVIOR THAT MAKES YOU A NATIONAL SECURITY RISK!
NONE OF YOU ARE ABOVE THE LAW! NOT EVEN CAPTAIN AMERICA--
LISTEN, PETEY. YOU'RE CLEARLY A TOP-NOTCH PENCIL PUSHER. AND WE LOVE THAT ABOUT YOU.
BUT THIS IS HOW THE BIG BOYS ROLL...
...FACE IT, TIGER, YOU'RE WAY OUTTA YOUR LEAGUE...!
KEEP TAUNTING ME BEAST...
...AND WE'L JUST SEE WH OUT OF THE LEAGUE HERE!

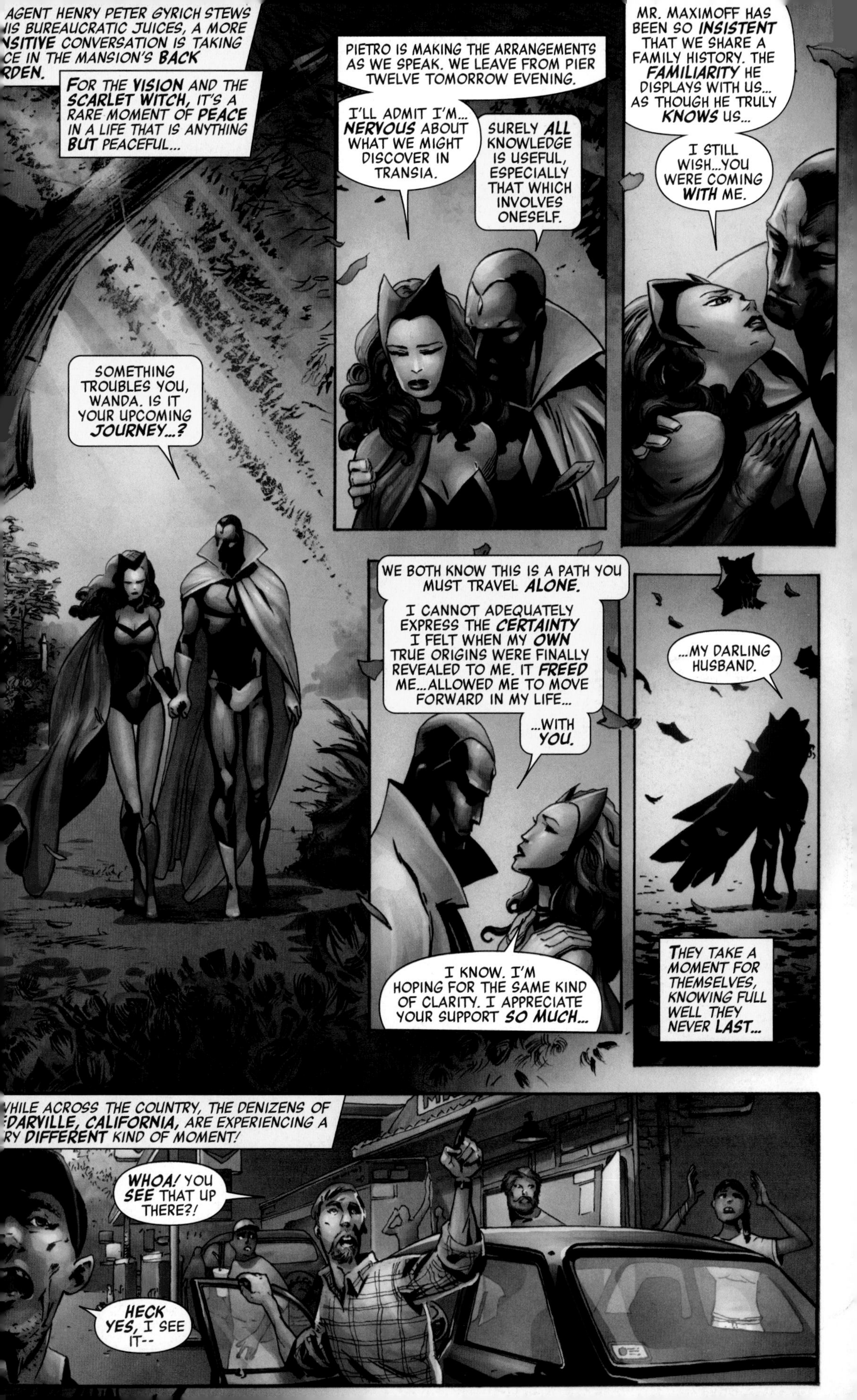
AGENT HENRY PETER GYRICH STEWS
IIS BUREAUCRATIC JUICES, A MORE
NSITIVE CONVERSATION IS TAKING
CE IN THE MANSION'S BACK
RDEN.
FOR THE VISION AND THE SCARLET WITCH, IT'S A RARE MOMENT OF PEACE IN A LIFE THAT IS ANYTHING BUT PEACEFUL...
SOMETHING TROUBLES YOU, WANDA. IS IT YOUR UPCOMING JOURNEY...?
PIETRO IS MAKING THE ARRANGEMENTS AS WE SPEAK. WE LEAVE FROM PIER TWELVE TOMORROW EVENING.
I'LL ADMIT I'M... NERVOUS ABOUT WHAT WE MIGHT DISCOVER IN TRANSIA.
SURELY ALL KNOWLEDGE IS USEFUL, ESPECIALLY THAT WHICH INVOLVES ONESELF.
MR. MAXIMOFF HAS BEEN SO INSISTENT THAT WE SHARE A FAMILY HISTORY. THE FAMILIARITY HE DISPLAYS WITH US... AS THOUGH HE TRULY KNOWS US...
I STILL WISH...YOU WERE COMING WITH ME.
WE BOTH KNOW THIS IS A PATH YOU MUST TRAVEL ALONE.
I CANNOT ADEQUATELY EXPRESS THE CERTAINTY I FELT WHEN MY OWN TRUE ORIGINS WERE FINALLY REVEALED TO ME. IT FREED ME...ALLOWED ME TO MOVE FORWARD IN MY LIFE...
...WITH YOU.
I KNOW. I'M HOPING FOR THE SAME KIND OF CLARITY. I APPRECIATE YOUR SUPPORT SO MUCH...
...MY DARLING HUSBAND.
THEY TAKE A MOMENT FOR THEMSELVES, KNOWING FULL WELL THEY NEVER LAST...
VHILE ACROSS THE COUNTRY, THE DENIZENS OF
EDARVILLE, CALIFORNIA, ARE EXPERIENCING A
RY DIFFERENT KIND OF MOMENT!
WHOA! YOU SEE THAT UP THERE?!
HECK YES, I SEE IT--

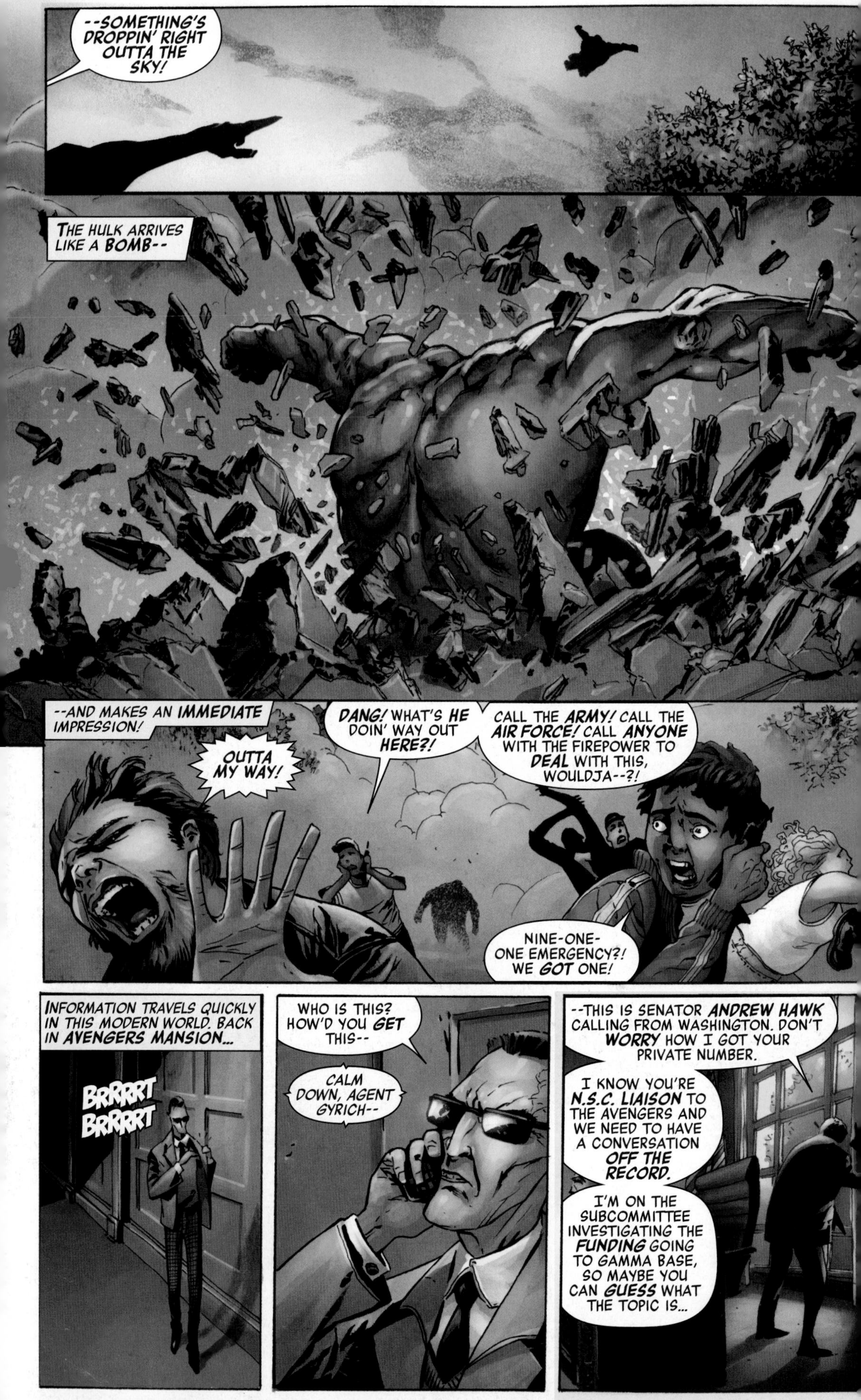

--SOMETHING'S DROPPIN' RIGHT OUTTA THE SKY!
THE HULK ARRIVES LIKE A BOMB--
--AND MAKES AN IMMEDIATE IMPRESSION!
OUTTA MY WAY!
DANG! WHAT'S HE DOIN' WAY OUT HERE?!
CALL THE ARMY! CALL THE AIR FORCE! CALL ANYONE WITH THE FIREPOWER TO DEAL WITH THIS, WOULDJA--?!
NINE-ONE-ONE EMERGENCY?! WE GOT ONE!
INFORMATION TRAVELS QUICKLY IN THIS MODERN WORLD. BACK IN AVENGERS MANSION...
BRRRRT BRRRRT
WHO IS THIS? HOW'D YOU GET THIS--
CALM DOWN, AGENT GYRICH--
--THIS IS SENATOR ANDREW HAWK CALLING FROM WASHINGTON. DON'T WORRY HOW I GOT YOUR PRIVATE NUMBER.
I KNOW YOU'RE N.S.C. LIAISON TO THE AVENGERS AND WE NEED TO HAVE A CONVERSATION OFF THE RECORD.
I'M ON THE SUBCOMMITTEE INVESTIGATING THE FUNDING GOING TO GAMMA BASE, SO MAYBE YOU CAN GUESS WHAT THE TOPIC IS...

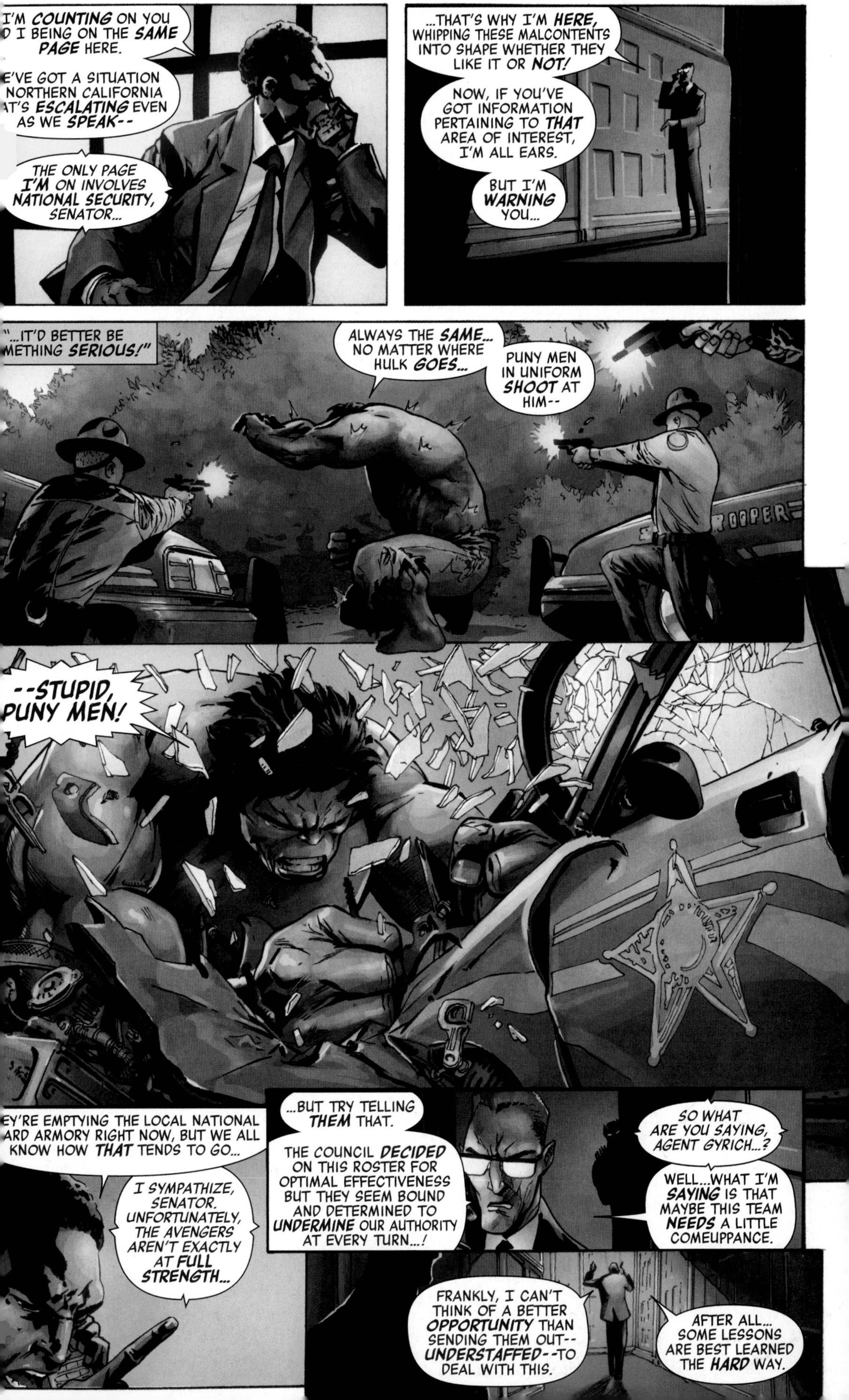
I'M COUNTING ON YOU D I BEING ON THE SAME PAGE HERE.
E'VE GOT A SITUATION NORTHERN CALIFORNIA AT'S ESCALATING EVEN AS WE SPEAK--
THE ONLY PAGE I'M ON INVOLVES NATIONAL SECURITY, SENATOR...
...THAT'S WHY I'M HERE, WHIPPING THESE MALCONTENTS INTO SHAPE WHETHER THEY LIKE IT OR NOT!
NOW, IF YOU'VE GOT INFORMATION PERTAINING TO THAT AREA OF INTEREST, I'M ALL EARS.
BUT I'M WARNING YOU...
"...IT'D BETTER BE METHING SERIOUS!"
ALWAYS THE SAME... NO MATTER WHERE HULK GOES...
PUNY MEN IN UNIFORM SHOOT AT HIM--
ROOPER
--STUPID, PUNY MEN!
EY'RE EMPTYING THE LOCAL NATIONAL ARD ARMORY RIGHT NOW, BUT WE ALL KNOW HOW THAT TENDS TO GO...
I SYMPATHIZE, SENATOR. UNFORTUNATELY, THE AVENGERS AREN'T EXACTLY AT FULL STRENGTH...
...BUT TRY TELLING THEM THAT.
THE COUNCIL DECIDED ON THIS ROSTER FOR OPTIMAL EFFECTIVENESS BUT THEY SEEM BOUND AND DETERMINED TO UNDERMINE OUR AUTHORITY AT EVERY TURN...!
SO WHAT ARE YOU SAYING, AGENT GYRICH...?
WELL...WHAT I'M SAYING IS THAT MAYBE THIS TEAM NEEDS A LITTLE COMEUPPANCE.
FRANKLY, I CAN'T THINK OF A BETTER OPPORTUNITY THAN SENDING THEM OUT--UNDERSTAFFED--TO DEAL WITH THIS.
AFTER ALL... SOME LESSONS ARE BEST LEARNED THE HARD WAY.

A FEW MOMENTS LATER, IN A NEARBY COMMUNICATIONS ROOM...

LADIES AND GENTLEMEN, LISTEN UP...

...THE *HULK* IS ON A RAMPAGE IN THE HILLS OUTSIDE CEDARVILLE, CALIFORNIA. RIGHT NOW, YOU COULD CONSIDER IT TO BE A *LOCAL* MATTER, BUT KNOWING THE HULK--

HOLD ON-- HOW DID *YOU* KNOW ABOUT THIS BEFORE *US?!*

ONE, BECAUSE I'M THE *GOVERNMENT.*

AND *TWO,* NO ONE WANTS TO CAUSE WIDER *PUBLIC PANIC.* THIS IS YOUR CHANCE TO GET IN, GET OUT AND KEEP THIS FROM BECOMING AN EVEN *BIGGER* NIGHTMARE.

THE HULK, HUH? DON'T WE CONSIDER HIM ONE OF THE *GOOD GUYS...?*

DEPENDS ON YOUR POINT OF VIEW, *BEAST.* OR, MORE SPECIFICALLY, DEPENDS ON THE *MOOD* HE'S IN...

FOR THE SAKE OF ARGUMENT, ASSUME IT'S A *BAD* ONE.

THE SCARLET WITCH AND QUICKSILVER HAVE ALREADY LEFT THE MANSION. SHOULD WE CALL IN REINFORCEMENTS?

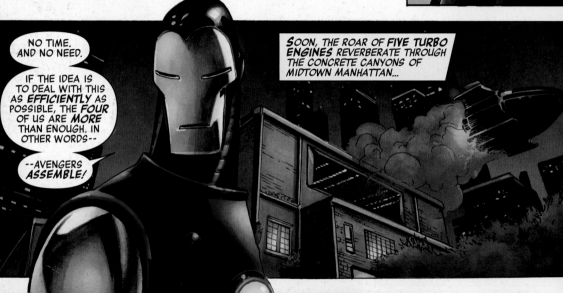

NO TIME. AND NO NEED.

IF THE IDEA IS TO DEAL WITH THIS AS *EFFICIENTLY* AS POSSIBLE, THE *FOUR* OF US ARE *MORE* THAN ENOUGH. IN OTHER WORDS--

--AVENGERS *ASSEMBLE!*

SOON, THE ROAR OF *FIVE TURBO ENGINES* REVERBERATE THROUGH THE *CONCRETE CANYONS* OF MIDTOWN MANHATTAN...

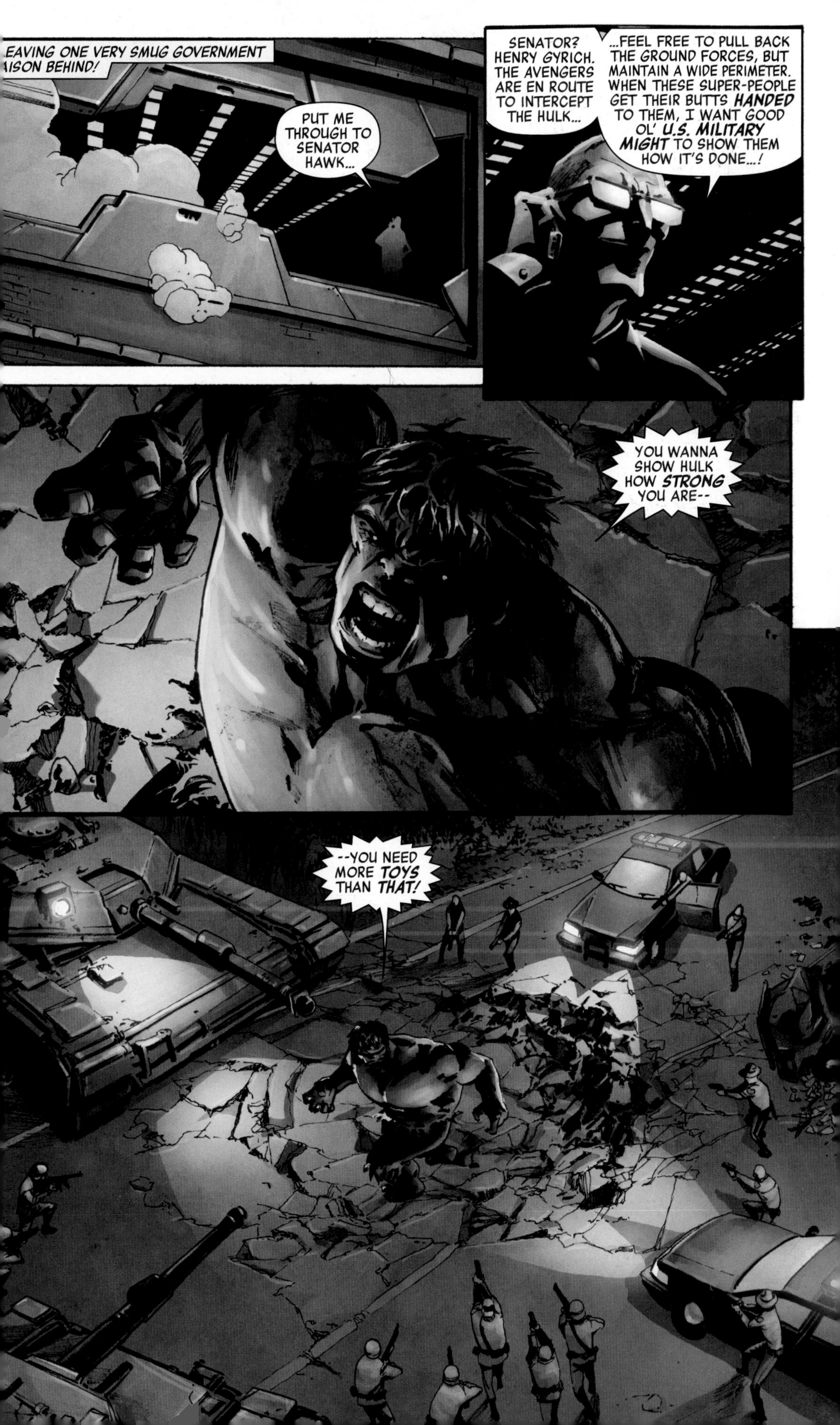
EAVING ONE VERY SMUG GOVERNMENT
AISON BEHIND!
PUT ME THROUGH TO SENATOR HAWK...
SENATOR? HENRY GYRICH. THE AVENGERS ARE EN ROUTE TO INTERCEPT THE HULK...
...FEEL FREE TO PULL BACK THE GROUND FORCES, BUT MAINTAIN A WIDE PERIMETER. WHEN THESE SUPER-PEOPLE GET THEIR BUTTS HANDED TO THEM, I WANT GOOD OL' U.S. MILITARY MIGHT TO SHOW THEM HOW IT'S DONE...!
YOU WANNA SHOW HULK HOW STRONG YOU ARE--
--YOU NEED MORE TOYS THAN THAT!

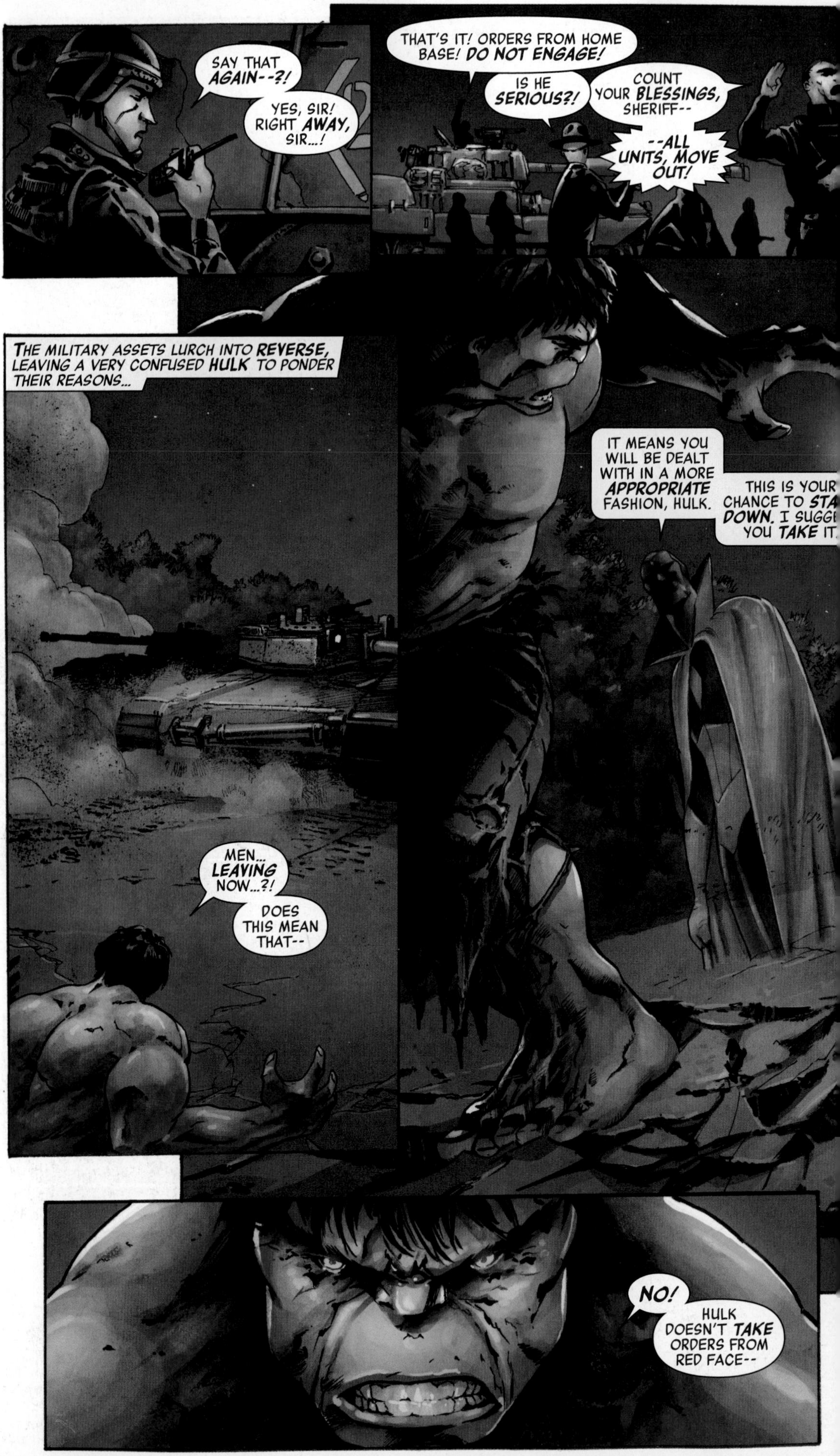
SAY THAT AGAIN--?!
YES, SIR! RIGHT AWAY, SIR...!
THAT'S IT! ORDERS FROM HOME BASE! DO NOT ENGAGE!
IS HE SERIOUS?!
COUNT YOUR BLESSINGS, SHERIFF--
--ALL UNITS, MOVE OUT!
THE MILITARY ASSETS LURCH INTO REVERSE, LEAVING A VERY CONFUSED HULK TO PONDER THEIR REASONS...
MEN... LEAVING NOW...?!
DOES THIS MEAN THAT--
IT MEANS YOU WILL BE DEALT WITH IN A MORE APPROPRIATE FASHION, HULK.
THIS IS YOUR CHANCE TO STA DOWN. I SUGG YOU TAKE IT.
NO!
HULK DOESN'T TAKE ORDERS FROM RED FACE--

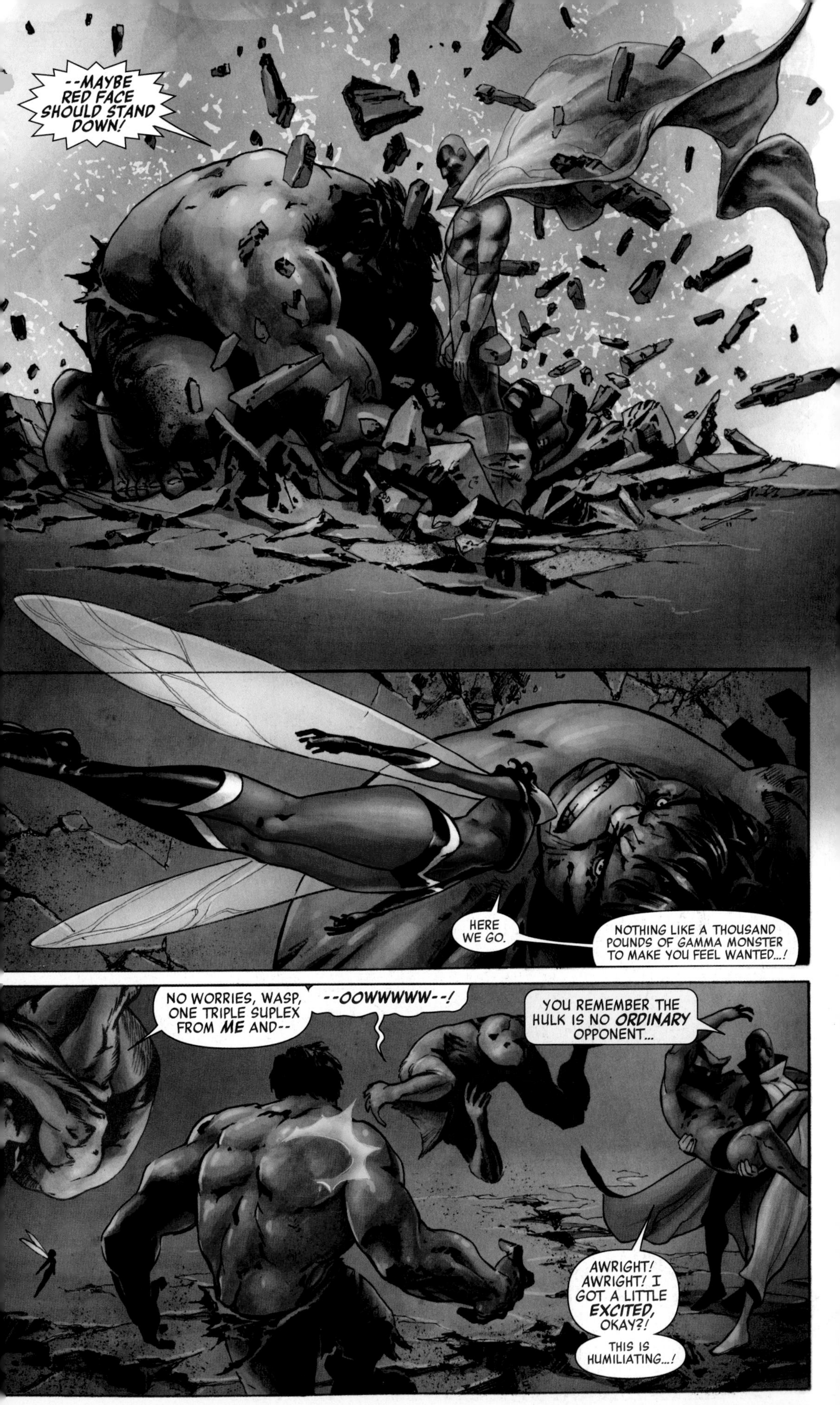
--MAYBE RED FACE SHOULD STAND DOWN!
HERE WE GO.
NOTHING LIKE A THOUSAND POUNDS OF GAMMA MONSTER TO MAKE YOU FEEL WANTED...!
NO WORRIES, WASP, ONE TRIPLE SUPLEX FROM ME AND--
--OOWWWWW--!
YOU REMEMBER THE HULK IS NO ORDINARY OPPONENT...
AWRIGHT! AWRIGHT! I GOT A LITTLE EXCITED, OKAY?!
THIS IS HUMILIATING...!

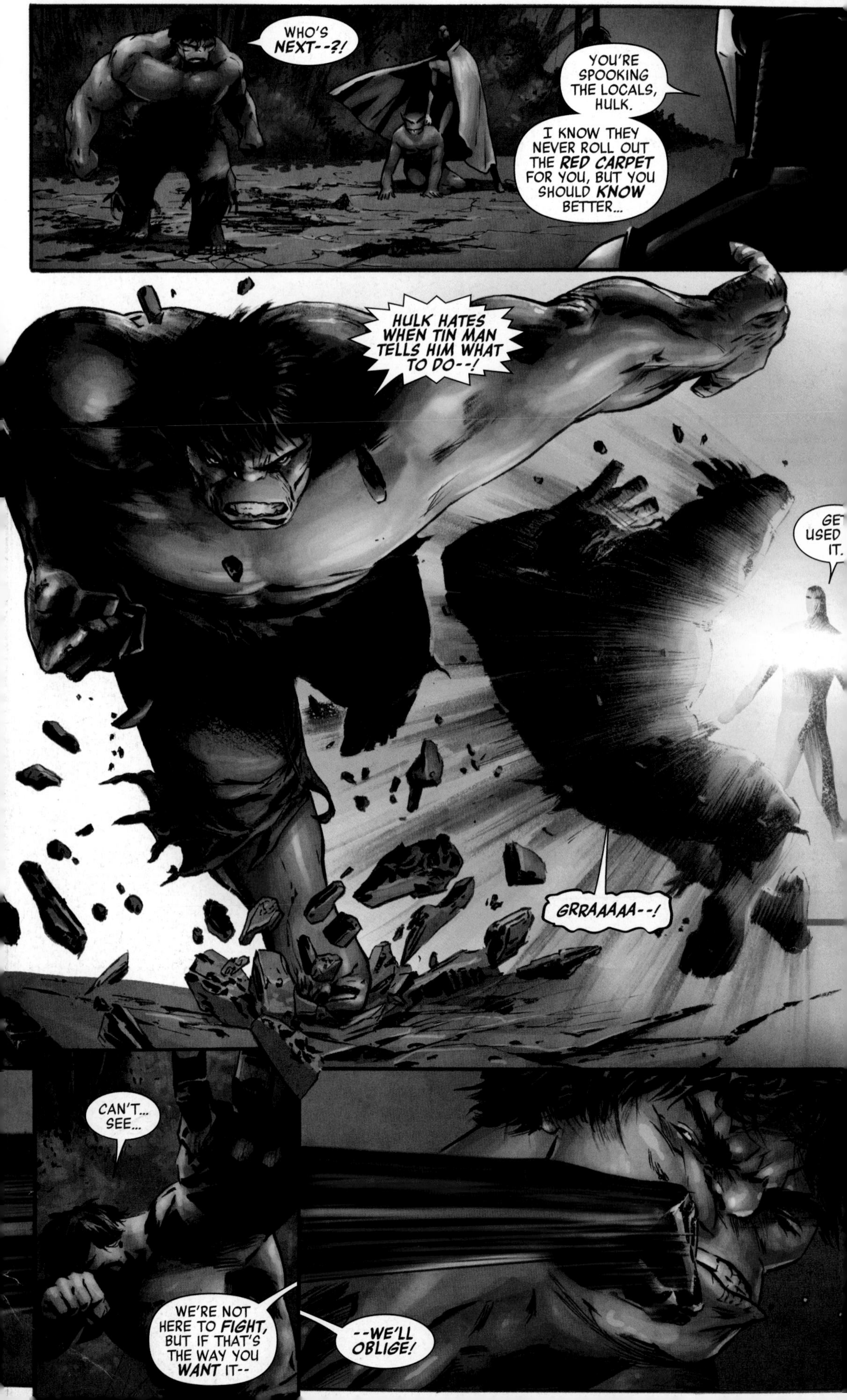
WHO'S NEXT--?!
YOU'RE SPOOKING THE LOCALS, HULK.
I KNOW THEY NEVER ROLL OUT THE RED CARPET FOR YOU, BUT YOU SHOULD KNOW BETTER...
HULK HATES WHEN TIN MAN TELLS HIM WHAT TO DO--!
GRRAAAAA--!
CAN'T... SEE...
WE'RE NOT HERE TO FIGHT, BUT IF THAT'S THE WAY YOU WANT IT--
--WE'LL OBLIGE!

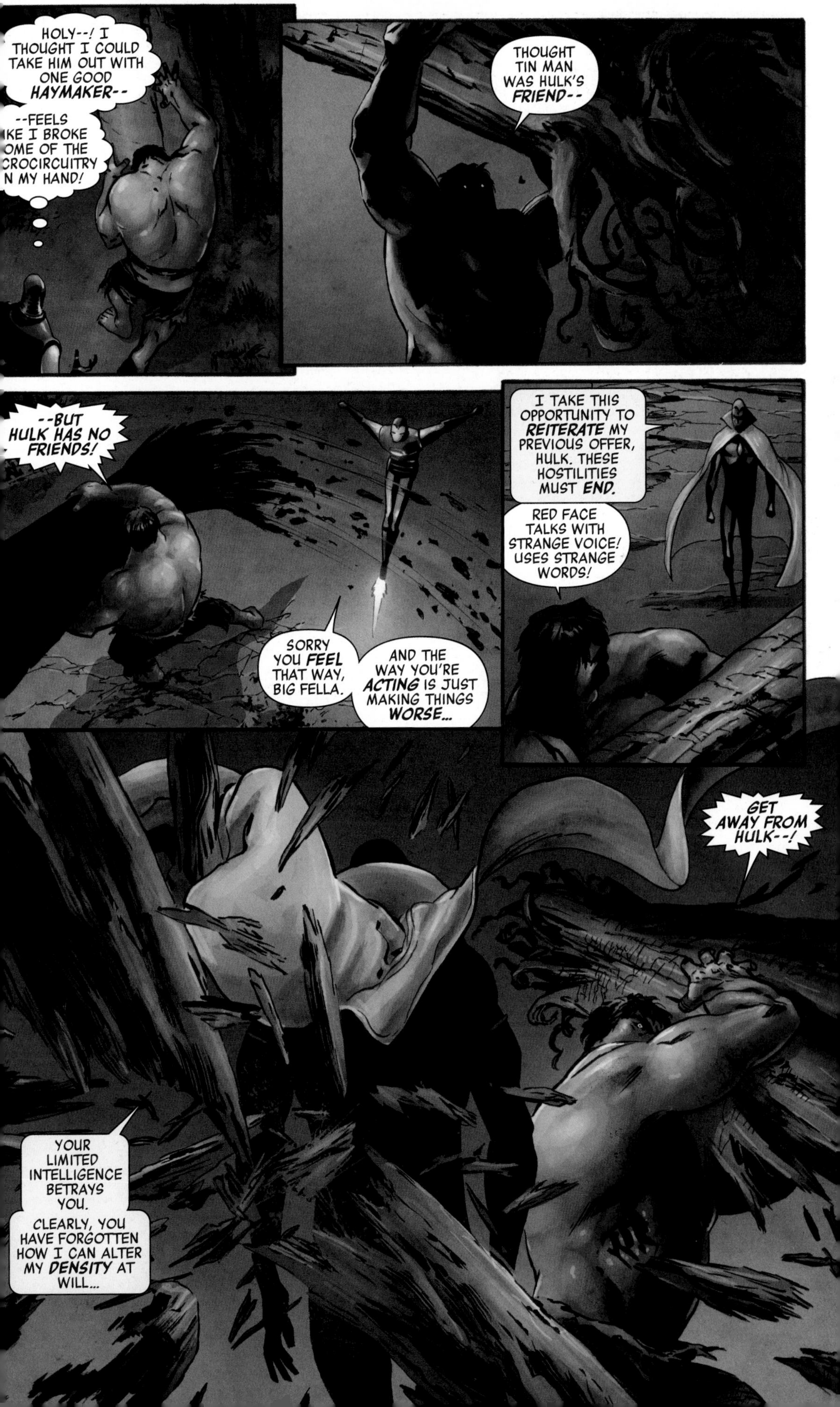
HOLY--! I THOUGHT I COULD TAKE HIM OUT WITH ONE GOOD HAYMAKER--
--FEELS KE I BROKE OME OF THE CROCIRCUITRY N MY HAND!
THOUGHT TIN MAN WAS HULK'S FRIEND--
--BUT HULK HAS NO FRIENDS!
SORRY YOU FEEL THAT WAY, BIG FELLA.
AND THE WAY YOU'RE ACTING IS JUST MAKING THINGS WORSE...
I TAKE THIS OPPORTUNITY TO REITERATE MY PREVIOUS OFFER, HULK. THESE HOSTILITIES MUST END.
RED FACE TALKS WITH STRANGE VOICE! USES STRANGE WORDS!
GET AWAY FROM HULK--!
YOUR LIMITED INTELLIGENCE BETRAYS YOU.
CLEARLY, YOU HAVE FORGOTTEN HOW I CAN ALTER MY DENSITY AT WILL...

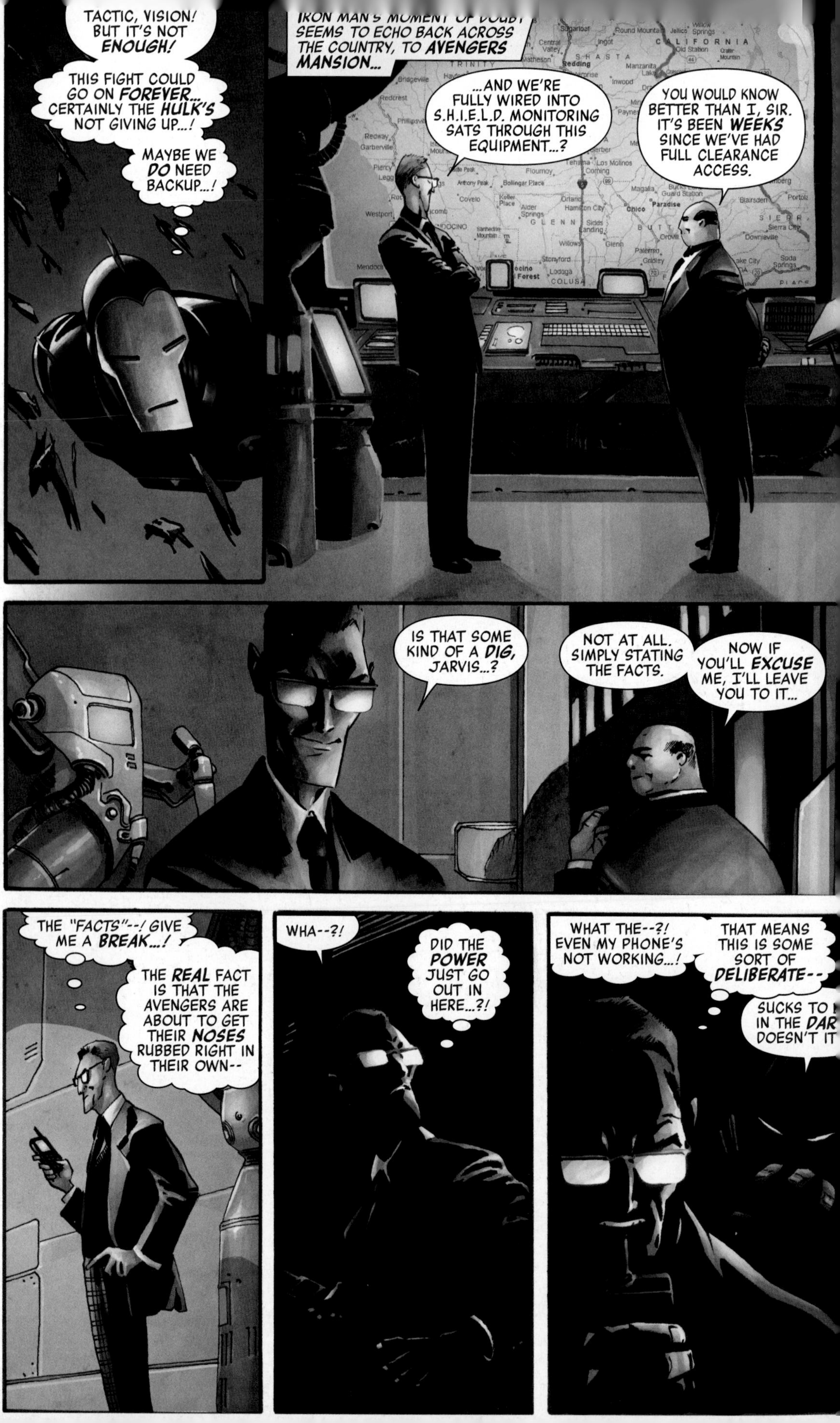
TACTIC, VISION! BUT IT'S NOT ENOUGH!
THIS FIGHT COULD GO ON FOREVER... CERTAINLY THE HULK'S NOT GIVING UP...!
MAYBE WE DO NEED BACKUP...!
IRON MAN'S MOMENT OF DOUBT SEEMS TO ECHO BACK ACROSS THE COUNTRY, TO AVENGERS MANSION...
...AND WE'RE FULLY WIRED INTO S.H.I.E.L.D. MONITORING SATS THROUGH THIS EQUIPMENT...?
YOU WOULD KNOW BETTER THAN I, SIR. IT'S BEEN WEEKS SINCE WE'VE HAD FULL CLEARANCE ACCESS.
IS THAT SOME KIND OF A DIG, JARVIS...?
NOT AT ALL. SIMPLY STATING THE FACTS.
NOW IF YOU'LL EXCUSE ME, I'LL LEAVE YOU TO IT...
THE "FACTS"--! GIVE ME A BREAK...!
THE REAL FACT IS THAT THE AVENGERS ARE ABOUT TO GET THEIR NOSES RUBBED RIGHT IN THEIR OWN--
WHA--?!
DID THE POWER JUST GO OUT IN HERE...?!
WHAT THE--?! EVEN MY PHONE'S NOT WORKING...!
THAT MEANS THIS IS SOME SORT OF DELIBERATE--
SUCKS TO
IN THE DAR
DOESN'T IT

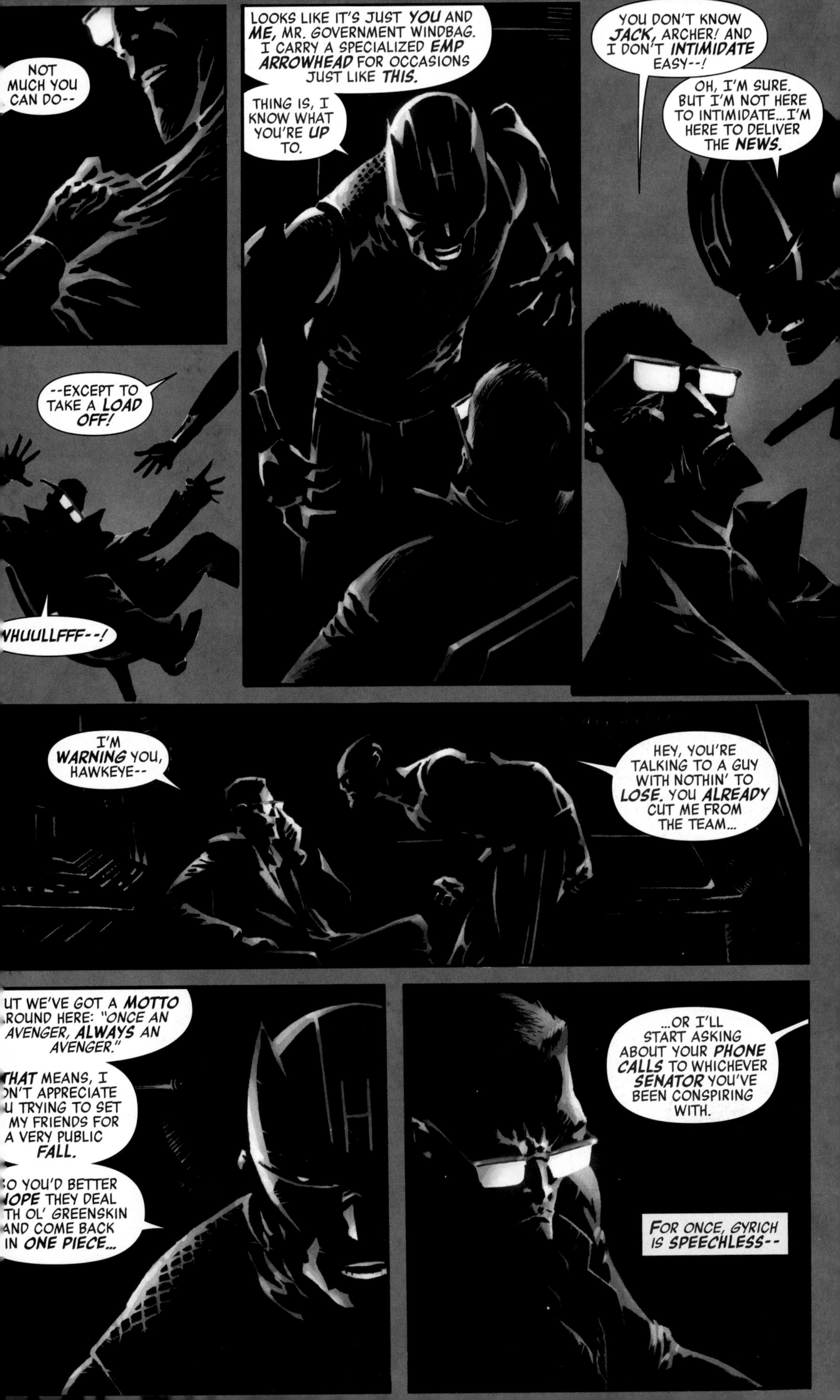
NOT MUCH YOU CAN DO--
LOOKS LIKE IT'S JUST YOU AND ME, MR. GOVERNMENT WINDBAG. I CARRY A SPECIALIZED EMP ARROWHEAD FOR OCCASIONS JUST LIKE THIS.
THING IS, I KNOW WHAT YOU'RE UP TO.
YOU DON'T KNOW JACK, ARCHER! AND I DON'T INTIMIDATE EASY--!
OH, I'M SURE. BUT I'M NOT HERE TO INTIMIDATE...I'M HERE TO DELIVER THE NEWS.
--EXCEPT TO TAKE A LOAD OFF!
WHUULLFFF--!
I'M WARNING YOU, HAWKEYE--
HEY, YOU'RE TALKING TO A GUY WITH NOTHIN' TO LOSE. YOU ALREADY CUT ME FROM THE TEAM...
UT WE'VE GOT A MOTTO ROUND HERE: "ONCE AN AVENGER, ALWAYS AN AVENGER."
THAT MEANS, I ON'T APPRECIATE U TRYING TO SET MY FRIENDS FOR A VERY PUBLIC FALL.
O YOU'D BETTER HOPE THEY DEAL TH OL' GREENSKIN AND COME BACK IN ONE PIECE...
...OR I'LL START ASKING ABOUT YOUR PHONE CALLS TO WHICHEVER SENATOR YOU'VE BEEN CONSPIRING WITH.
FOR ONCE, GYRICH IS SPEECHLESS--

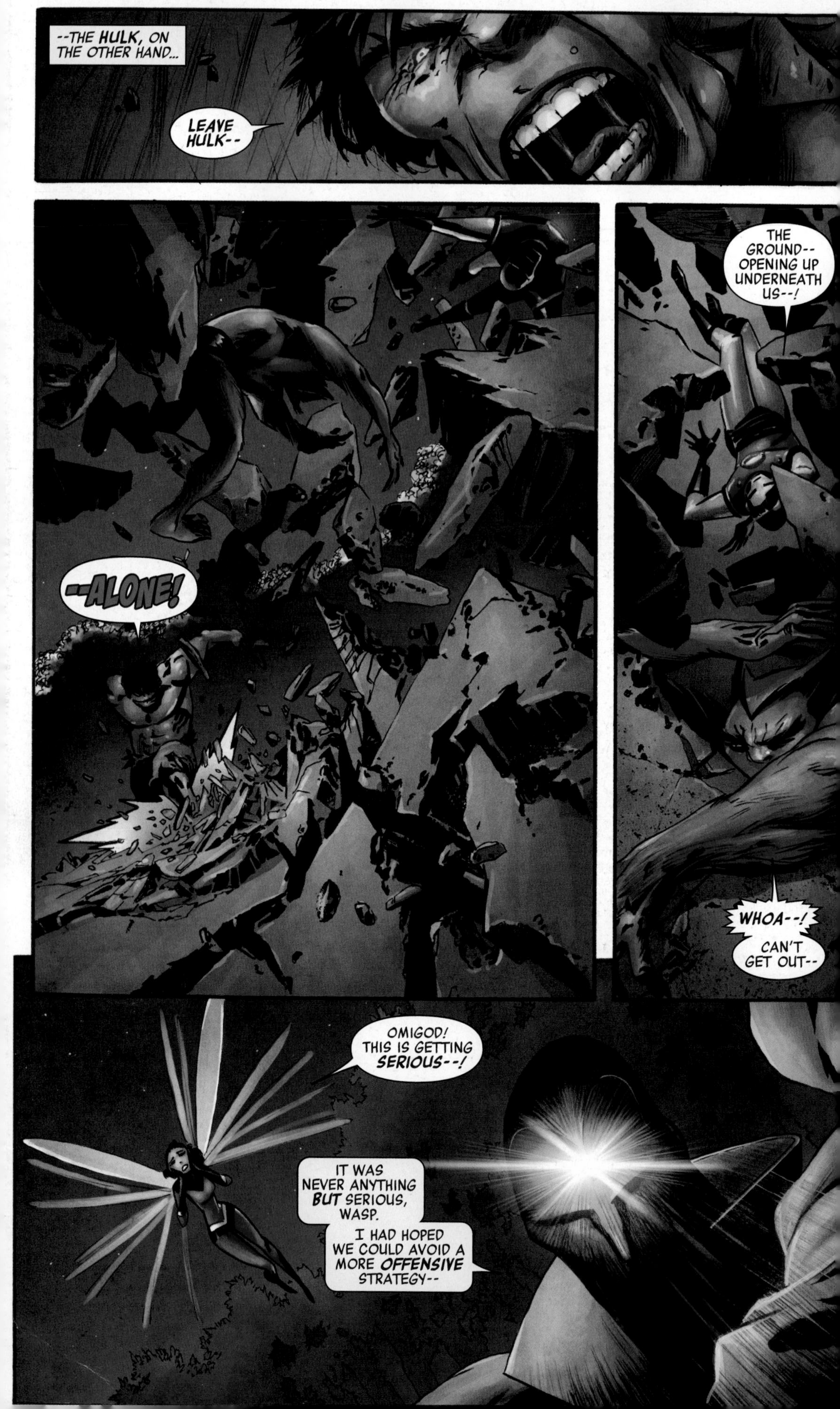

--THE **HULK**, ON THE OTHER HAND...
LEAVE HULK--
--ALONE!
THE GROUND--OPENING UP UNDERNEATH US--!
WHOA--! CAN'T GET OUT--
OMIGOD! THIS IS GETTING **SERIOUS**--!
IT WAS NEVER ANYTHING **BUT** SERIOUS, WASP.
I HAD HOPED WE COULD AVOID A MORE **OFFENSIVE** STRATEGY--

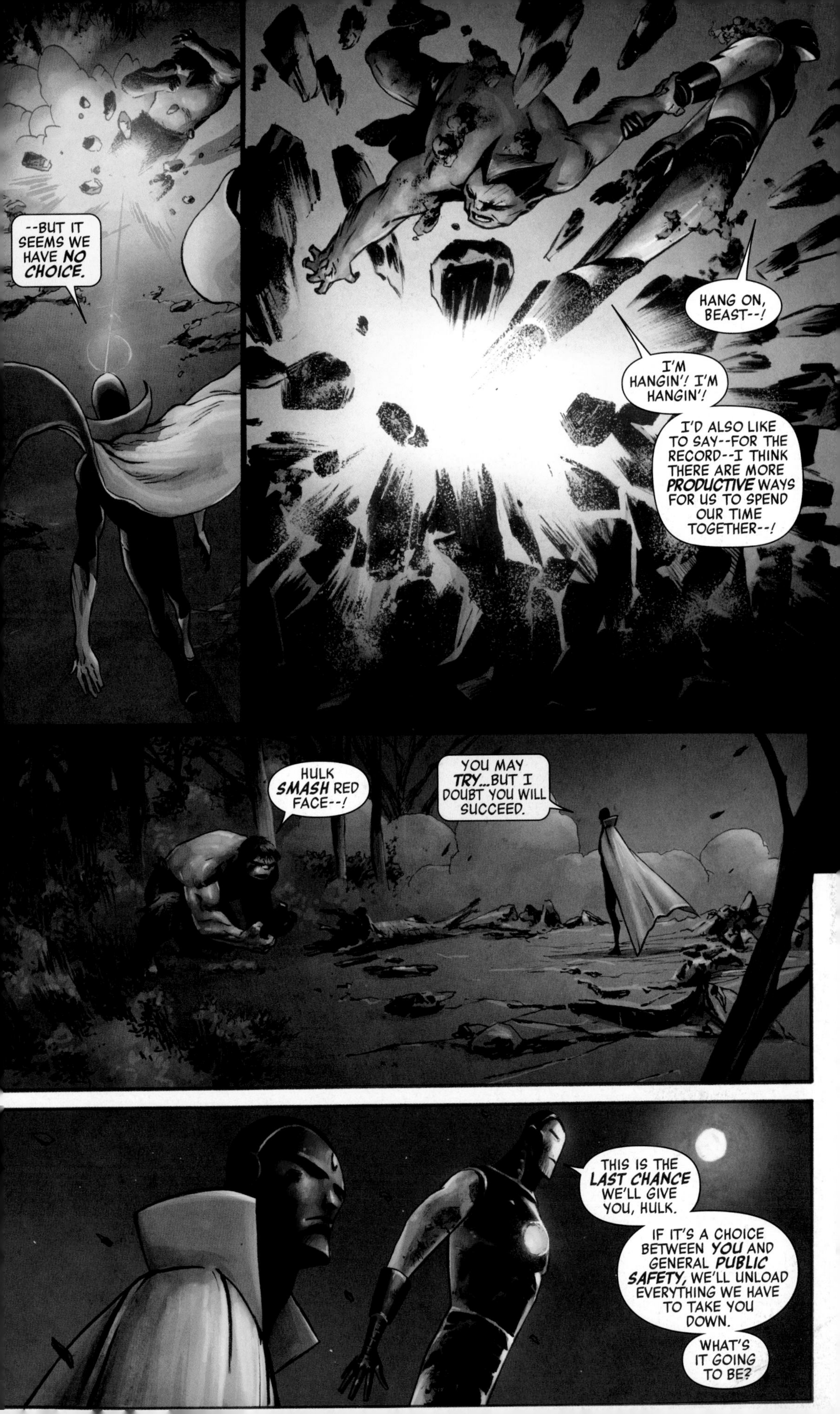
--BUT IT SEEMS WE HAVE NO CHOICE.
HANG ON, BEAST--!
I'M HANGIN'! I'M HANGIN'!
I'D ALSO LIKE TO SAY--FOR THE RECORD--I THINK THERE ARE MORE PRODUCTIVE WAYS FOR US TO SPEND OUR TIME TOGETHER--!
HULK SMASH RED FACE--!
YOU MAY TRY...BUT I DOUBT YOU WILL SUCCEED.
THIS IS THE LAST CHANCE WE'LL GIVE YOU, HULK.
IF IT'S A CHOICE BETWEEN YOU AND GENERAL PUBLIC SAFETY, WE'LL UNLOAD EVERYTHING WE HAVE TO TAKE YOU DOWN.
WHAT'S IT GOING TO BE?

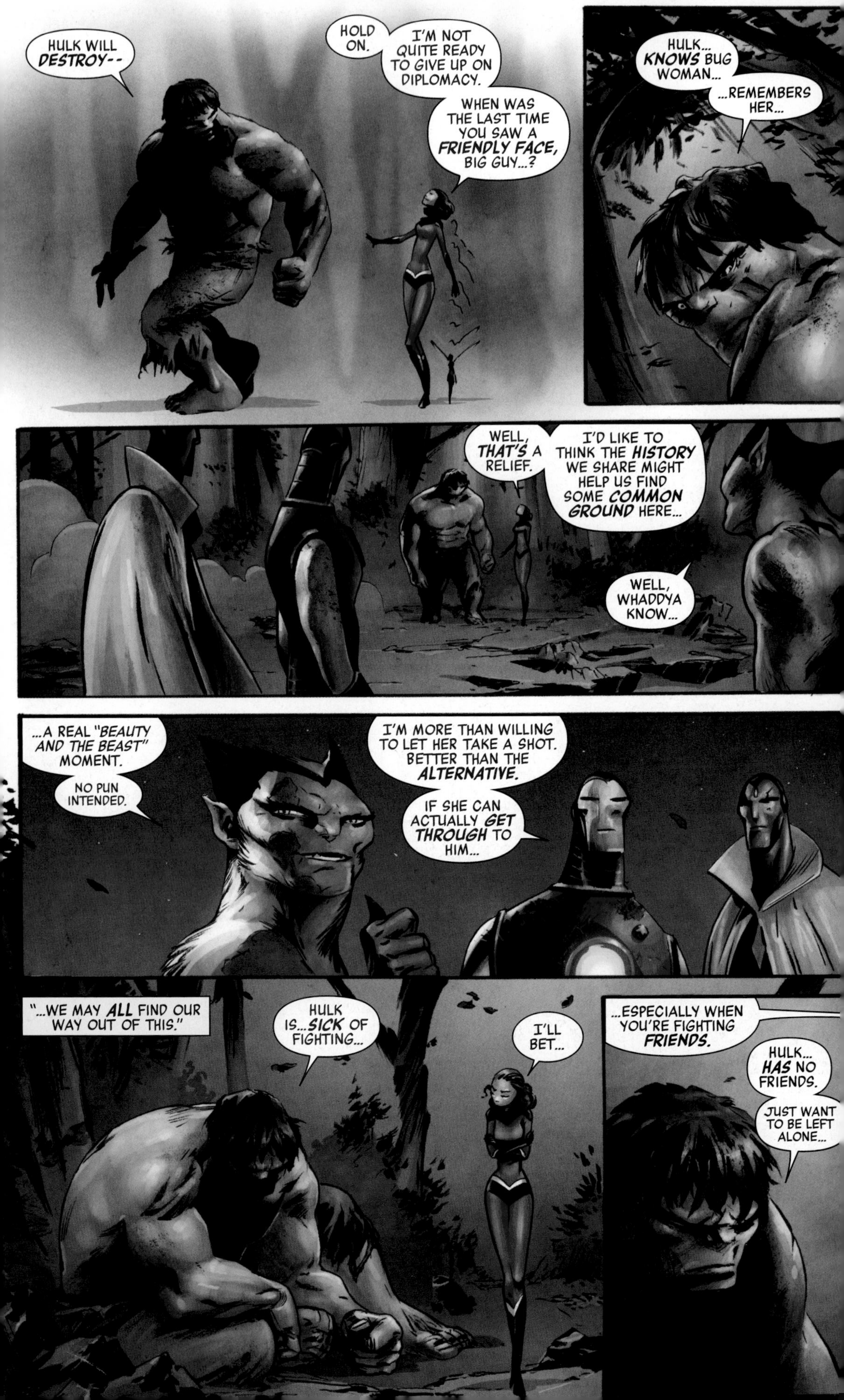
HULK WILL DESTROY--
HOLD ON.
I'M NOT QUITE READY TO GIVE UP ON DIPLOMACY.
WHEN WAS THE LAST TIME YOU SAW A FRIENDLY FACE, BIG GUY...?
HULK... KNOWS BUG WOMAN...
...REMEMBERS HER...
WELL, THAT'S A RELIEF.
I'D LIKE TO THINK THE HISTORY WE SHARE MIGHT HELP US FIND SOME COMMON GROUND HERE...
WELL, WHADDYA KNOW...
...A REAL "BEAUTY AND THE BEAST" MOMENT.
NO PUN INTENDED.
I'M MORE THAN WILLING TO LET HER TAKE A SHOT. BETTER THAN THE ALTERNATIVE.
IF SHE CAN ACTUALLY GET THROUGH TO HIM...
"...WE MAY ALL FIND OUR WAY OUT OF THIS."
HULK IS...SICK OF FIGHTING...
I'LL BET...
...ESPECIALLY WHEN YOU'RE FIGHTING FRIENDS.
HULK... HAS NO FRIENDS.
JUST WANT TO BE LEFT ALONE...

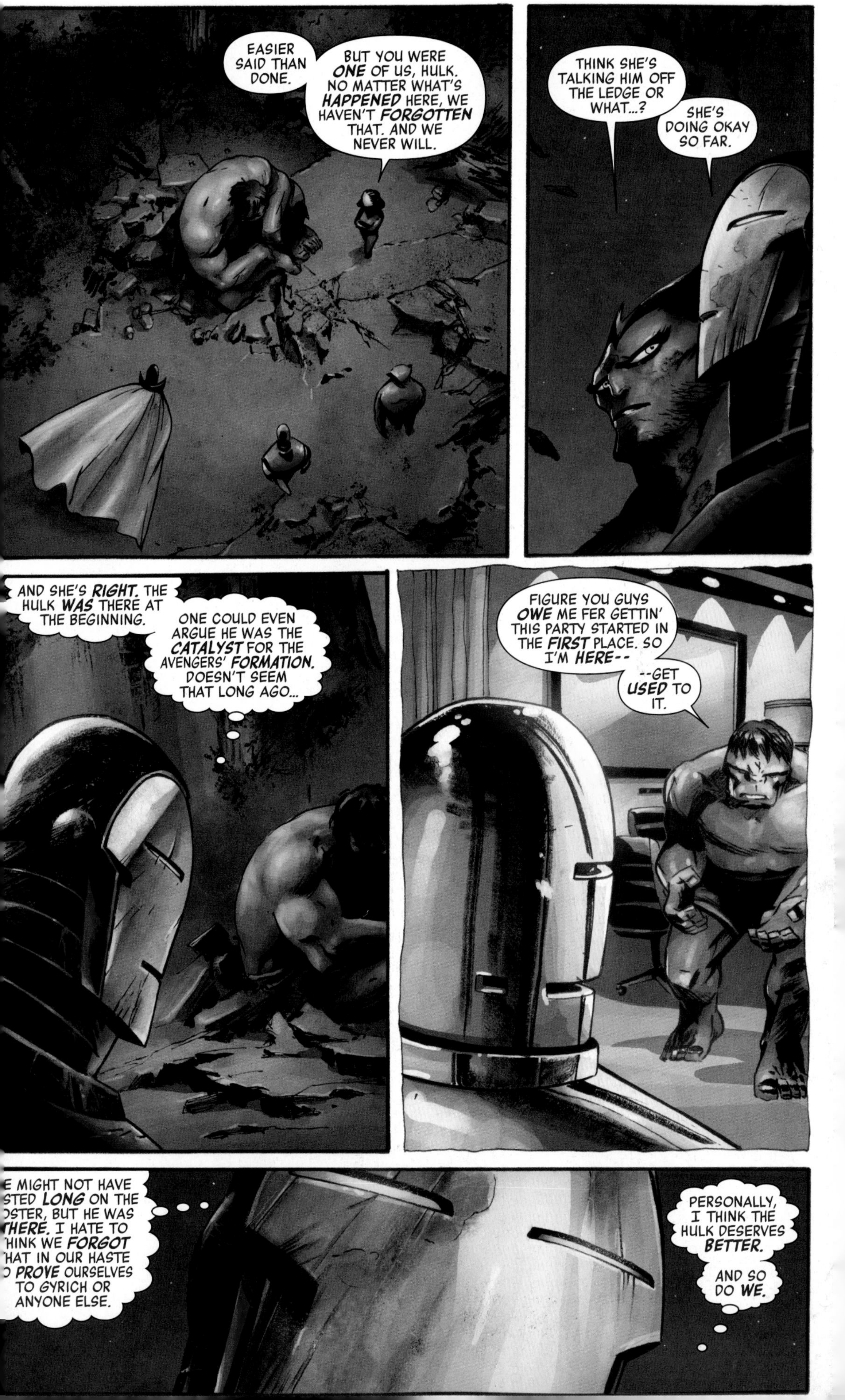
EASIER SAID THAN DONE.
BUT YOU WERE ONE OF US, HULK. NO MATTER WHAT'S HAPPENED HERE, WE HAVEN'T FORGOTTEN THAT. AND WE NEVER WILL.
THINK SHE'S TALKING HIM OFF THE LEDGE OR WHAT...?
SHE'S DOING OKAY SO FAR.
AND SHE'S RIGHT. THE HULK WAS THERE AT THE BEGINNING.
ONE COULD EVEN ARGUE HE WAS THE CATALYST FOR THE AVENGERS' FORMATION. DOESN'T SEEM THAT LONG AGO...
FIGURE YOU GUYS OWE ME FER GETTIN' THIS PARTY STARTED IN THE FIRST PLACE. SO I'M HERE--
--GET USED TO IT.
E MIGHT NOT HAVE STED LONG ON THE OSTER, BUT HE WAS THERE. I HATE TO HINK WE FORGOT THAT IN OUR HASTE PROVE OURSELVES TO GYRICH OR ANYONE ELSE.
PERSONALLY, I THINK THE HULK DESERVES BETTER.
AND SO DO WE.

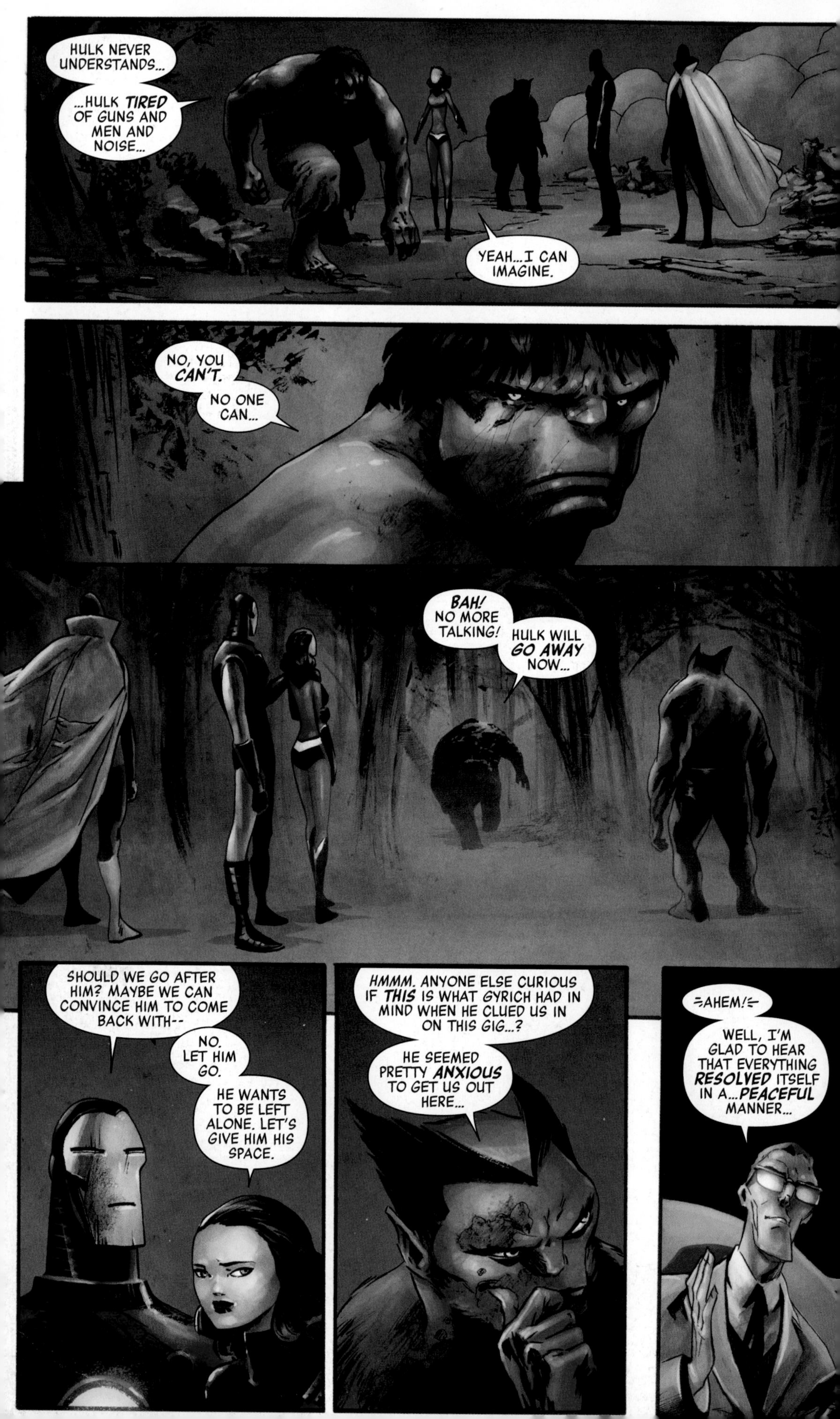
HULK NEVER UNDERSTANDS...
...HULK TIRED OF GUNS AND MEN AND NOISE...
YEAH...I CAN IMAGINE.
NO, YOU CAN'T.
NO ONE CAN...
BAH! NO MORE TALKING!
HULK WILL GO AWAY NOW...
SHOULD WE GO AFTER HIM? MAYBE WE CAN CONVINCE HIM TO COME BACK WITH--
NO. LET HIM GO.
HE WANTS TO BE LEFT ALONE. LET'S GIVE HIM HIS SPACE.
HMMM. ANYONE ELSE CURIOUS IF THIS IS WHAT GYRICH HAD IN MIND WHEN HE CLUED US IN ON THIS GIG...?
HE SEEMED PRETTY ANXIOUS TO GET US OUT HERE...
AHEM!
WELL, I'M GLAD TO HEAR THAT EVERYTHING RESOLVED ITSELF IN A...PEACEFUL MANNER...

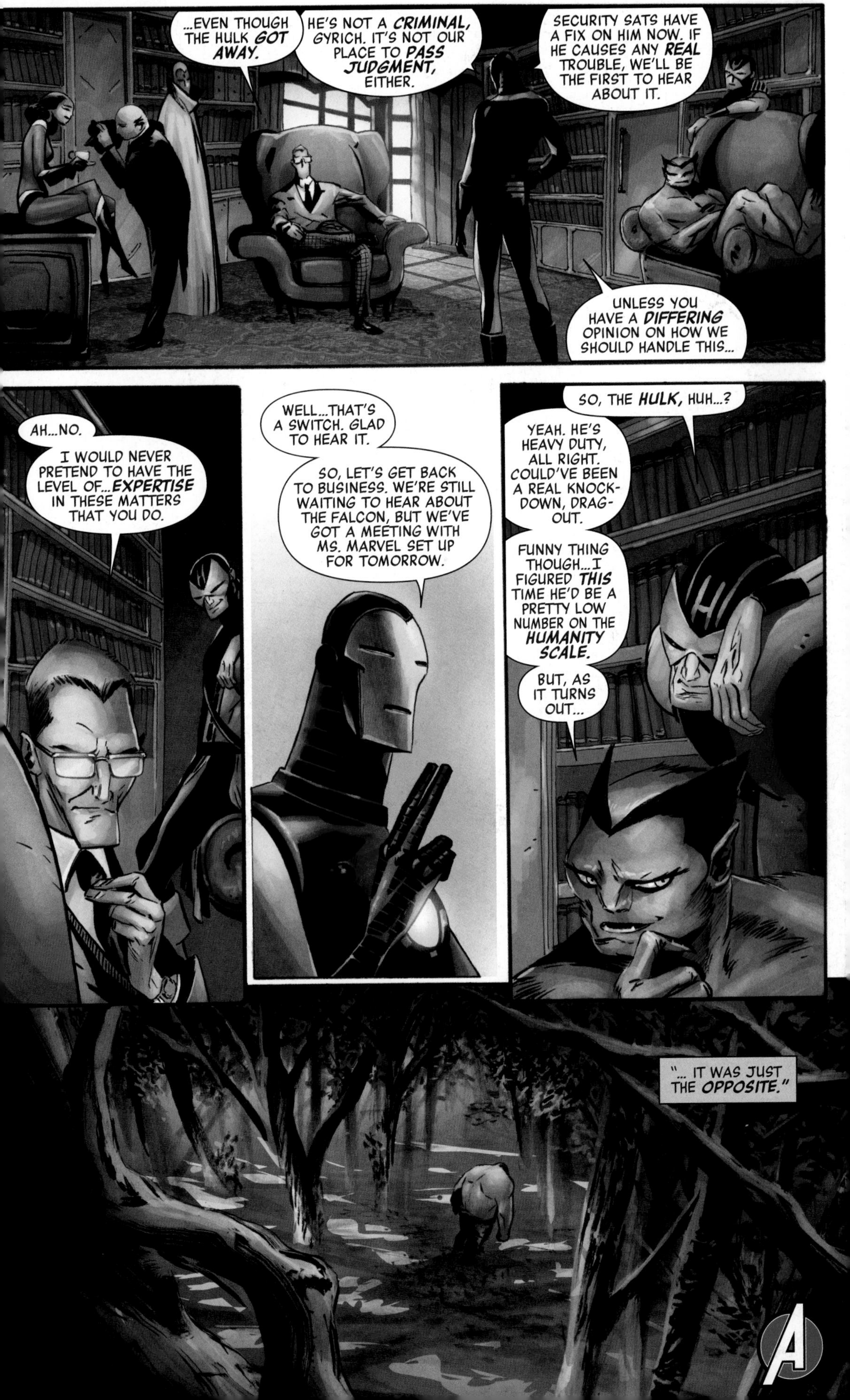
...EVEN THOUGH THE HULK GOT AWAY.
HE'S NOT A CRIMINAL, GYRICH. IT'S NOT OUR PLACE TO PASS JUDGMENT, EITHER.
SECURITY SATS HAVE A FIX ON HIM NOW. IF HE CAUSES ANY REAL TROUBLE, WE'LL BE THE FIRST TO HEAR ABOUT IT.
UNLESS YOU HAVE A DIFFERING OPINION ON HOW WE SHOULD HANDLE THIS...
AH...NO.
I WOULD NEVER PRETEND TO HAVE THE LEVEL OF...EXPERTISE IN THESE MATTERS THAT YOU DO.
WELL...THAT'S A SWITCH. GLAD TO HEAR IT.
SO, LET'S GET BACK TO BUSINESS. WE'RE STILL WAITING TO HEAR ABOUT THE FALCON, BUT WE'VE GOT A MEETING WITH MS. MARVEL SET UP FOR TOMORROW.
SO, THE HULK, HUH...?
YEAH. HE'S HEAVY DUTY, ALL RIGHT. COULD'VE BEEN A REAL KNOCK-DOWN, DRAG-OUT.
FUNNY THING THOUGH...I FIGURED THIS TIME HE'D BE A PRETTY LOW NUMBER ON THE HUMANITY SCALE.
BUT, AS IT TURNS OUT...
"... IT WAS JUST THE OPPOSITE."

#3

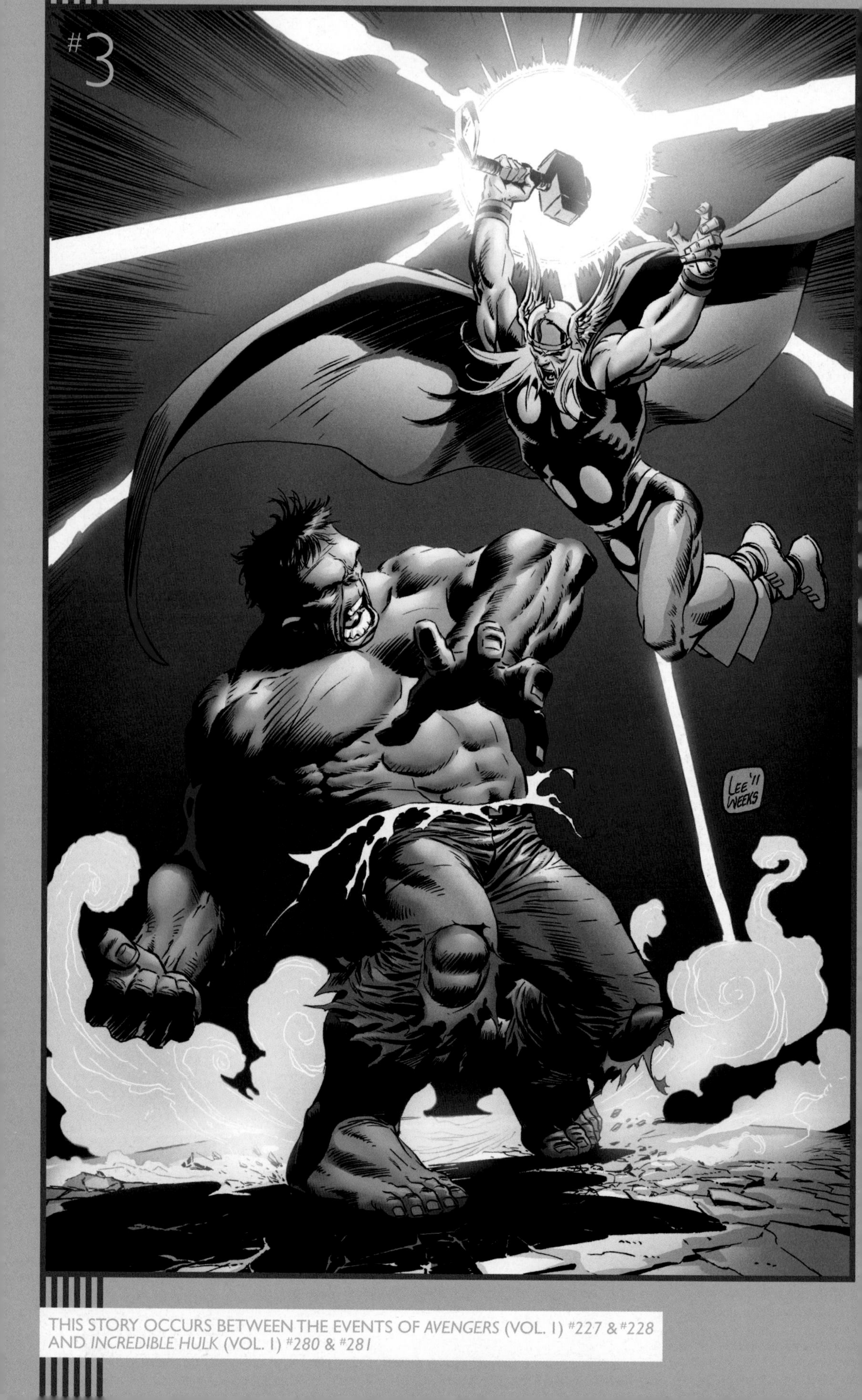
LEE '11
WEEKS

THIS STORY OCCURS BETWEEN THE EVENTS OF *AVENGERS* (VOL. 1) #227 & #228 AND *INCREDIBLE HULK* (VOL. 1) #280 & #281

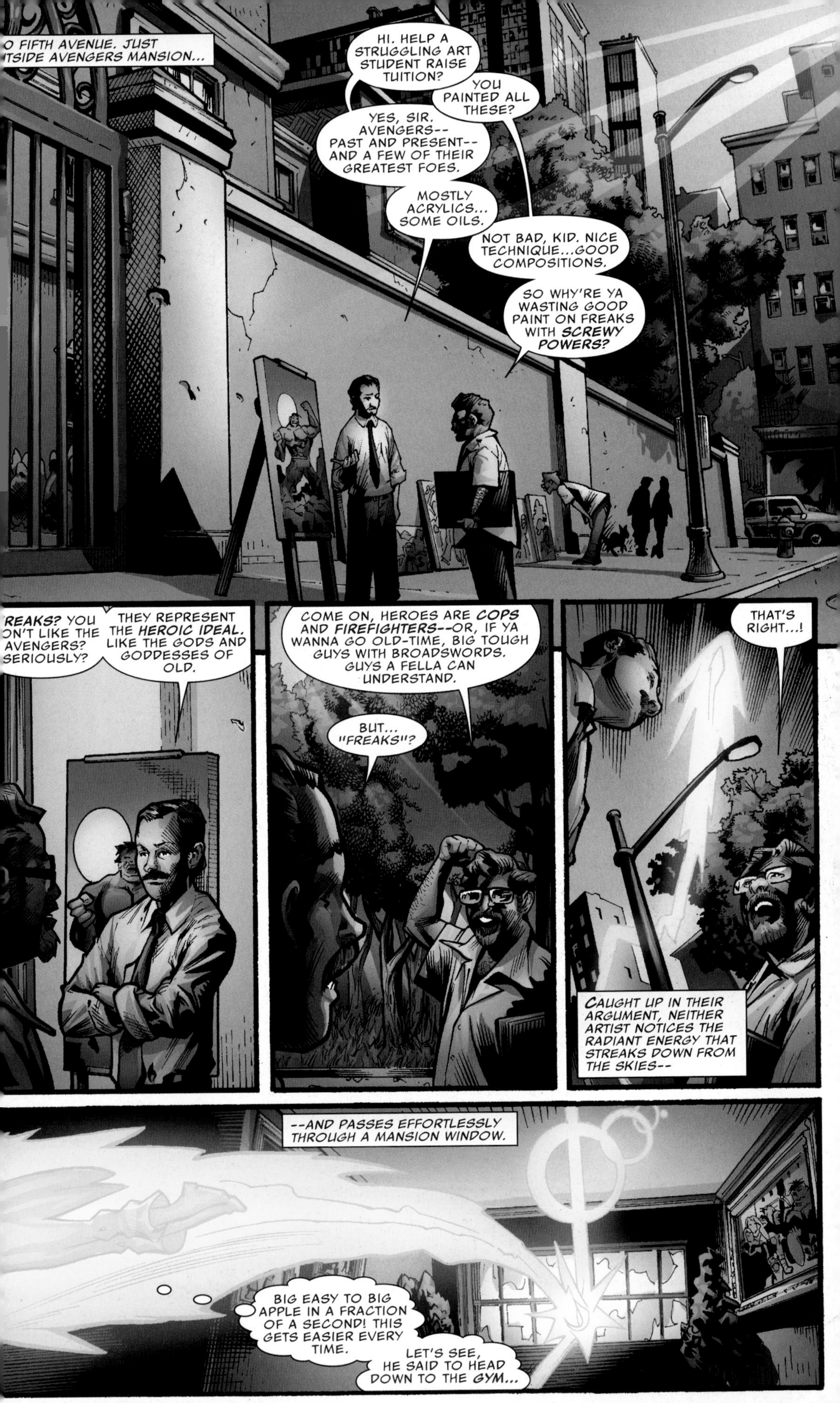
O FIFTH AVENUE. JUST
TSIDE AVENGERS MANSION...
HI. HELP A STRUGGLING ART STUDENT RAISE TUITION?
YOU PAINTED ALL THESE?
YES, SIR. AVENGERS-- PAST AND PRESENT-- AND A FEW OF THEIR GREATEST FOES.
MOSTLY ACRYLICS... SOME OILS.
NOT BAD, KID. NICE TECHNIQUE...GOOD COMPOSITIONS.
SO WHY'RE YA WASTING GOOD PAINT ON FREAKS WITH SCREWY POWERS?
REAKS? YOU ON'T LIKE THE AVENGERS? SERIOUSLY?
THEY REPRESENT THE HEROIC IDEAL. LIKE THE GODS AND GODDESSES OF OLD.
COME ON, HEROES ARE COPS AND FIREFIGHTERS--OR, IF YA WANNA GO OLD-TIME, BIG TOUGH GUYS WITH BROADSWORDS. GUYS A FELLA CAN UNDERSTAND.
BUT... "FREAKS"?
THAT'S RIGHT...!
CAUGHT UP IN THEIR ARGUMENT, NEITHER ARTIST NOTICES THE RADIANT ENERGY THAT STREAKS DOWN FROM THE SKIES--
--AND PASSES EFFORTLESSLY THROUGH A MANSION WINDOW.
BIG EASY TO BIG APPLE IN A FRACTION OF A SECOND! THIS GETS EASIER EVERY TIME.
LET'S SEE, HE SAID TO HEAD DOWN TO THE GYM...

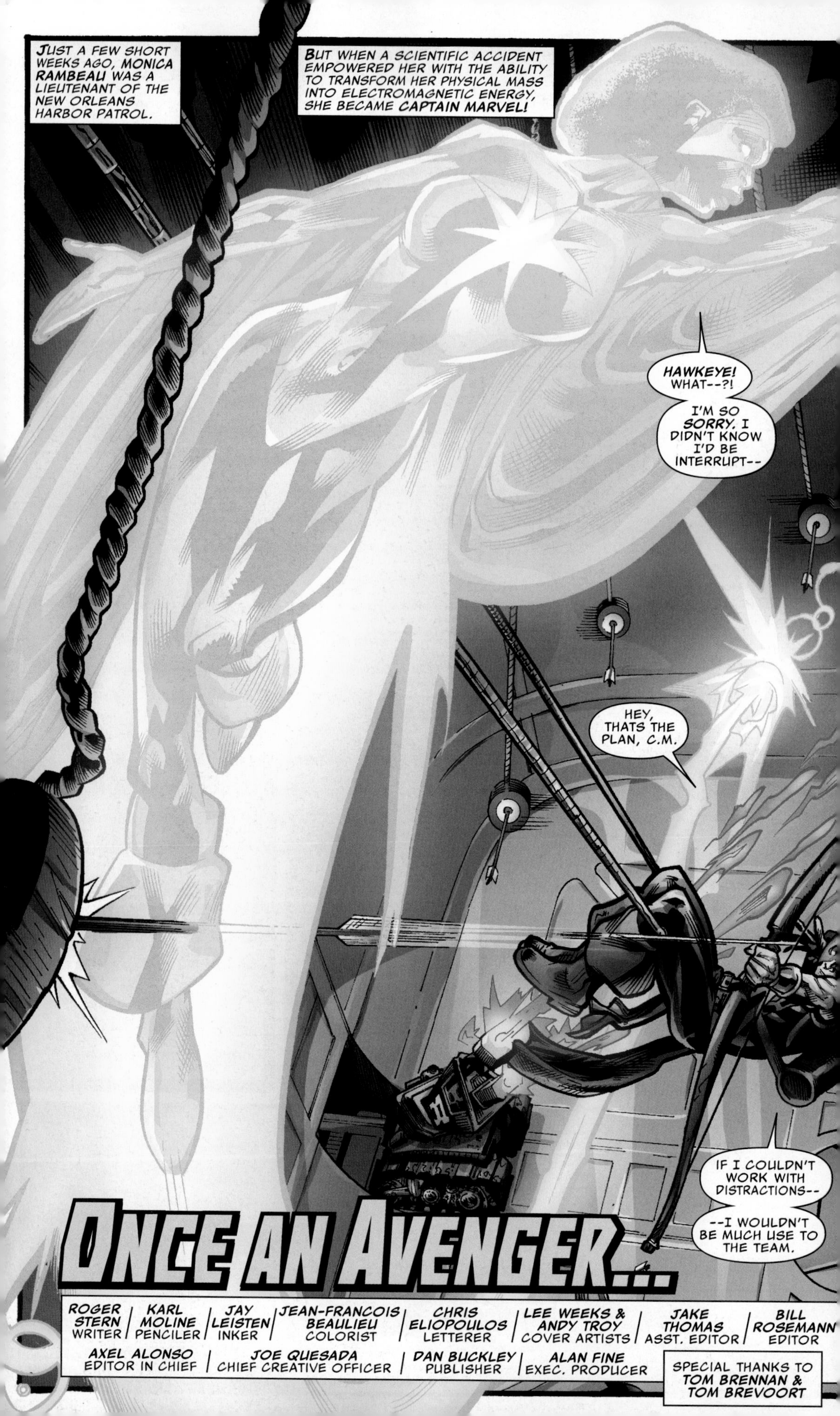
JUST A FEW SHORT WEEKS AGO, MONICA RAMBEAU WAS A LIEUTENANT OF THE NEW ORLEANS HARBOR PATROL.
BUT WHEN A SCIENTIFIC ACCIDENT EMPOWERED HER WITH THE ABILITY TO TRANSFORM HER PHYSICAL MASS INTO ELECTROMAGNETIC ENERGY, SHE BECAME CAPTAIN MARVEL!
HAWKEYE! WHAT--?!
I'M SO SORRY. I DIDN'T KNOW I'D BE INTERRUPT--
HEY, THATS THE PLAN, C.M.
IF I COULDN'T WORK WITH DISTRACTIONS--
--I WOULDN'T BE MUCH USE TO THE TEAM.
ONCE AN AVENGER...
ROGER STERN WRITER
KARL MOLINE PENCILER
JAY LEISTEN INKER
JEAN-FRANCOIS BEAULIEU COLORIST
CHRIS ELIOPOULOS LETTERER
LEE WEEKS & ANDY TROY COVER ARTISTS
JAKE THOMAS ASST. EDITOR
BILL ROSEMANN EDITOR
AXEL ALONSO EDITOR IN CHIEF
JOE QUESADA CHIEF CREATIVE OFFICER
DAN BUCKLEY PUBLISHER
ALAN FINE EXEC. PRODUCER
SPECIAL THANKS TO TOM BRENNAN & TOM BREVOORT

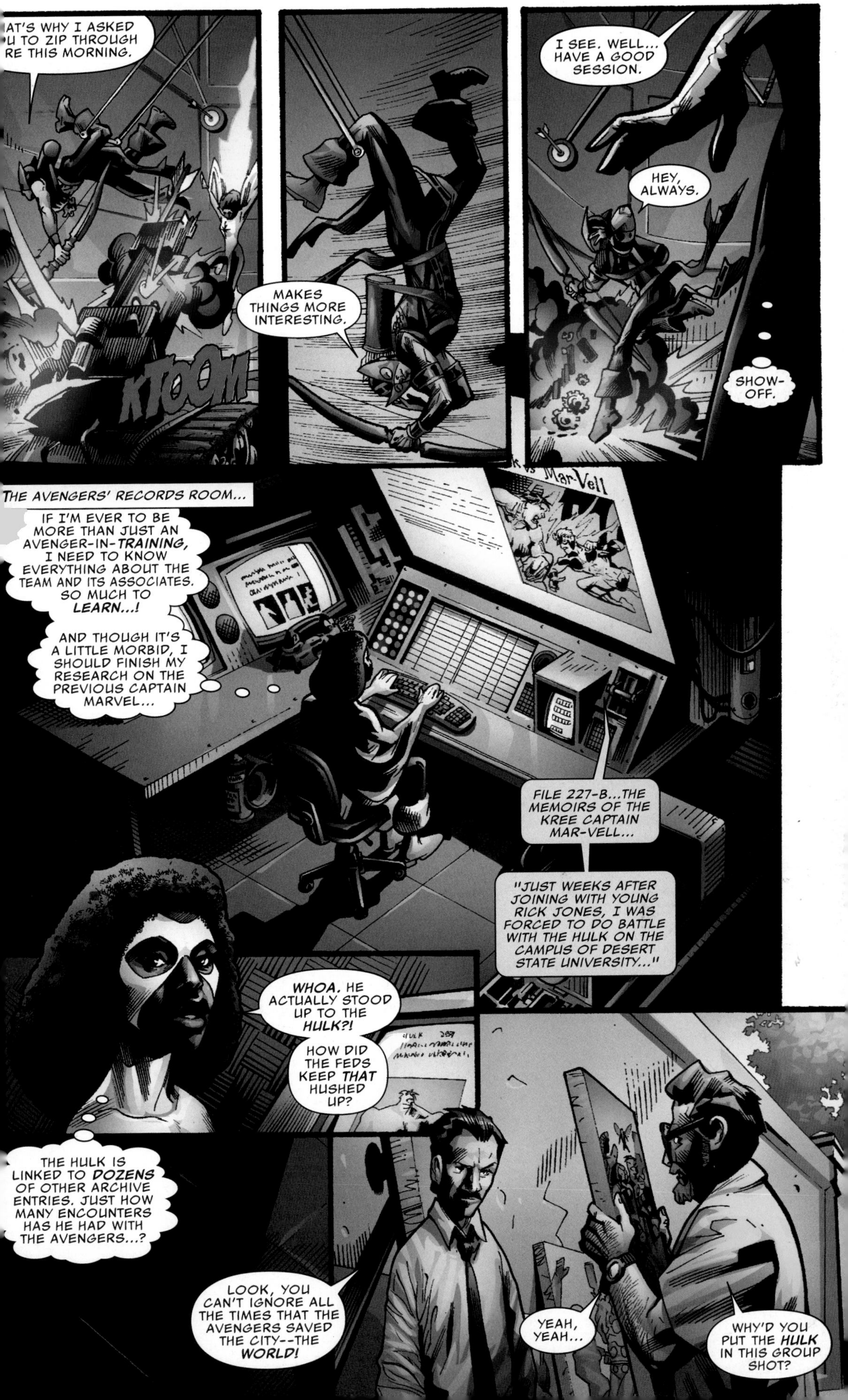
AT'S WHY I ASKED
U TO ZIP THROUGH
RE THIS MORNING.
KTOOM
MAKES THINGS MORE INTERESTING.
I SEE. WELL... HAVE A GOOD SESSION.
HEY, ALWAYS.
SHOW-OFF.
THE AVENGERS' RECORDS ROOM...
IF I'M EVER TO BE MORE THAN JUST AN AVENGER-IN-TRAINING, I NEED TO KNOW EVERYTHING ABOUT THE TEAM AND ITS ASSOCIATES. SO MUCH TO LEARN...!
AND THOUGH IT'S A LITTLE MORBID, I SHOULD FINISH MY RESEARCH ON THE PREVIOUS CAPTAIN MARVEL...
Mar-Vell
FILE 227-B...THE MEMOIRS OF THE KREE CAPTAIN MAR-VELL...
"JUST WEEKS AFTER JOINING WITH YOUNG RICK JONES, I WAS FORCED TO DO BATTLE WITH THE HULK ON THE CAMPUS OF DESERT STATE UNIVERSITY..."
WHOA. HE ACTUALLY STOOD UP TO THE HULK?!
HOW DID THE FEDS KEEP THAT HUSHED UP?
THE HULK IS LINKED TO DOZENS OF OTHER ARCHIVE ENTRIES. JUST HOW MANY ENCOUNTERS HAS HE HAD WITH THE AVENGERS...?
LOOK, YOU CAN'T IGNORE ALL THE TIMES THAT THE AVENGERS SAVED THE CITY--THE WORLD!
YEAH, YEAH...
WHY'D YOU PUT THE HULK IN THIS GROUP SHOT?

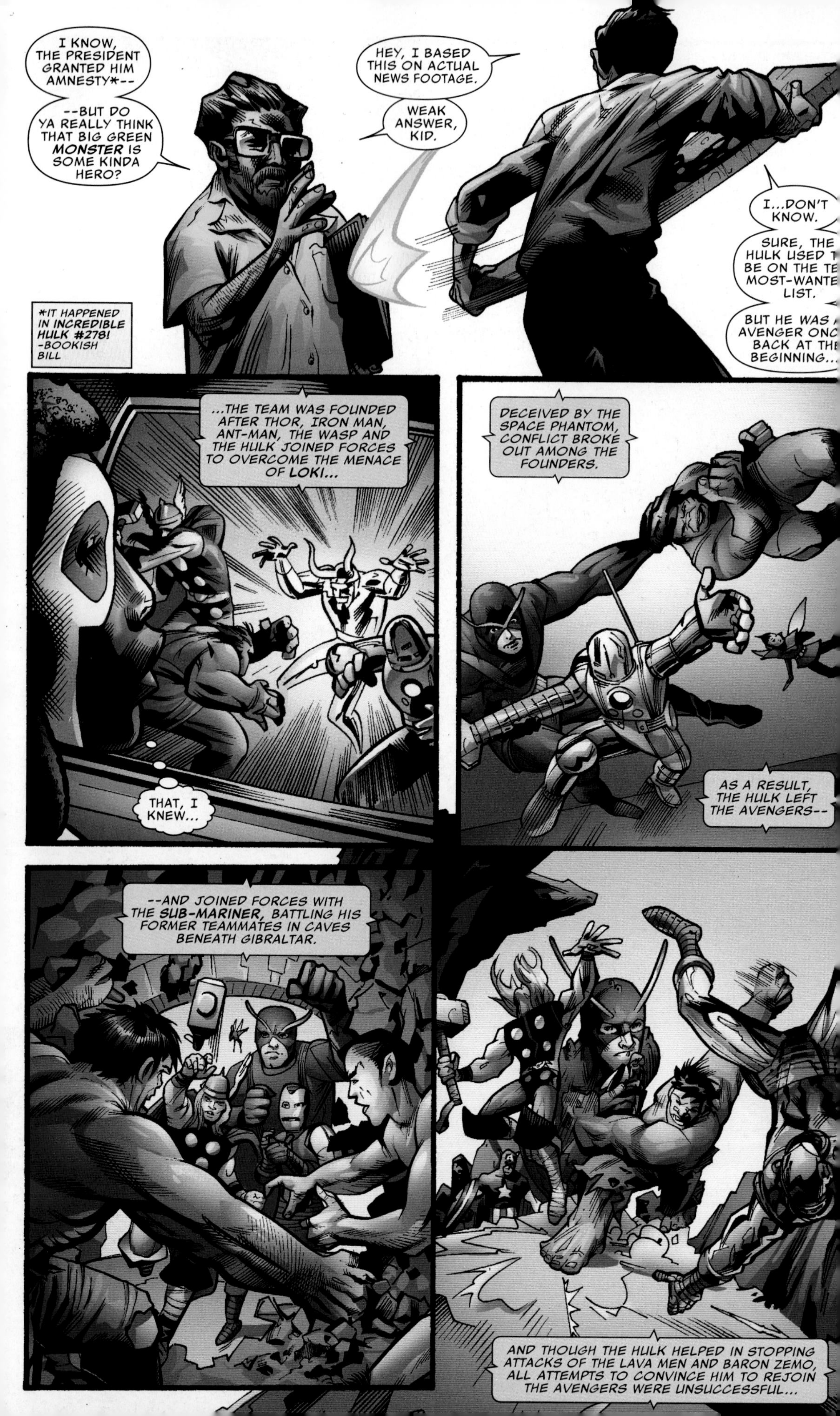
I KNOW, THE PRESIDENT GRANTED HIM AMNESTY*--
--BUT DO YA REALLY THINK THAT BIG GREEN MONSTER IS SOME KINDA HERO?
HEY, I BASED THIS ON ACTUAL NEWS FOOTAGE.
WEAK ANSWER, KID.
I...DON'T KNOW.
SURE, THE HULK USED T BE ON THE TE MOST-WANTE LIST.
BUT HE WAS AVENGER ONC BACK AT TH BEGINNING...
*IT HAPPENED IN INCREDIBLE HULK #278! -BOOKISH BILL
...THE TEAM WAS FOUNDED AFTER THOR, IRON MAN, ANT-MAN, THE WASP AND THE HULK JOINED FORCES TO OVERCOME THE MENACE OF LOKI...
THAT, I KNEW...
DECEIVED BY THE SPACE PHANTOM, CONFLICT BROKE OUT AMONG THE FOUNDERS.
AS A RESULT, THE HULK LEFT THE AVENGERS--
--AND JOINED FORCES WITH THE SUB-MARINER, BATTLING HIS FORMER TEAMMATES IN CAVES BENEATH GIBRALTAR.
AND THOUGH THE HULK HELPED IN STOPPING ATTACKS OF THE LAVA MEN AND BARON ZEMO, ALL ATTEMPTS TO CONVINCE HIM TO REJOIN THE AVENGERS WERE UNSUCCESSFUL...

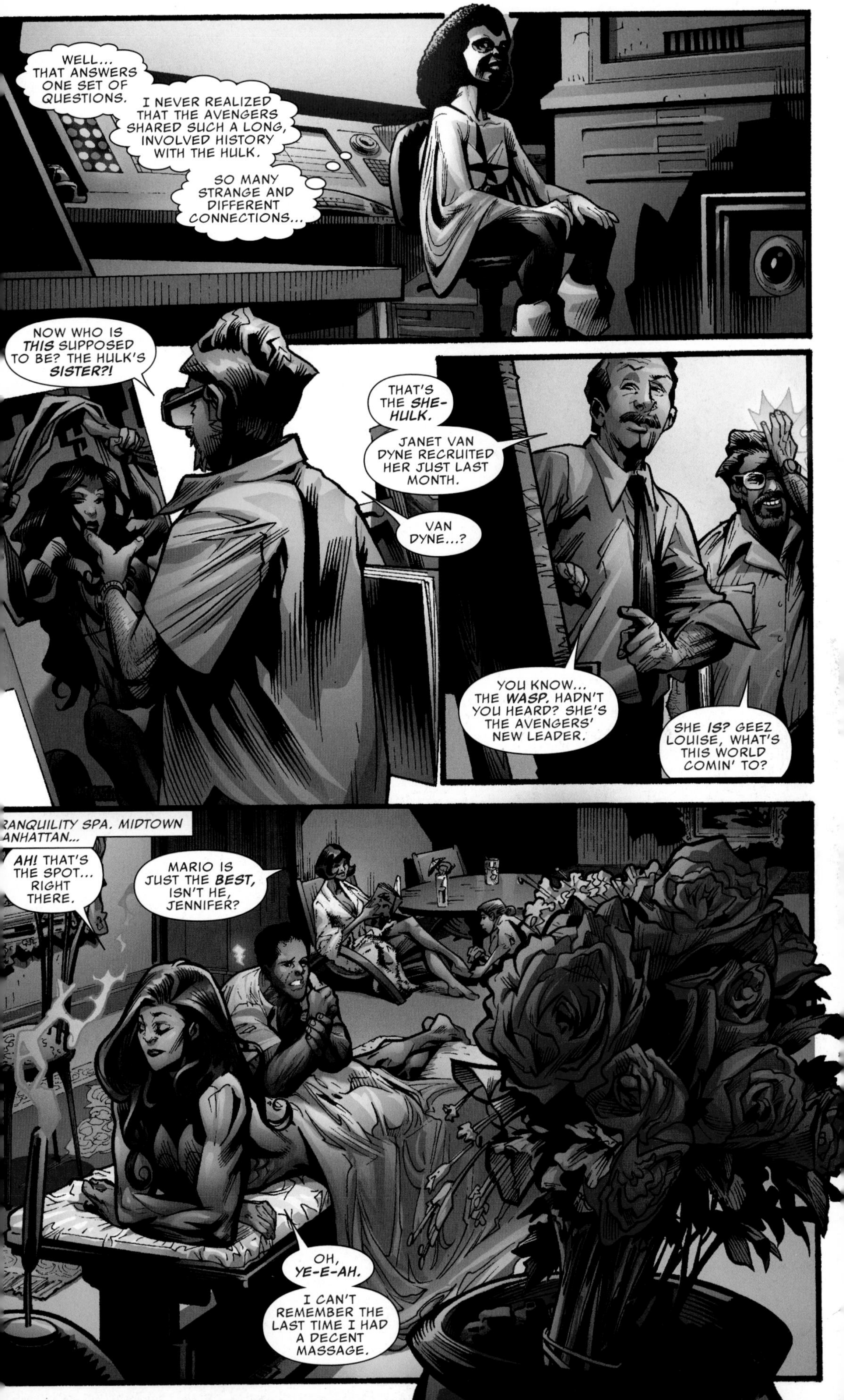

WELL... THAT ANSWERS ONE SET OF QUESTIONS.
I NEVER REALIZED THAT THE AVENGERS SHARED SUCH A LONG, INVOLVED HISTORY WITH THE HULK.
SO MANY STRANGE AND DIFFERENT CONNECTIONS...
NOW WHO IS THIS SUPPOSED TO BE? THE HULK'S SISTER?!
THAT'S THE SHE-HULK.
JANET VAN DYNE RECRUITED HER JUST LAST MONTH.
VAN DYNE...?
YOU KNOW... THE WASP. HADN'T YOU HEARD? SHE'S THE AVENGERS' NEW LEADER.
SHE IS? GEEZ LOUISE, WHAT'S THIS WORLD COMIN' TO?
RANQUILITY SPA. MIDTOWN ANHATTAN...
AH! THAT'S THE SPOT... RIGHT THERE.
MARIO IS JUST THE BEST, ISN'T HE, JENNIFER?
OH, YE-E-AH.
I CAN'T REMEMBER THE LAST TIME I HAD A DECENT MASSAGE.

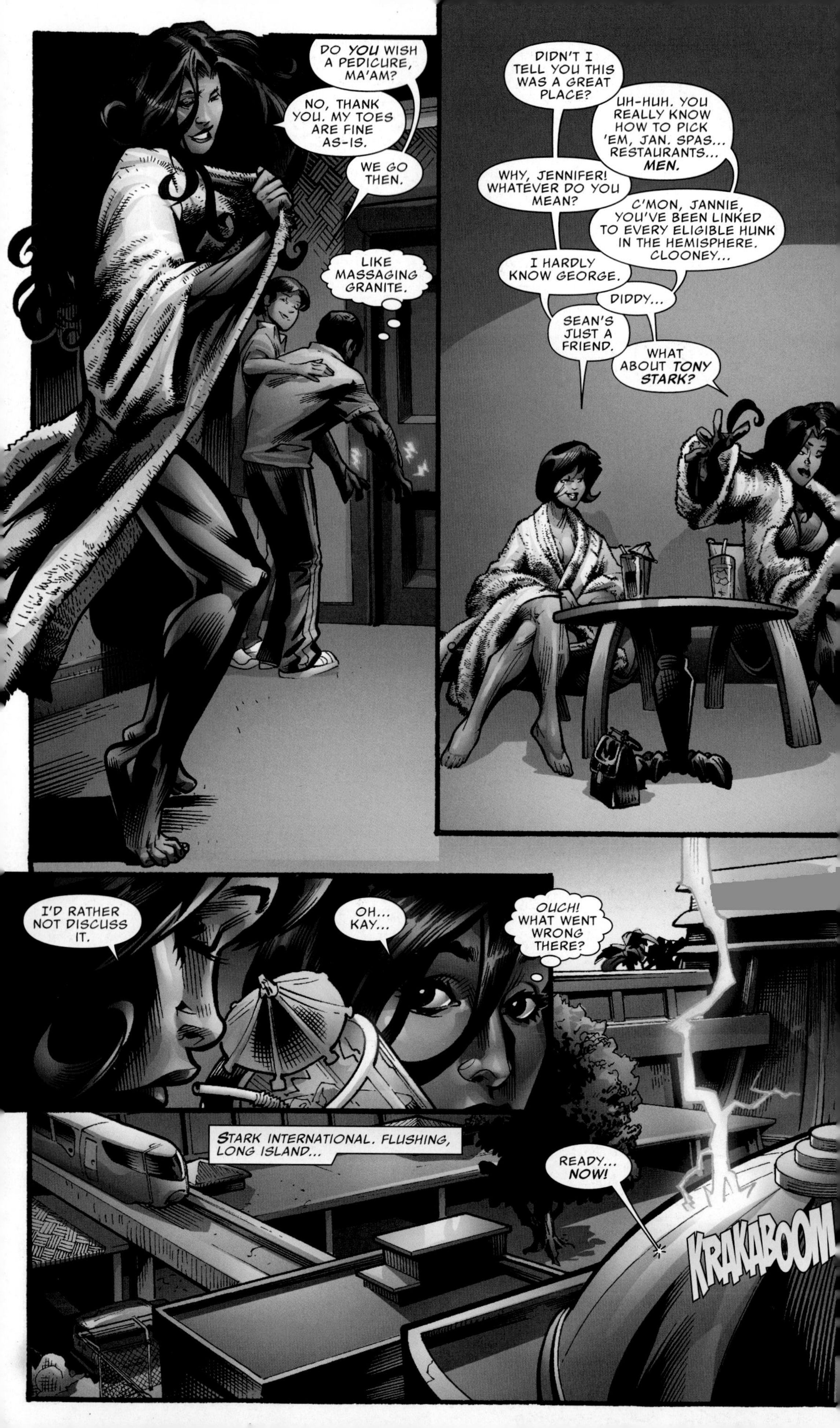
DO YOU WISH A PEDICURE, MA'AM?
NO, THANK YOU. MY TOES ARE FINE AS-IS.
WE GO THEN.
LIKE MASSAGING GRANITE.
DIDN'T I TELL YOU THIS WAS A GREAT PLACE?
UH-HUH. YOU REALLY KNOW HOW TO PICK 'EM, JAN. SPAS... RESTAURANTS... MEN.
WHY, JENNIFER! WHATEVER DO YOU MEAN?
C'MON, JANNIE, YOU'VE BEEN LINKED TO EVERY ELIGIBLE HUNK IN THE HEMISPHERE. CLOONEY...
I HARDLY KNOW GEORGE.
DIDDY...
SEAN'S JUST A FRIEND.
WHAT ABOUT TONY STARK?
I'D RATHER NOT DISCUSS IT.
OH... KAY...
OUCH! WHAT WENT WRONG THERE?
STARK INTERNATIONAL. FLUSHING, LONG ISLAND...
READY... NOW!
KRAKABOOM

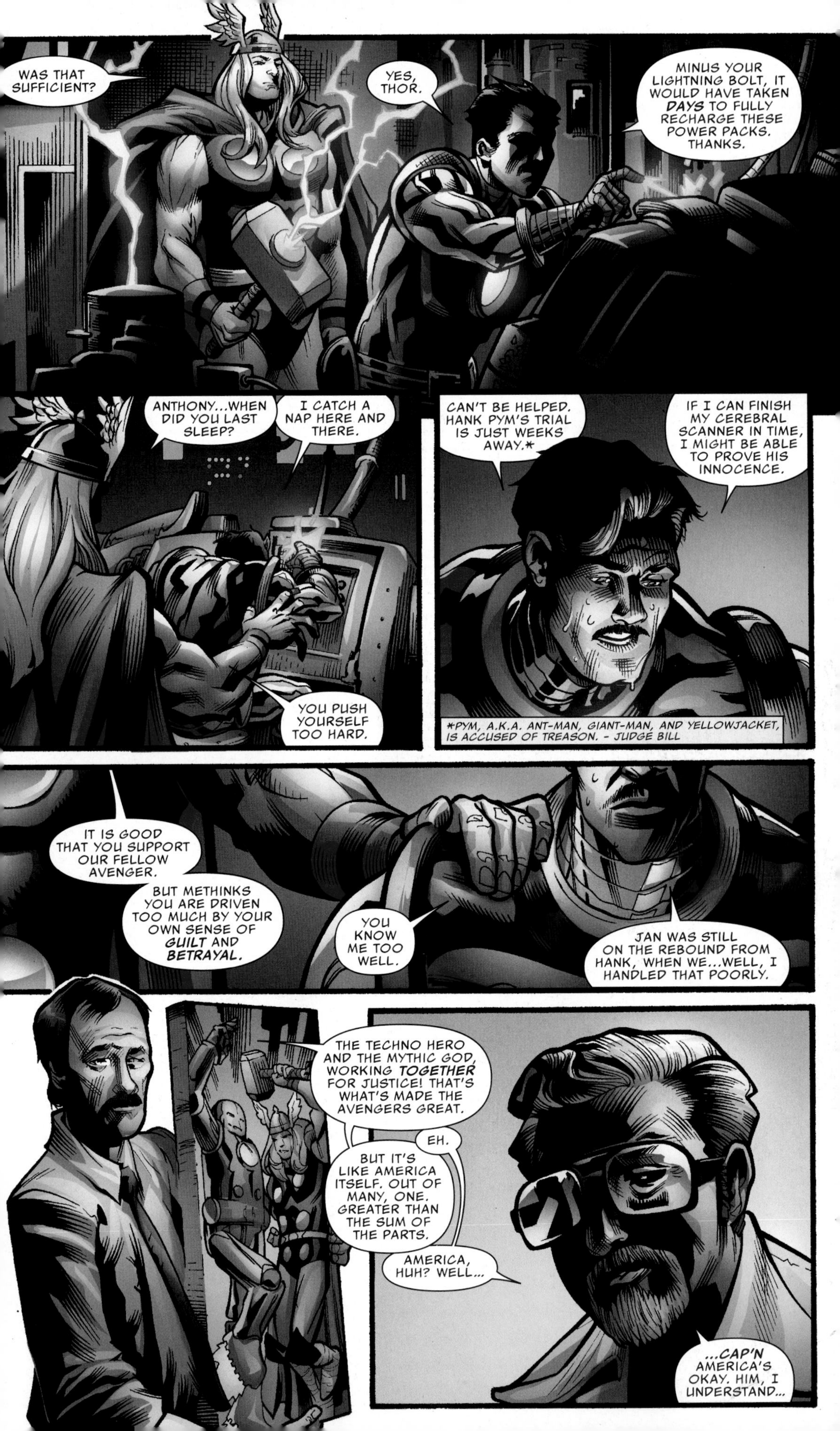
WAS THAT SUFFICIENT?
YES, THOR.
MINUS YOUR LIGHTNING BOLT, IT WOULD HAVE TAKEN DAYS TO FULLY RECHARGE THESE POWER PACKS. THANKS.
ANTHONY...WHEN DID YOU LAST SLEEP?
I CATCH A NAP HERE AND THERE.
YOU PUSH YOURSELF TOO HARD.
CAN'T BE HELPED. HANK PYM'S TRIAL IS JUST WEEKS AWAY.*
IF I CAN FINISH MY CEREBRAL SCANNER IN TIME, I MIGHT BE ABLE TO PROVE HIS INNOCENCE.
*PYM, A.K.A. ANT-MAN, GIANT-MAN, AND YELLOWJACKET, IS ACCUSED OF TREASON. - JUDGE BILL
IT IS GOOD THAT YOU SUPPORT OUR FELLOW AVENGER.
BUT METHINKS YOU ARE DRIVEN TOO MUCH BY YOUR OWN SENSE OF GUILT AND BETRAYAL.
YOU KNOW ME TOO WELL.
JAN WAS STILL ON THE REBOUND FROM HANK, WHEN WE...WELL, I HANDLED THAT POORLY.
THE TECHNO HERO AND THE MYTHIC GOD, WORKING TOGETHER FOR JUSTICE! THAT'S WHAT'S MADE THE AVENGERS GREAT.
EH.
BUT IT'S LIKE AMERICA ITSELF. OUT OF MANY, ONE. GREATER THAN THE SUM OF THE PARTS.
AMERICA, HUH? WELL...
...CAP'N AMERICA'S OKAY. HIM, I UNDERSTAND...

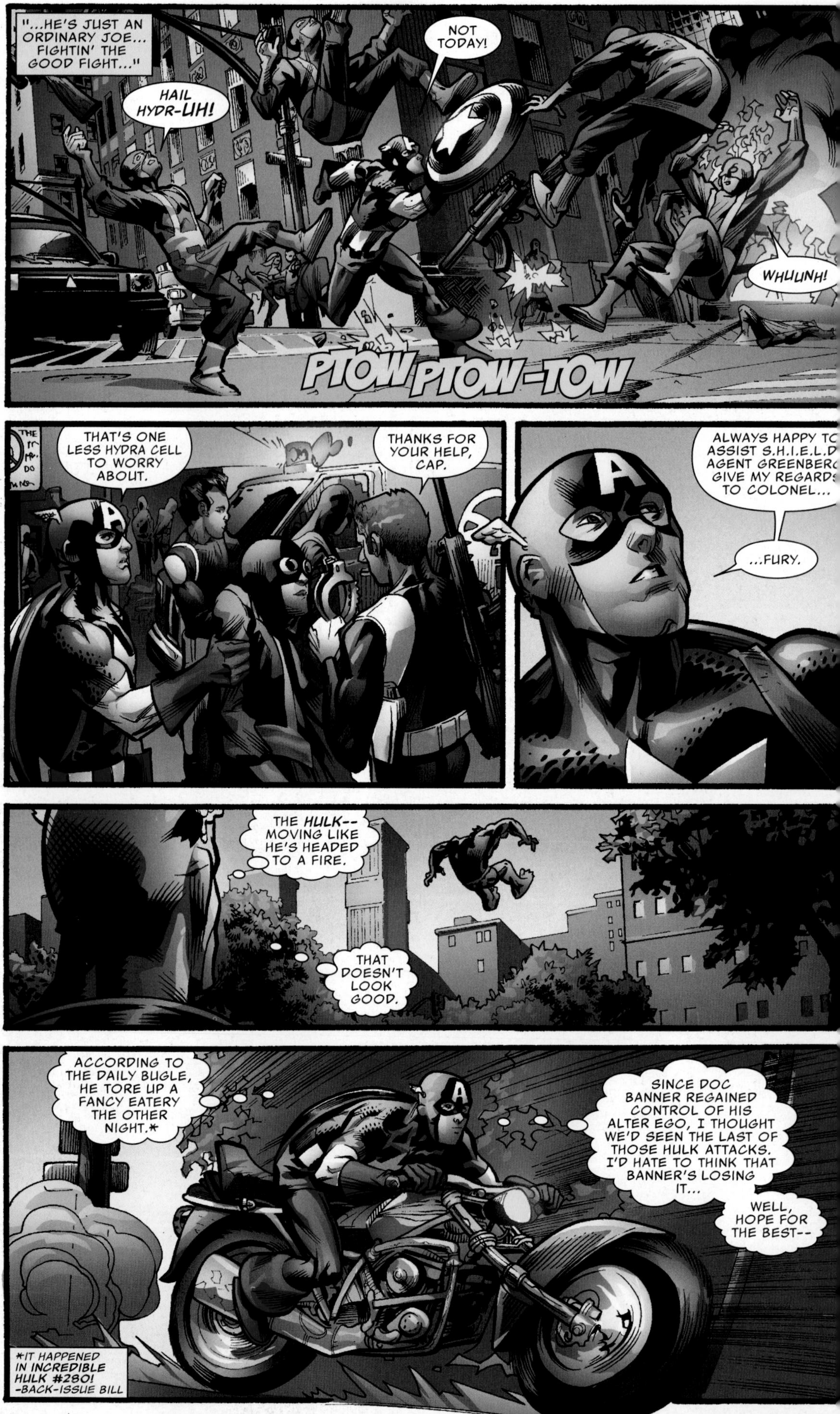
"...HE'S JUST AN ORDINARY JOE... FIGHTIN' THE GOOD FIGHT..."
HAIL HYDR-UH!
NOT TODAY!
WHUUNH!
PTOW PTOW-TOW
THAT'S ONE LESS HYDRA CELL TO WORRY ABOUT.
THANKS FOR YOUR HELP, CAP.
ALWAYS HAPPY TO ASSIST S.H.I.E.L.D. AGENT GREENBERG. GIVE MY REGARDS TO COLONEL...
...FURY.
THE HULK-- MOVING LIKE HE'S HEADED TO A FIRE.
THAT DOESN'T LOOK GOOD.
ACCORDING TO THE DAILY BUGLE, HE TORE UP A FANCY EATERY THE OTHER NIGHT.*
SINCE DOC BANNER REGAINED CONTROL OF HIS ALTER EGO, I THOUGHT WE'D SEEN THE LAST OF THOSE HULK ATTACKS. I'D HATE TO THINK THAT BANNER'S LOSING IT...
WELL, HOPE FOR THE BEST--
*IT HAPPENED IN INCREDIBLE HULK #280! -BACK-ISSUE BILL

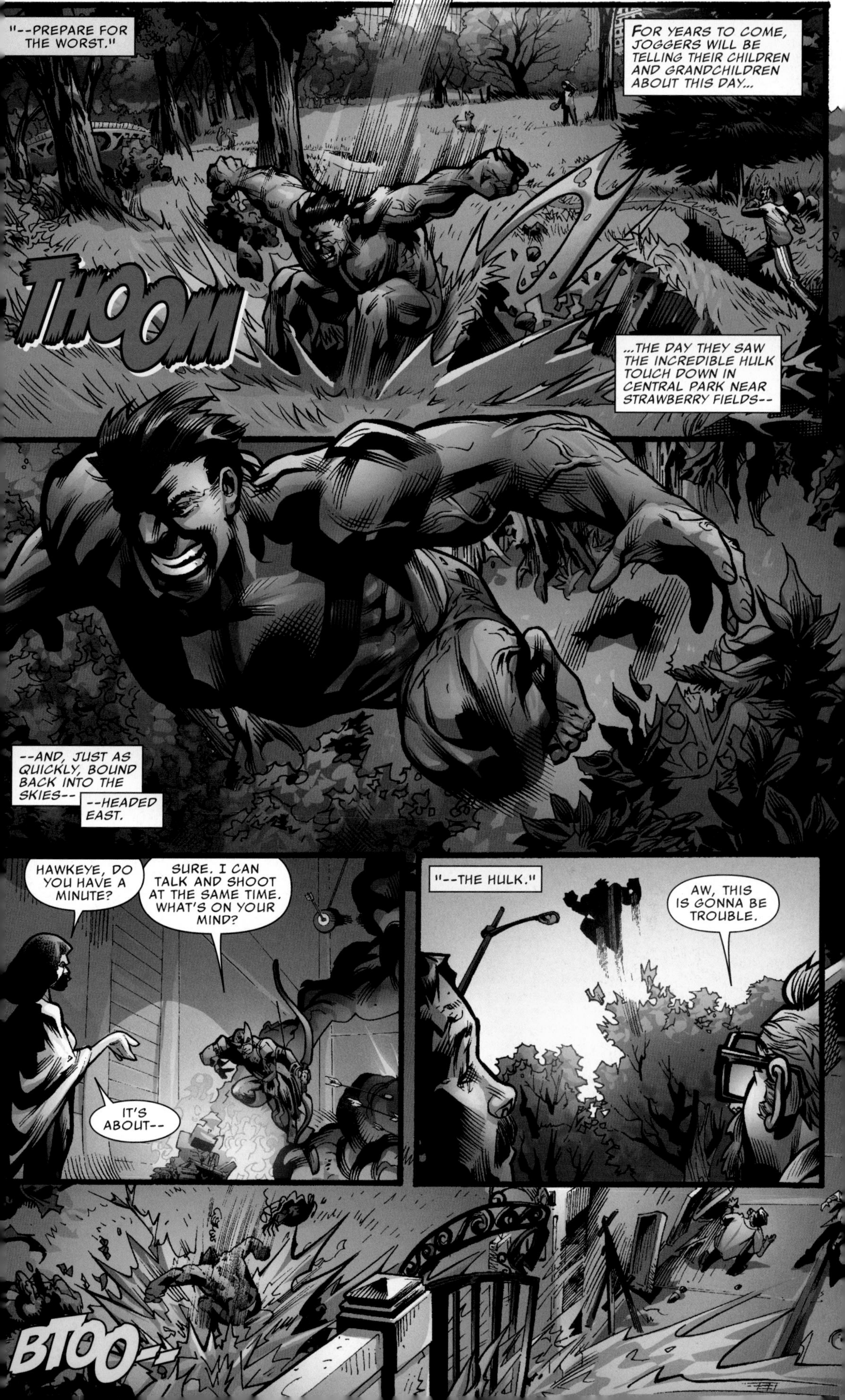
"--PREPARE FOR THE WORST."
FOR YEARS TO COME, JOGGERS WILL BE TELLING THEIR CHILDREN AND GRANDCHILDREN ABOUT THIS DAY...
THOOM
...THE DAY THEY SAW THE INCREDIBLE HULK TOUCH DOWN IN CENTRAL PARK NEAR STRAWBERRY FIELDS--
--AND, JUST AS QUICKLY, BOUND BACK INTO THE SKIES--
--HEADED EAST.
HAWKEYE, DO YOU HAVE A MINUTE?
SURE. I CAN TALK AND SHOOT AT THE SAME TIME. WHAT'S ON YOUR MIND?
IT'S ABOUT--
"--THE HULK."
AW, THIS IS GONNA BE TROUBLE.
BTOO-

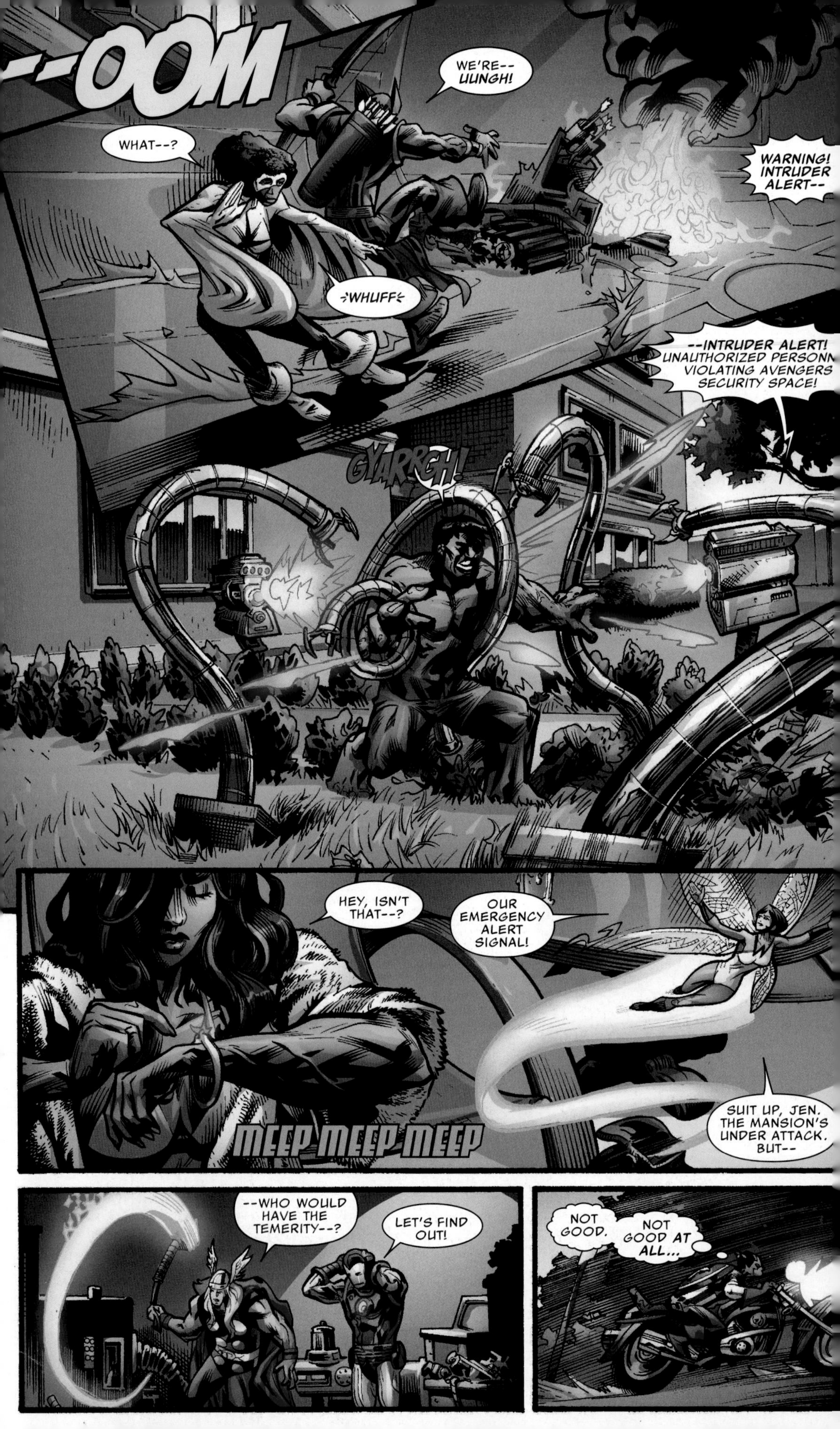
--OOM
WE'RE-- UUNGH!
WHAT--?
WARNING! INTRUDER ALERT--
WHUFF
--INTRUDER ALERT! UNAUTHORIZED PERSONN VIOLATING AVENGERS SECURITY SPACE!
GYARRGH!
HEY, ISN'T THAT--?
OUR EMERGENCY ALERT SIGNAL!
MEEP MEEP MEEP
SUIT UP, JEN. THE MANSION'S UNDER ATTACK. BUT--
--WHO WOULD HAVE THE TEMERITY--?
LET'S FIND OUT!
NOT GOOD.
NOT GOOD AT ALL...

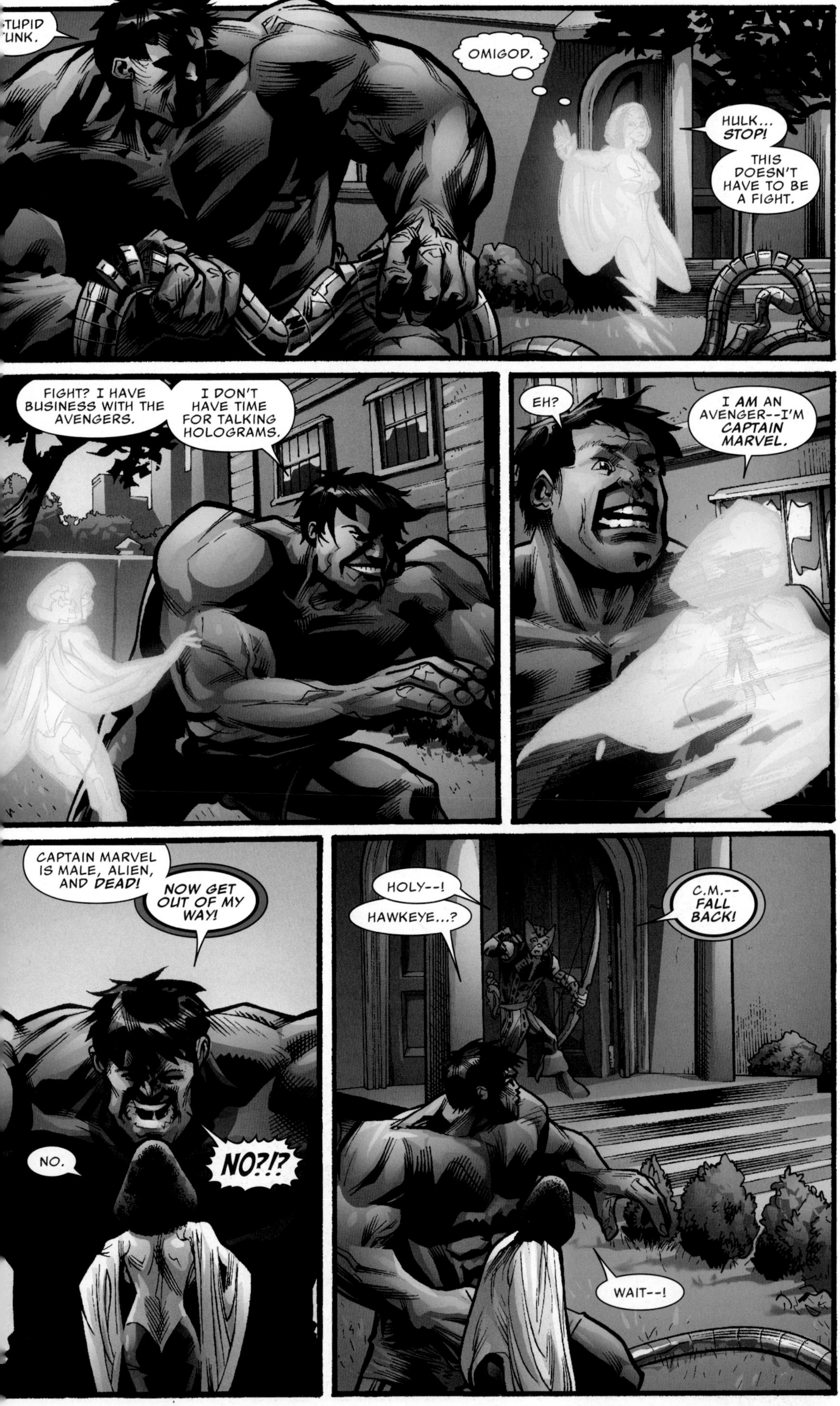
STUPID
TUNK.
OMIGOD.
HULK... STOP!
THIS DOESN'T HAVE TO BE A FIGHT.
FIGHT? I HAVE BUSINESS WITH THE AVENGERS.
I DON'T HAVE TIME FOR TALKING HOLOGRAMS.
EH?
I AM AN AVENGER--I'M CAPTAIN MARVEL.
CAPTAIN MARVEL IS MALE, ALIEN, AND DEAD!
NOW GET OUT OF MY WAY!
NO.
NO?!?
HOLY--!
HAWKEYE...?
C.M.-- FALL BACK!
WAIT--!

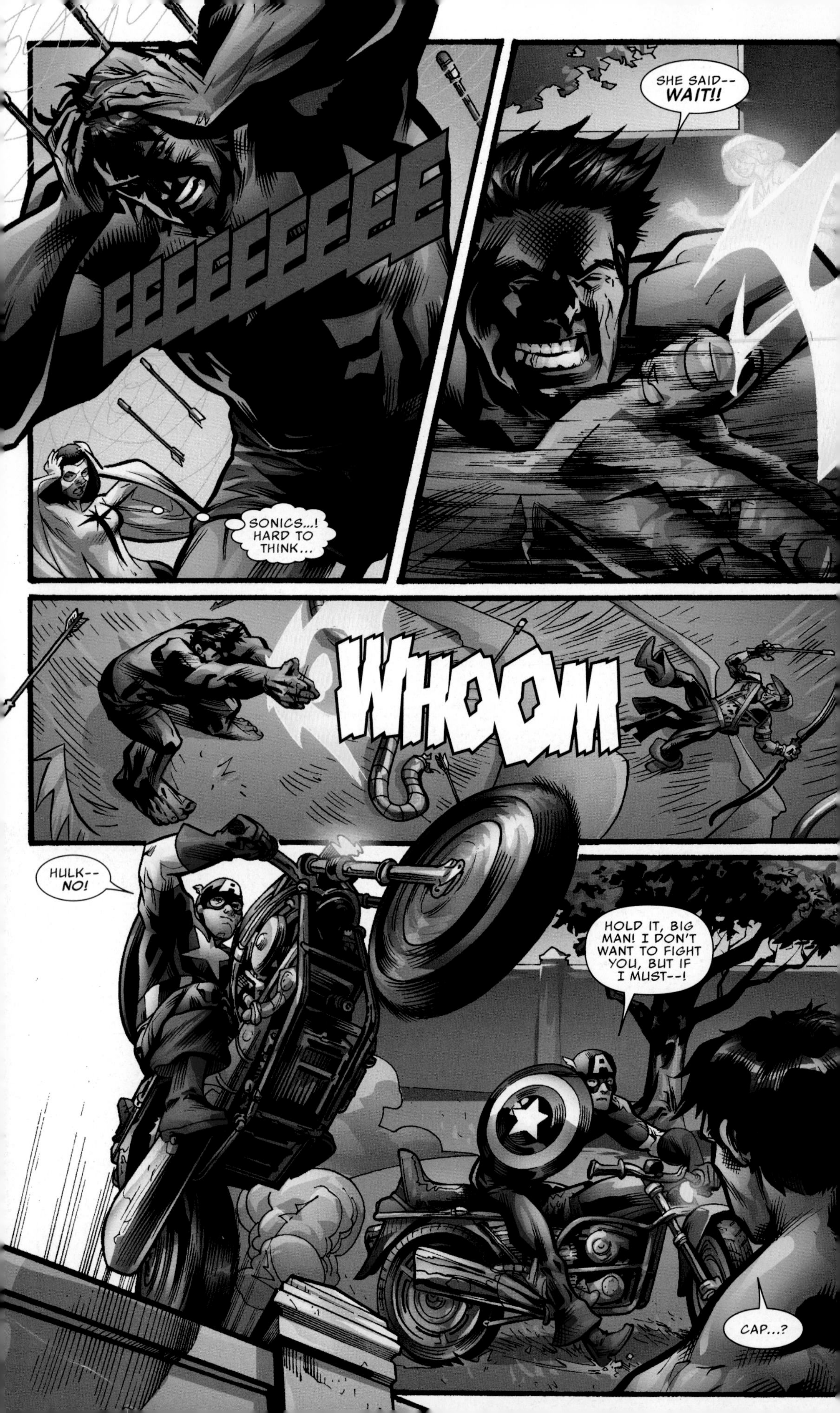
EEEEEEEEEE
SONICS...! HARD TO THINK...
SHE SAID-- WAIT!!
WHOOM
HULK-- NO!
HOLD IT, BIG MAN! I DON'T WANT TO FIGHT YOU, BUT IF I MUST--!
CAP...?

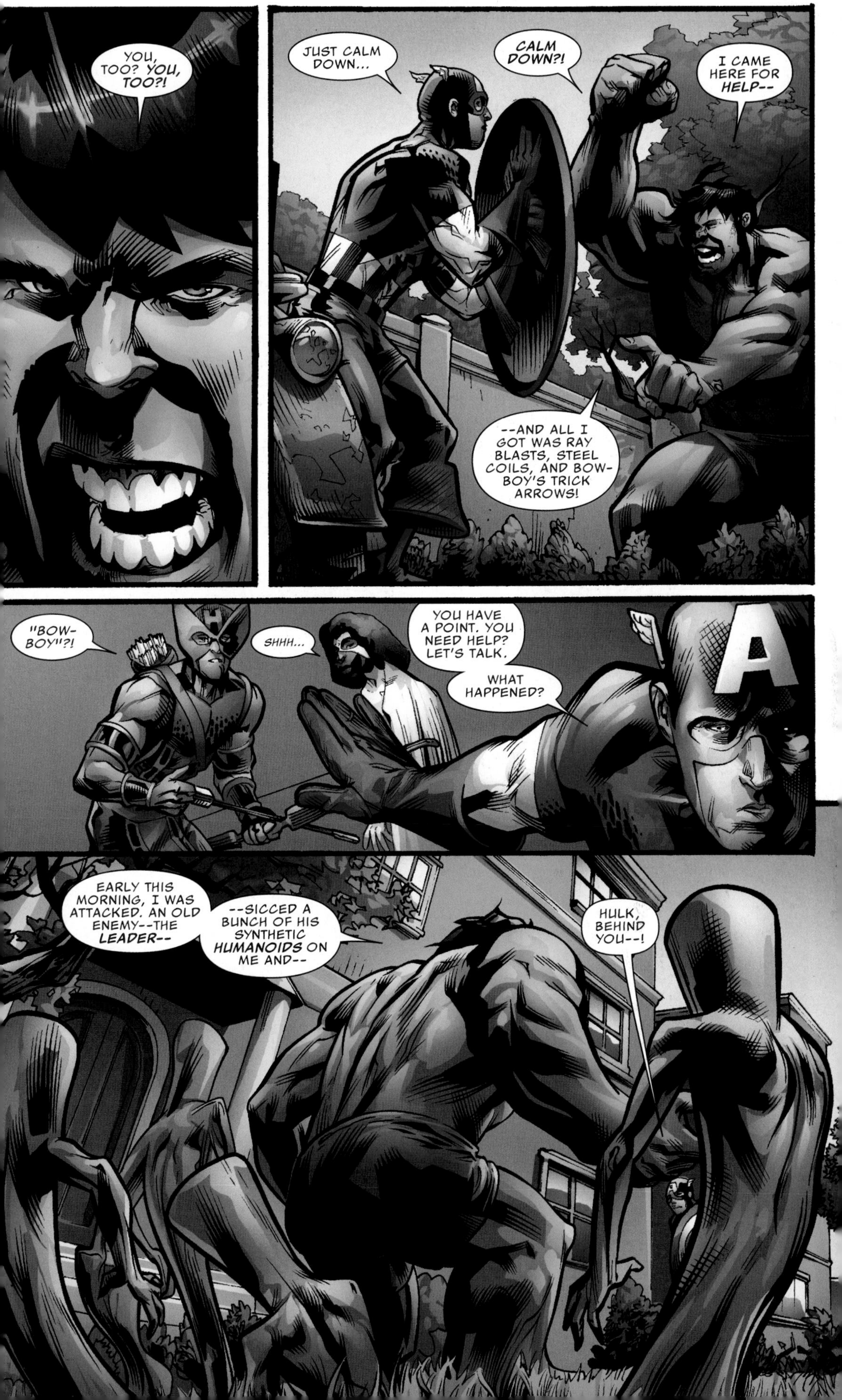
YOU, TOO? *YOU, TOO?!*
JUST CALM DOWN...
CALM DOWN?!
I CAME HERE FOR *HELP--*
--AND ALL I GOT WAS RAY BLASTS, STEEL COILS, AND BOW-BOY'S TRICK ARROWS!
"BOW-BOY"?!
SHHH...
YOU HAVE A POINT. YOU NEED HELP? LET'S TALK.
WHAT HAPPENED?
EARLY THIS MORNING, I WAS ATTACKED. AN OLD ENEMY--THE *LEADER--*
--SICCED A BUNCH OF HIS SYNTHETIC *HUMANOIDS* ON ME AND--
HULK, BEHIND YOU--!

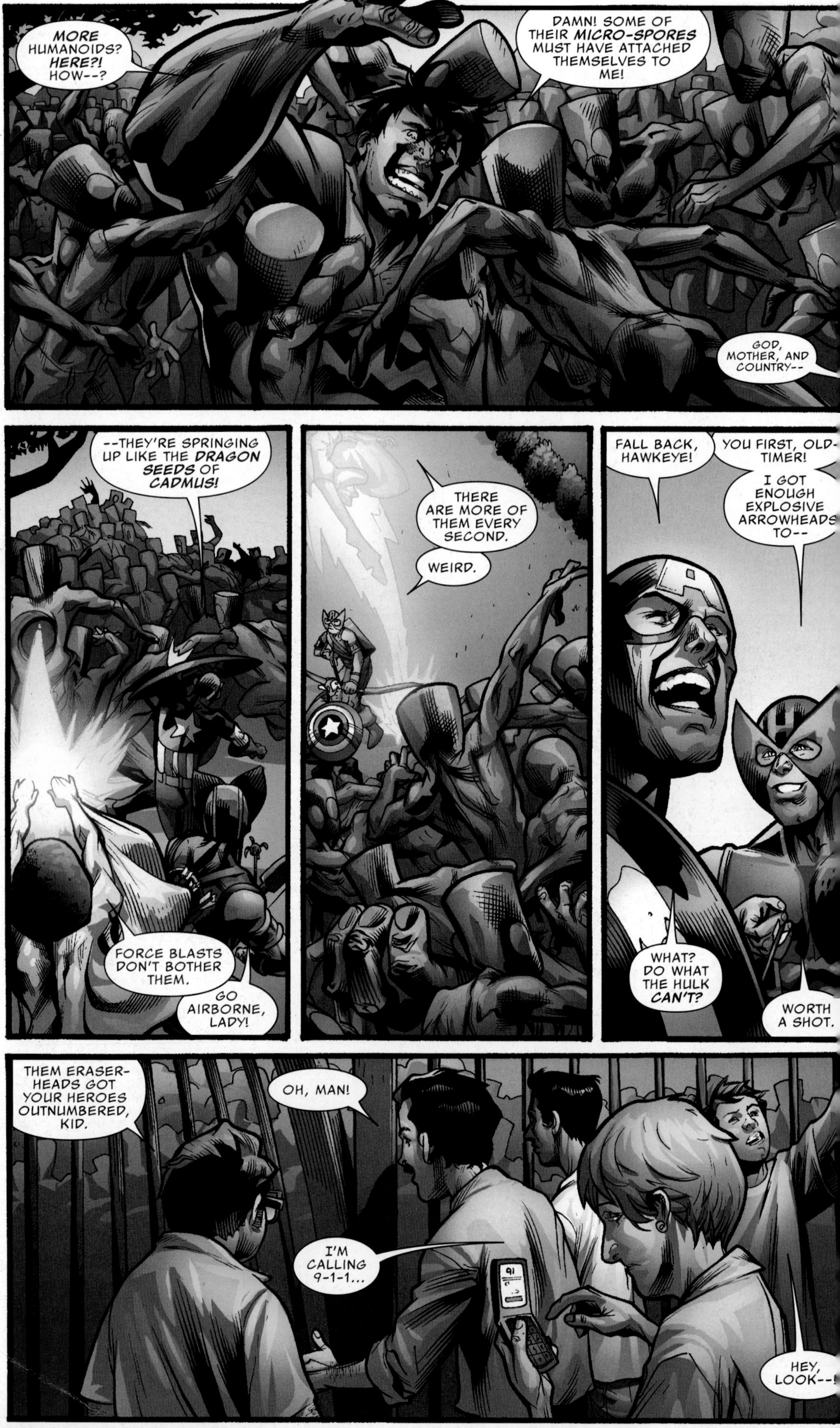
MORE HUMANOIDS? HERE?! HOW--?
DAMN! SOME OF THEIR MICRO-SPORES MUST HAVE ATTACHED THEMSELVES TO ME!
GOD, MOTHER, AND COUNTRY--
--THEY'RE SPRINGING UP LIKE THE DRAGON SEEDS OF CADMUS!
FORCE BLASTS DON'T BOTHER THEM.
GO AIRBORNE, LADY!
THERE ARE MORE OF THEM EVERY SECOND.
WEIRD.
FALL BACK, HAWKEYE!
YOU FIRST, OLD-TIMER!
I GOT ENOUGH EXPLOSIVE ARROWHEADS TO--
WHAT? DO WHAT THE HULK CAN'T?
WORTH A SHOT.
THEM ERASER-HEADS GOT YOUR HEROES OUTNUMBERED, KID.
OH, MAN!
I'M CALLING 9-1-1...
HEY, LOOK--!

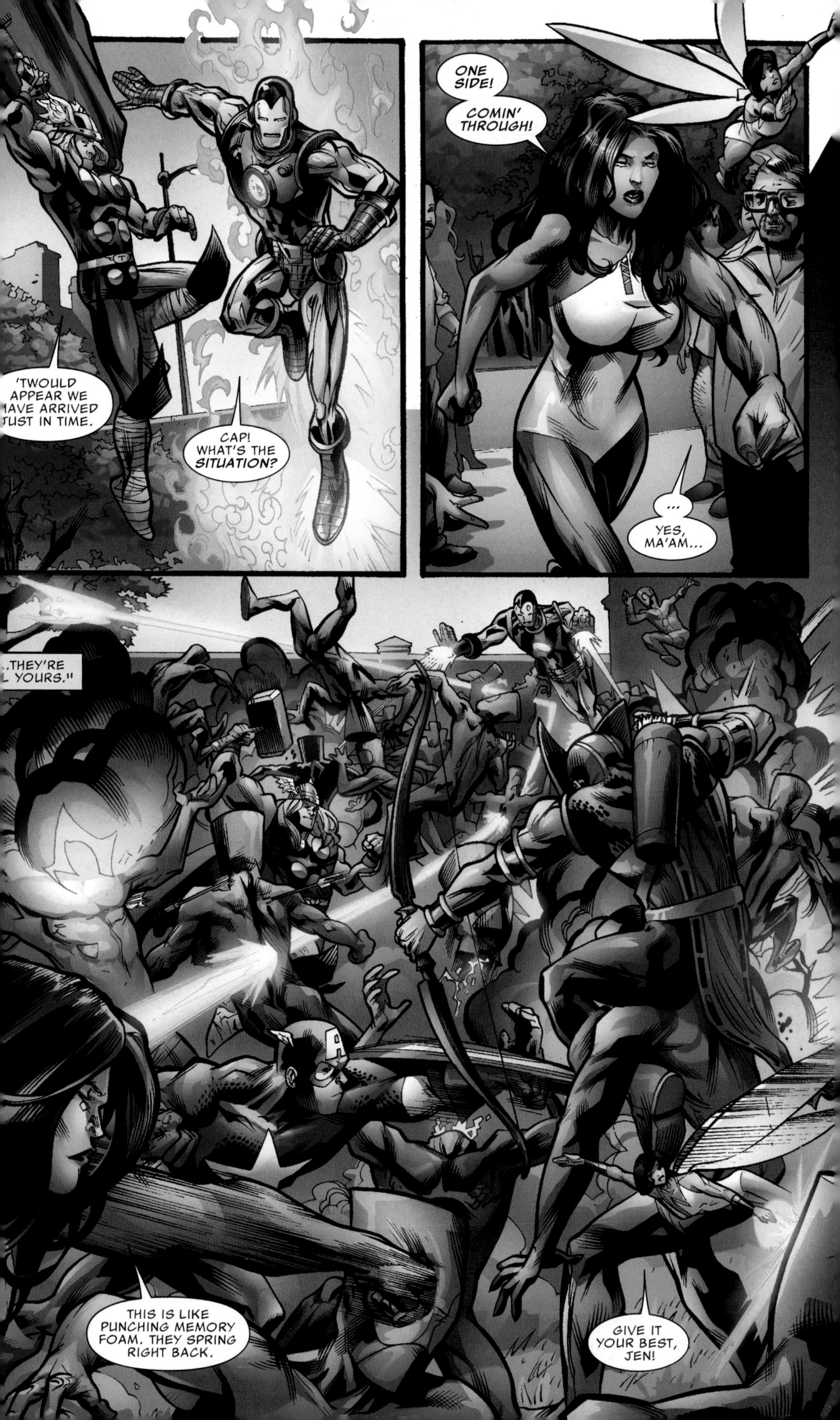
'TWOULD APPEAR WE HAVE ARRIVED JUST IN TIME.
CAP! WHAT'S THE SITUATION?
ONE SIDE!
COMIN' THROUGH!
...
YES, MA'AM...
..THEY'RE L YOURS."
THIS IS LIKE PUNCHING MEMORY FOAM. THEY SPRING RIGHT BACK.
GIVE IT YOUR BEST, JEN!

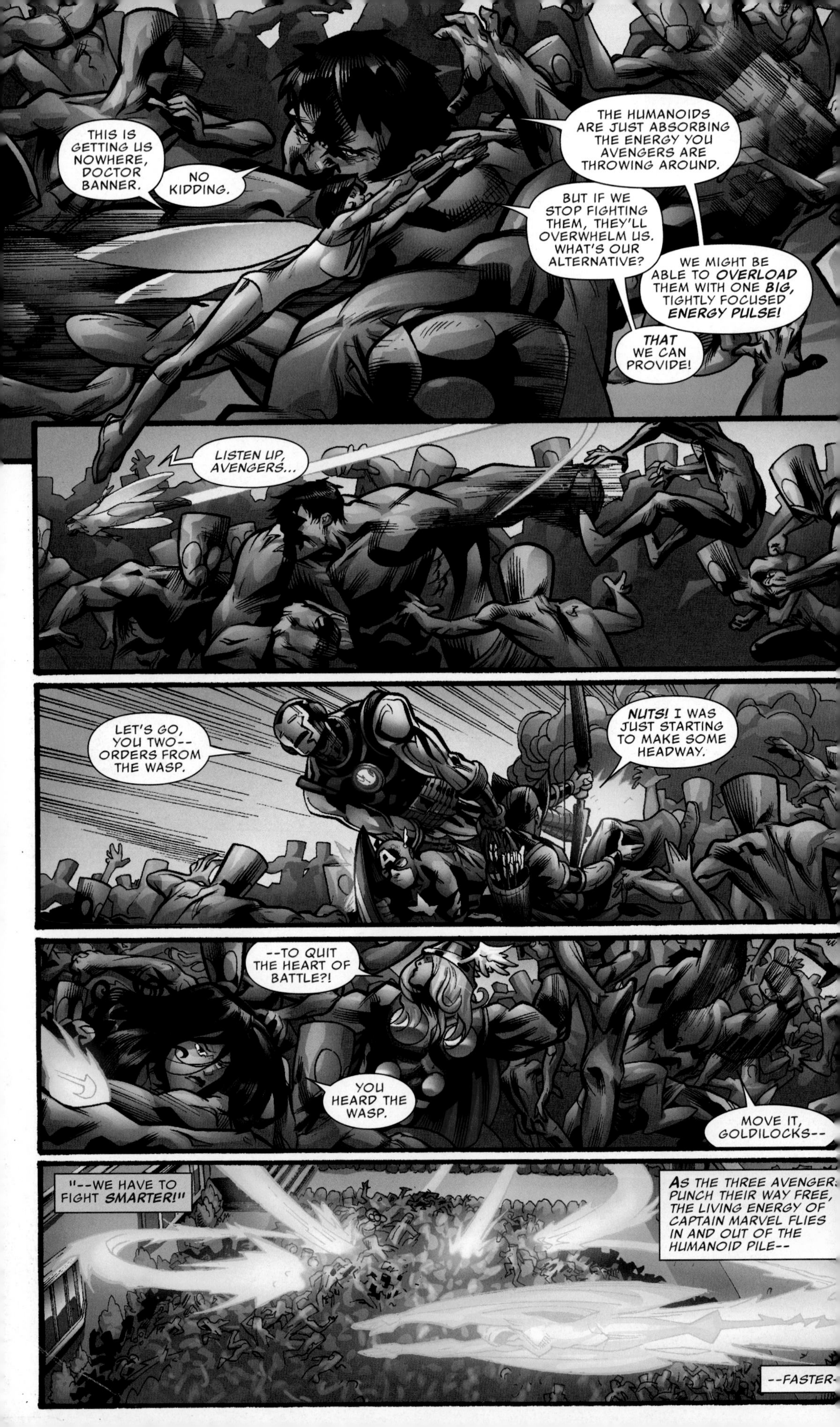
THIS IS GETTING US NOWHERE, DOCTOR BANNER.
NO KIDDING.
THE HUMANOIDS ARE JUST ABSORBING THE ENERGY YOU AVENGERS ARE THROWING AROUND.
BUT IF WE STOP FIGHTING THEM, THEY'LL OVERWHELM US. WHAT'S OUR ALTERNATIVE?
WE MIGHT BE ABLE TO OVERLOAD THEM WITH ONE BIG, TIGHTLY FOCUSED ENERGY PULSE!
THAT WE CAN PROVIDE!
LISTEN UP, AVENGERS...
LET'S GO, YOU TWO-- ORDERS FROM THE WASP.
NUTS! I WAS JUST STARTING TO MAKE SOME HEADWAY.
--TO QUIT THE HEART OF BATTLE?!
YOU HEARD THE WASP.
MOVE IT, GOLDILOCKS--
"--WE HAVE TO FIGHT SMARTER!"
AS THE THREE AVENGERS PUNCH THEIR WAY FREE, THE LIVING ENERGY OF CAPTAIN MARVEL FLIES IN AND OUT OF THE HUMANOID PILE--
--FASTER--

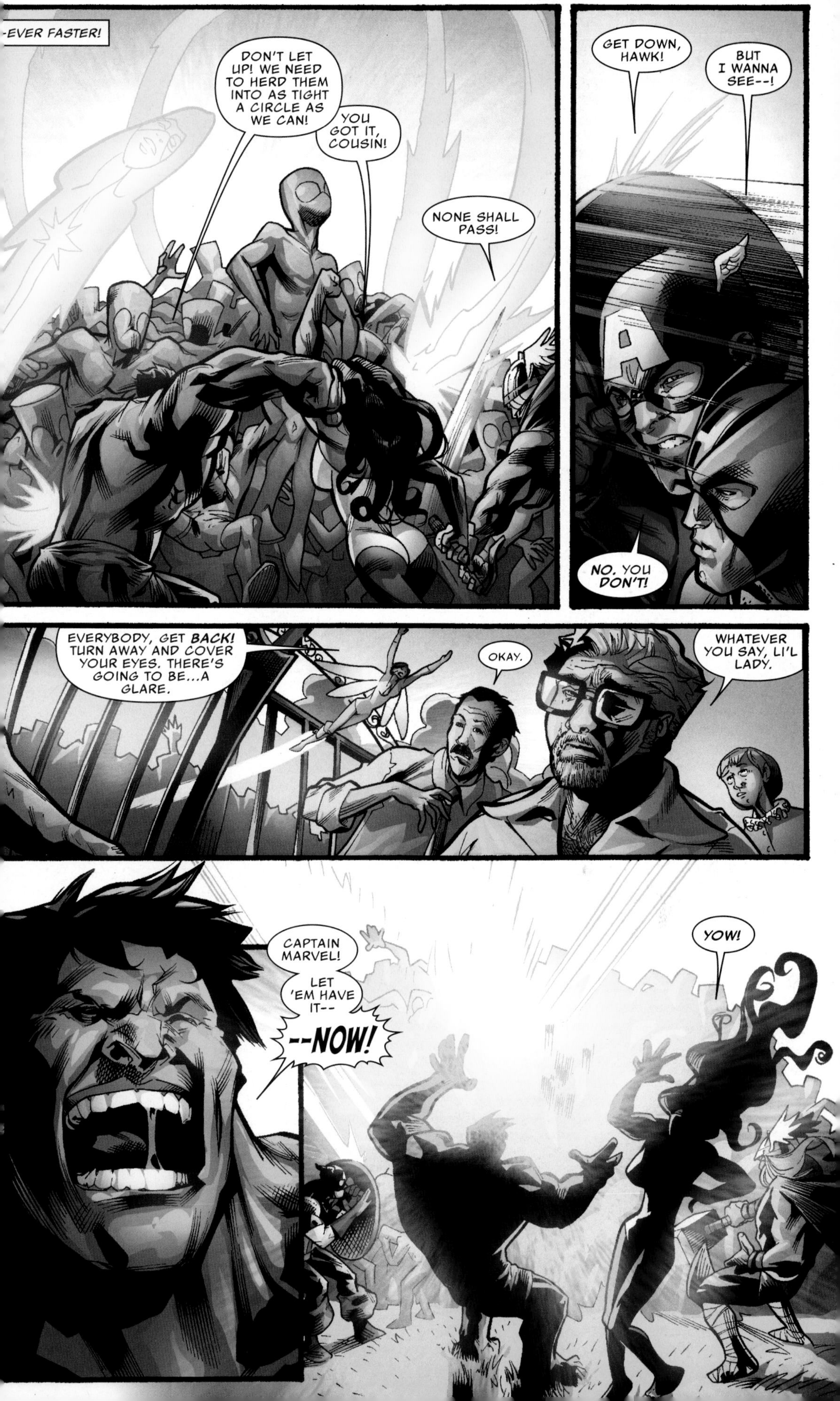
-EVER FASTER!
DON'T LET UP! WE NEED TO HERD THEM INTO AS TIGHT A CIRCLE AS WE CAN!
YOU GOT IT, COUSIN!
NONE SHALL PASS!
GET DOWN, HAWK!
BUT I WANNA SEE--!
NO. YOU DON'T!
EVERYBODY, GET BACK! TURN AWAY AND COVER YOUR EYES. THERE'S GOING TO BE...A GLARE.
OKAY.
WHATEVER YOU SAY, LI'L LADY.
CAPTAIN MARVEL!
LET 'EM HAVE IT--
--NOW!
YOW!

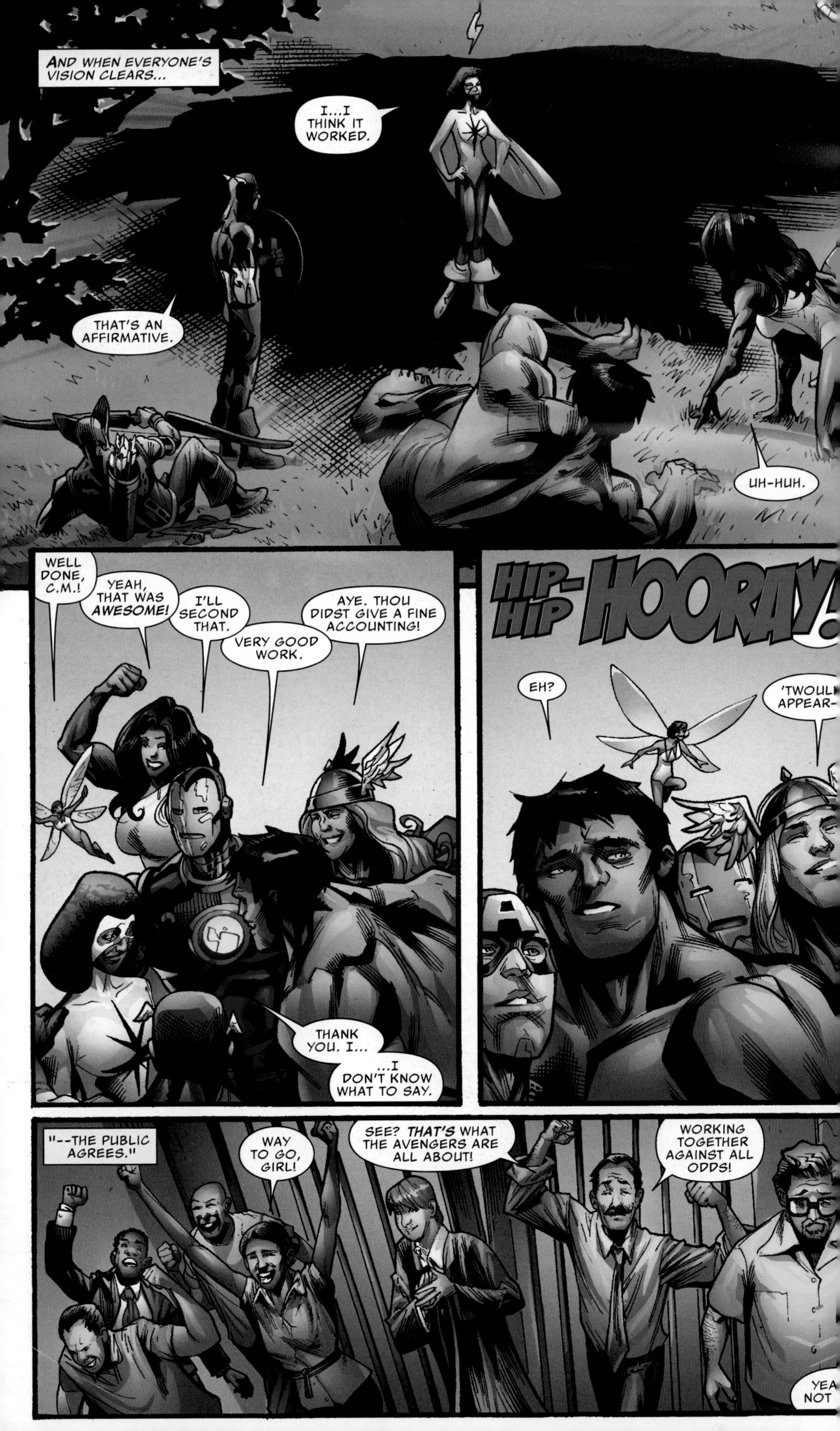
AND WHEN EVERYONE'S VISION CLEARS...
I...I THINK IT WORKED.
THAT'S AN AFFIRMATIVE.
UH-HUH.
WELL DONE, C.M.!
YEAH, THAT WAS AWESOME!
I'LL SECOND THAT.
VERY GOOD WORK.
AYE. THOU DIDST GIVE A FINE ACCOUNTING!
THANK YOU. I...
...I DON'T KNOW WHAT TO SAY.
HIP-HIP HOORAY!
EH?
"--THE PUBLIC AGREES."
WAY TO GO, GIRL!
SEE? THAT'S WHAT THE AVENGERS ARE ALL ABOUT!
WORKING TOGETHER AGAINST ALL ODDS!

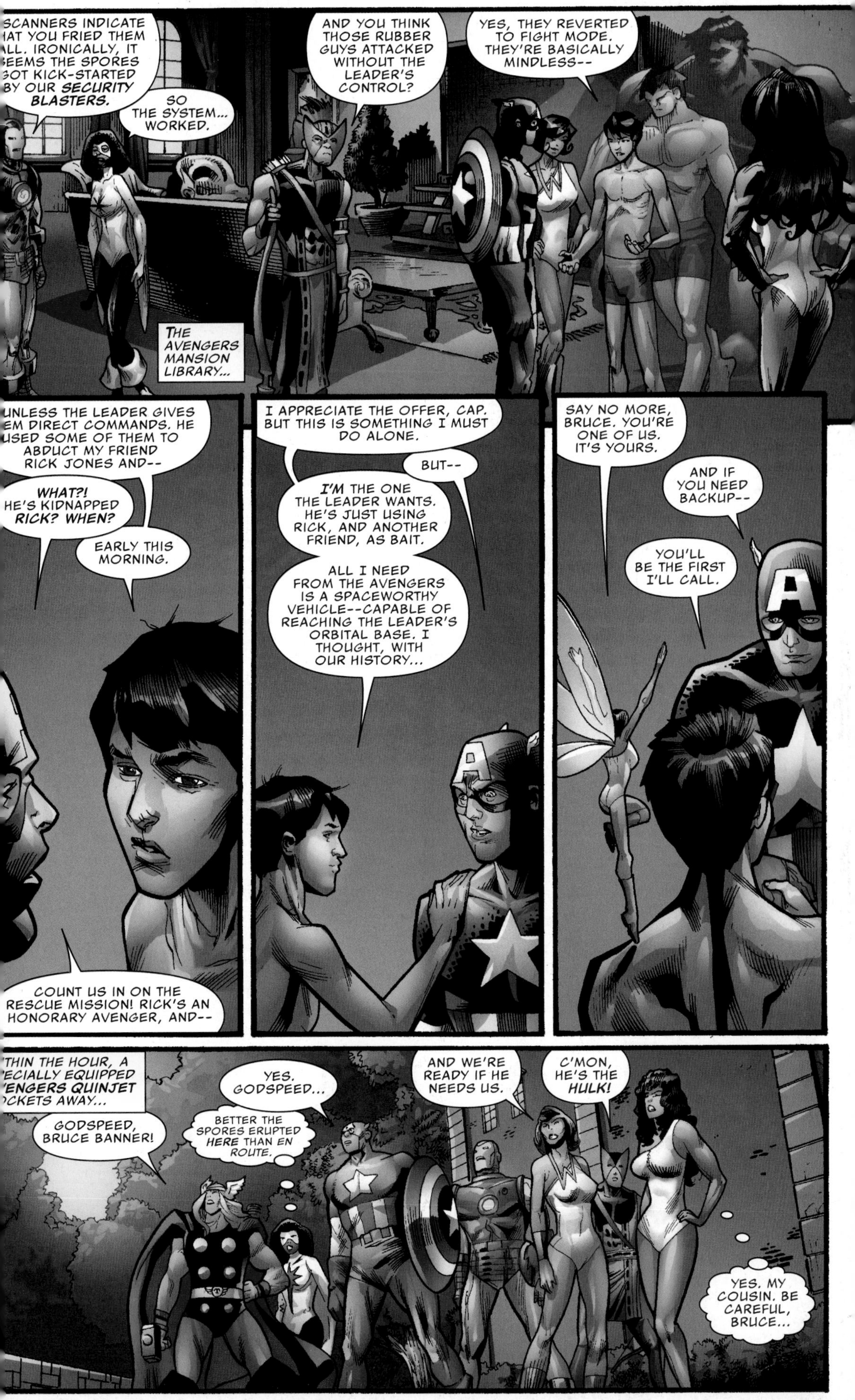

SCANNERS INDICATE
HAT YOU FRIED THEM
LL. IRONICALLY, IT
EEMS THE SPORES
GOT KICK-STARTED
BY OUR SECURITY BLASTERS.
SO THE SYSTEM... WORKED.
AND YOU THINK THOSE RUBBER GUYS ATTACKED WITHOUT THE LEADER'S CONTROL?
YES, THEY REVERTED TO FIGHT MODE. THEY'RE BASICALLY MINDLESS--
THE AVENGERS MANSION LIBRARY...
UNLESS THE LEADER GIVES
EM DIRECT COMMANDS. HE
USED SOME OF THEM TO
ABDUCT MY FRIEND RICK JONES AND--
WHAT?! HE'S KIDNAPPED RICK? WHEN?
EARLY THIS MORNING.
COUNT US IN ON THE RESCUE MISSION! RICK'S AN HONORARY AVENGER, AND--
I APPRECIATE THE OFFER, CAP. BUT THIS IS SOMETHING I MUST DO ALONE.
BUT--
I'M THE ONE THE LEADER WANTS. HE'S JUST USING RICK, AND ANOTHER FRIEND, AS BAIT.
ALL I NEED FROM THE AVENGERS IS A SPACEWORTHY VEHICLE--CAPABLE OF REACHING THE LEADER'S ORBITAL BASE. I THOUGHT, WITH OUR HISTORY...
SAY NO MORE, BRUCE. YOU'RE ONE OF US. IT'S YOURS.
AND IF YOU NEED BACKUP--
YOU'LL BE THE FIRST I'LL CALL.
THIN THE HOUR, A
ECIALLY EQUIPPED
VENGERS QUINJET
CKETS AWAY...
GODSPEED, BRUCE BANNER!
YES. GODSPEED...
BETTER THE SPORES ERUPTED HERE THAN EN ROUTE.
AND WE'RE READY IF HE NEEDS US.
C'MON, HE'S THE HULK!
YES, MY COUSIN. BE CAREFUL, BRUCE...

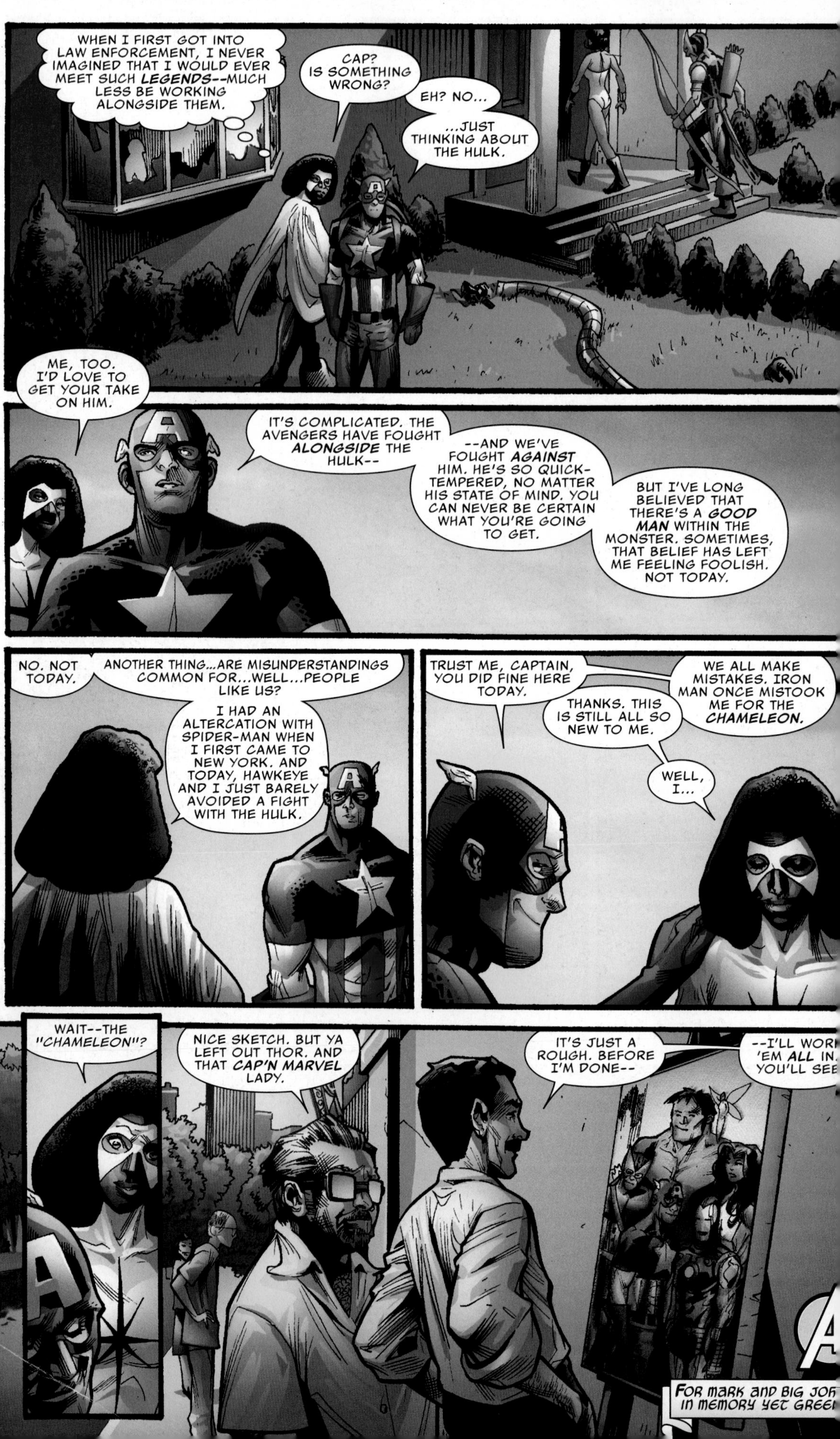
WHEN I FIRST GOT INTO LAW ENFORCEMENT, I NEVER IMAGINED THAT I WOULD EVER MEET SUCH LEGENDS--MUCH LESS BE WORKING ALONGSIDE THEM.
CAP? IS SOMETHING WRONG?
EH? NO...
...JUST THINKING ABOUT THE HULK.
ME, TOO. I'D LOVE TO GET YOUR TAKE ON HIM.
IT'S COMPLICATED. THE AVENGERS HAVE FOUGHT ALONGSIDE THE HULK--
--AND WE'VE FOUGHT AGAINST HIM. HE'S SO QUICK-TEMPERED, NO MATTER HIS STATE OF MIND. YOU CAN NEVER BE CERTAIN WHAT YOU'RE GOING TO GET.
BUT I'VE LONG BELIEVED THAT THERE'S A GOOD MAN WITHIN THE MONSTER. SOMETIMES, THAT BELIEF HAS LEFT ME FEELING FOOLISH. NOT TODAY.
NO. NOT TODAY.
ANOTHER THING...ARE MISUNDERSTANDINGS COMMON FOR...WELL...PEOPLE LIKE US?
I HAD AN ALTERCATION WITH SPIDER-MAN WHEN I FIRST CAME TO NEW YORK. AND TODAY, HAWKEYE AND I JUST BARELY AVOIDED A FIGHT WITH THE HULK.
TRUST ME, CAPTAIN, YOU DID FINE HERE TODAY.
THANKS. THIS IS STILL ALL SO NEW TO ME.
WE ALL MAKE MISTAKES. IRON MAN ONCE MISTOOK ME FOR THE CHAMELEON.
WELL, I...
WAIT--THE "CHAMELEON"?
NICE SKETCH. BUT YA LEFT OUT THOR. AND THAT CAP'N MARVEL LADY.
IT'S JUST A ROUGH. BEFORE I'M DONE--
--I'LL WORK 'EM ALL IN. YOU'LL SEE
FOR MARK AND BIG JOH IN MEMORY YET GREE

#4

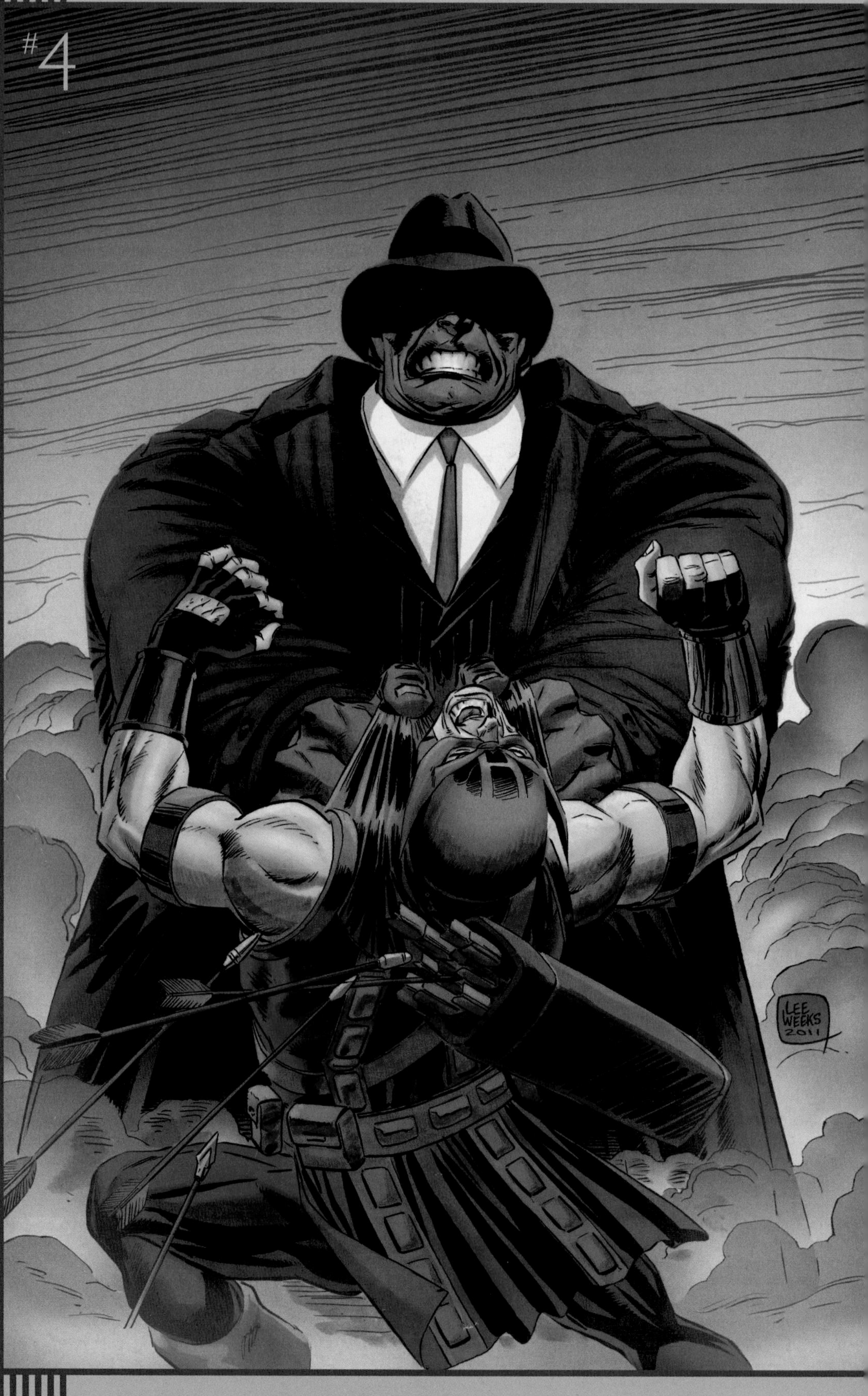
LEE WEEKS 2011

THIS STORY OCCURS IMMEDIATELY PRIOR TO THE EVENTS OF *WEST COAST AVENGERS* #5 AND *INCREDIBLE HULK* (VOL. 1) #347.

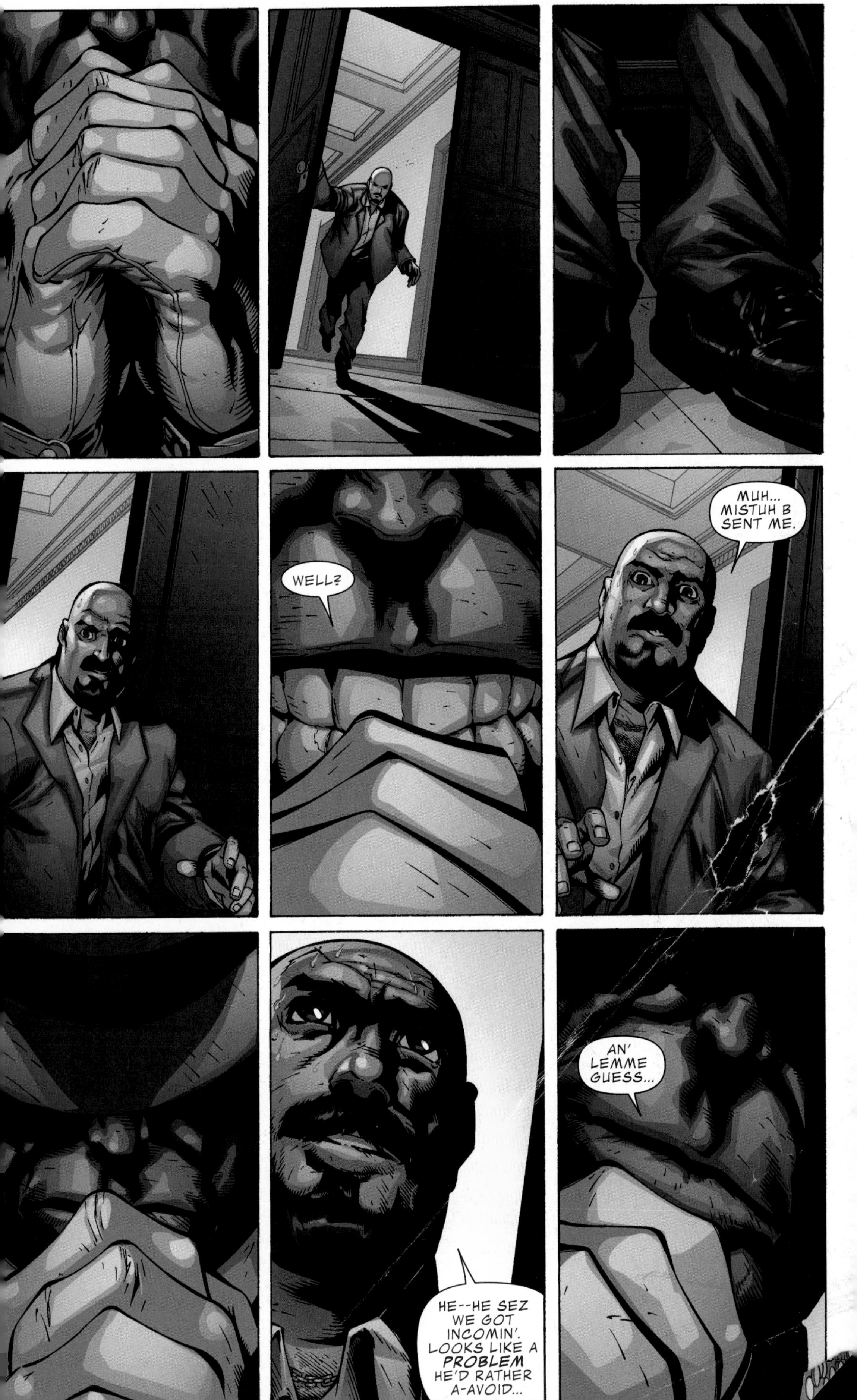
WELL?
MUH... MISTUH B SENT ME.
HE--HE SEZ WE GOT INCOMIN'. LOOKS LIKE A *PROBLEM* HE'D RATHER A-AVOID...
AN' LEMME GUESS...

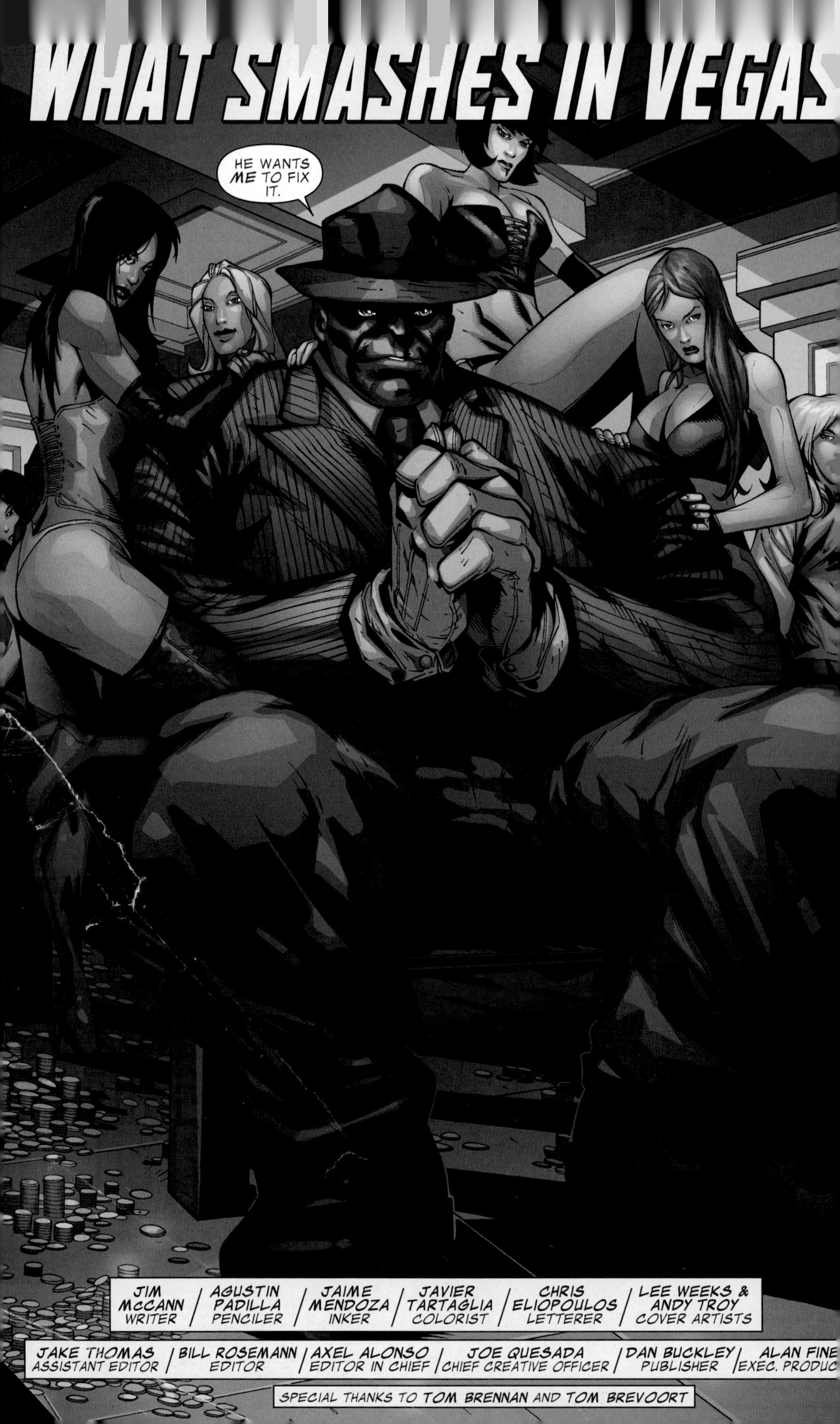
WHAT SMASHES IN VEGAS
HE WANTS ME TO FIX IT.
JIM McCANN WRITER
AGUSTIN PADILLA PENCILER
JAIME MENDOZA INKER
JAVIER TARTAGLIA COLORIST
CHRIS ELIOPOULOS LETTERER
LEE WEEKS & ANDY TROY COVER ARTISTS
JAKE THOMAS ASSISTANT EDITOR
BILL ROSEMANN EDITOR
AXEL ALONSO EDITOR IN CHIEF
JOE QUESADA CHIEF CREATIVE OFFICER
DAN BUCKLEY PUBLISHER
ALAN FINE EXEC. PRODUC
SPECIAL THANKS TO TOM BRENNAN AND TOM BREVOORT

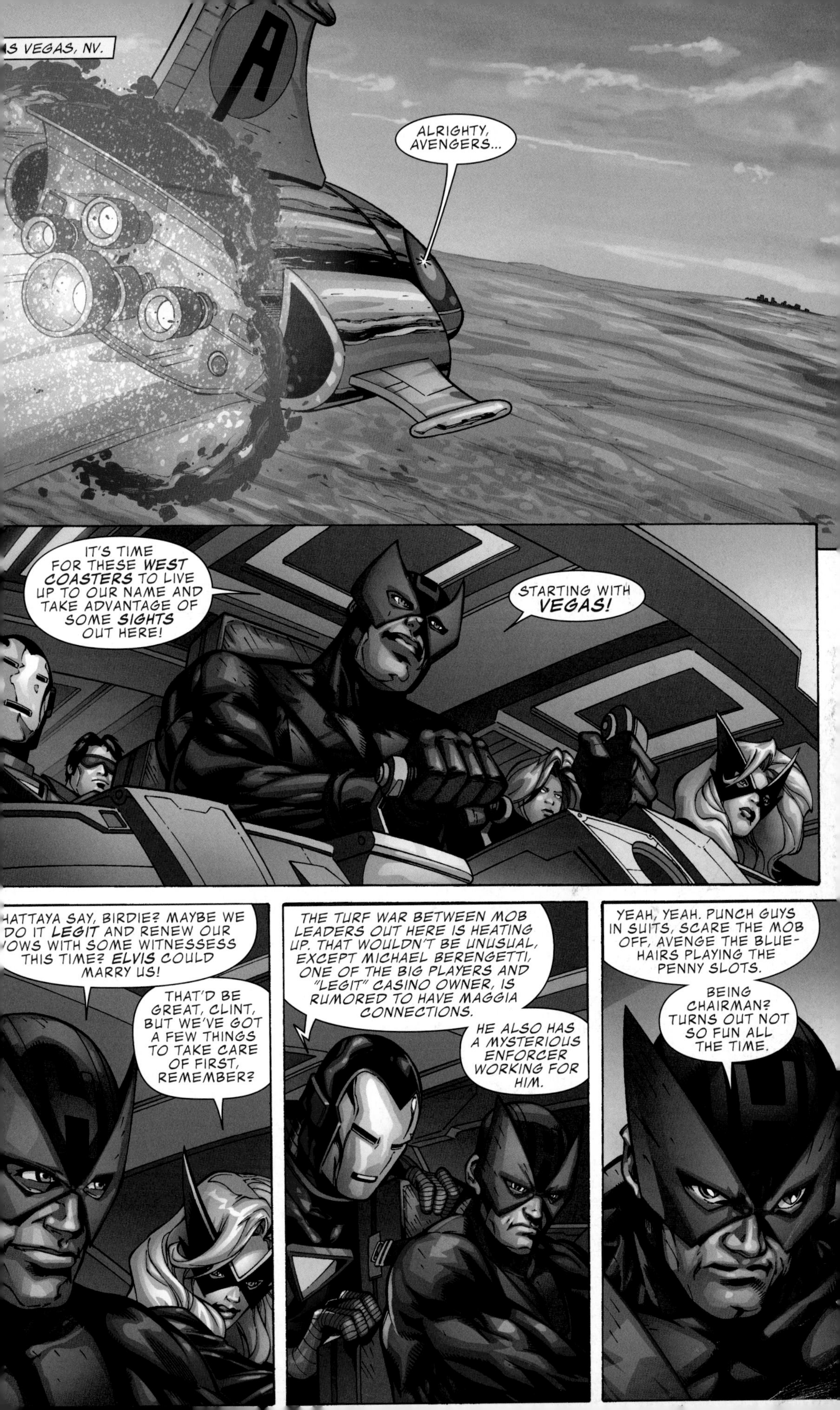

S VEGAS, NV.
ALRIGHTY, AVENGERS...
IT'S TIME FOR THESE WEST COASTERS TO LIVE UP TO OUR NAME AND TAKE ADVANTAGE OF SOME SIGHTS OUT HERE!
STARTING WITH VEGAS!
HATTAYA SAY, BIRDIE? MAYBE WE DO IT LEGIT AND RENEW OUR VOWS WITH SOME WITNESSESS THIS TIME? ELVIS COULD MARRY US!
THAT'D BE GREAT, CLINT, BUT WE'VE GOT A FEW THINGS TO TAKE CARE OF FIRST, REMEMBER?
THE TURF WAR BETWEEN MOB LEADERS OUT HERE IS HEATING UP. THAT WOULDN'T BE UNUSUAL, EXCEPT MICHAEL BERENGETTI, ONE OF THE BIG PLAYERS AND "LEGIT" CASINO OWNER, IS RUMORED TO HAVE MAGGIA CONNECTIONS.
HE ALSO HAS A MYSTERIOUS ENFORCER WORKING FOR HIM.
YEAH, YEAH. PUNCH GUYS IN SUITS, SCARE THE MOB OFF, AVENGE THE BLUE-HAIRS PLAYING THE PENNY SLOTS.
BEING CHAIRMAN? TURNS OUT NOT SO FUN ALL THE TIME.

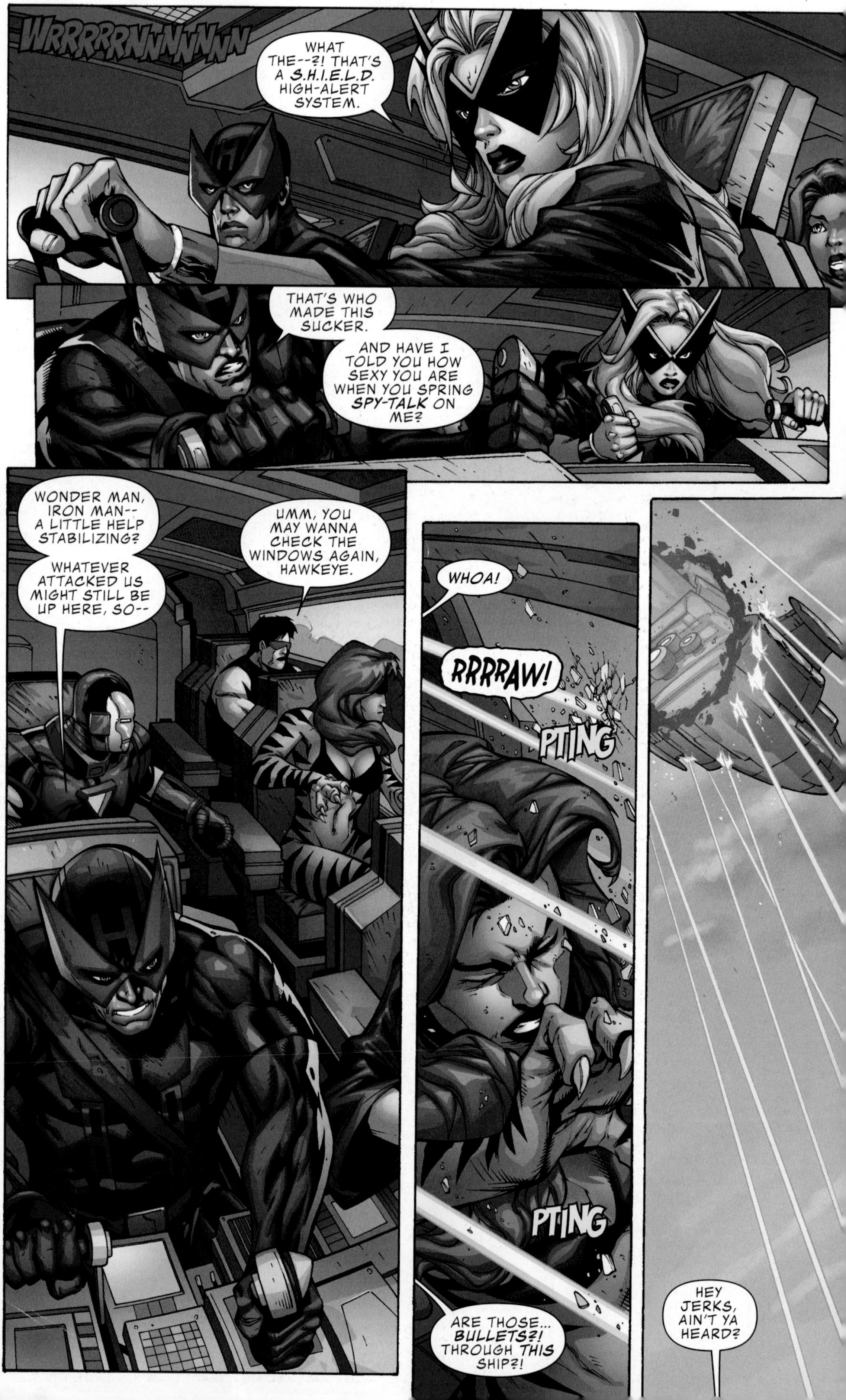
WRRRRRNNNNNNN
WHAT THE--?! THAT'S A S.H.I.E.L.D. HIGH-ALERT SYSTEM.
THAT'S WHO MADE THIS SUCKER.
AND HAVE I TOLD YOU HOW SEXY YOU ARE WHEN YOU SPRING SPY-TALK ON ME?
WONDER MAN, IRON MAN-- A LITTLE HELP STABILIZING?
WHATEVER ATTACKED US MIGHT STILL BE UP HERE, SO--
UMM, YOU MAY WANNA CHECK THE WINDOWS AGAIN, HAWKEYE.
WHOA!
RRRRAW!
PTING
PTING
ARE THOSE... BULLETS?! THROUGH THIS SHIP?!
HEY JERKS, AIN'T YA HEARD?

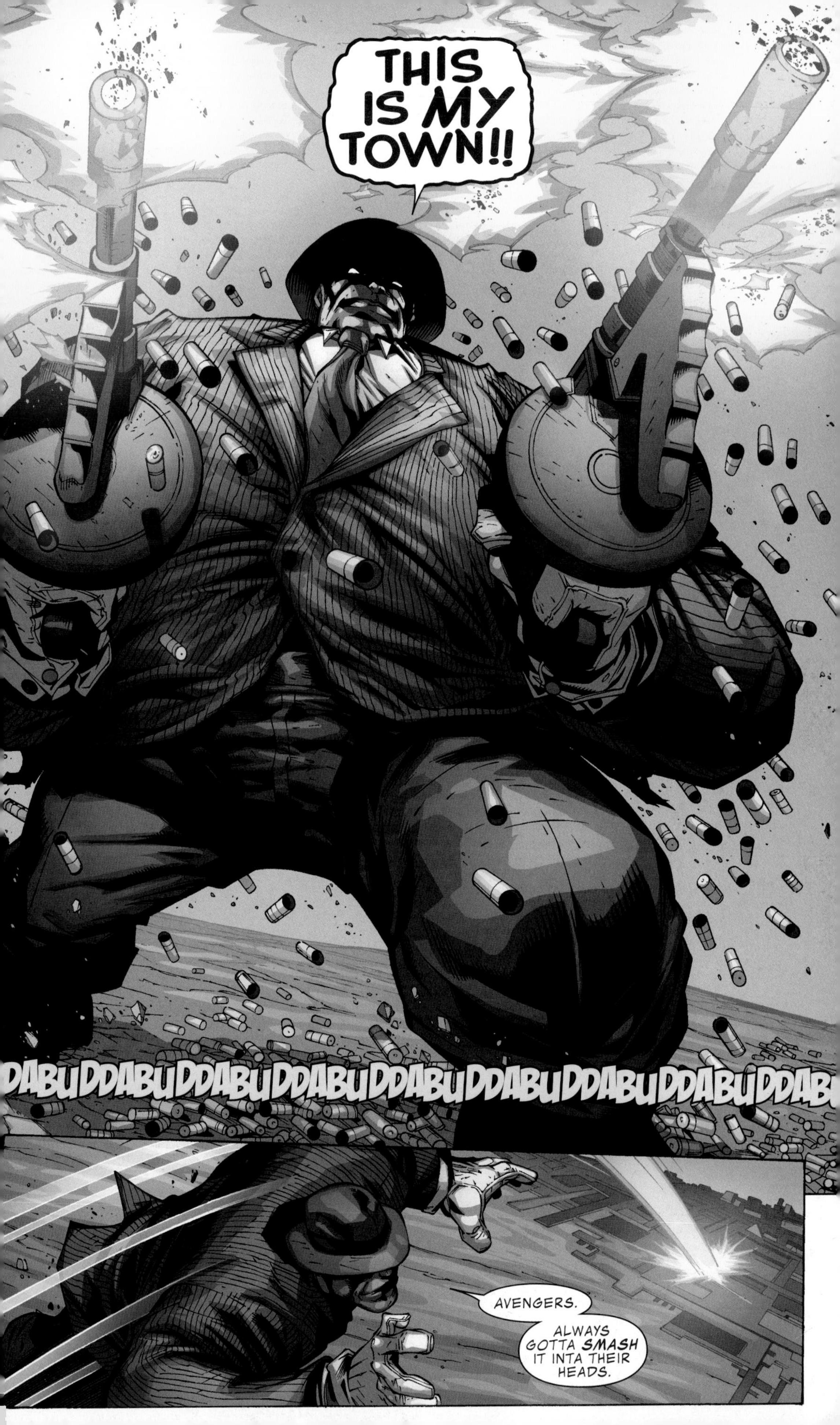
THIS IS MY TOWN!!
DABUDDABUDDABUDDABUDDABUDDABUDDABUDDABUDDABI
AVENGERS.
ALWAYS GOTTA SMASH IT INTA THEIR HEADS.

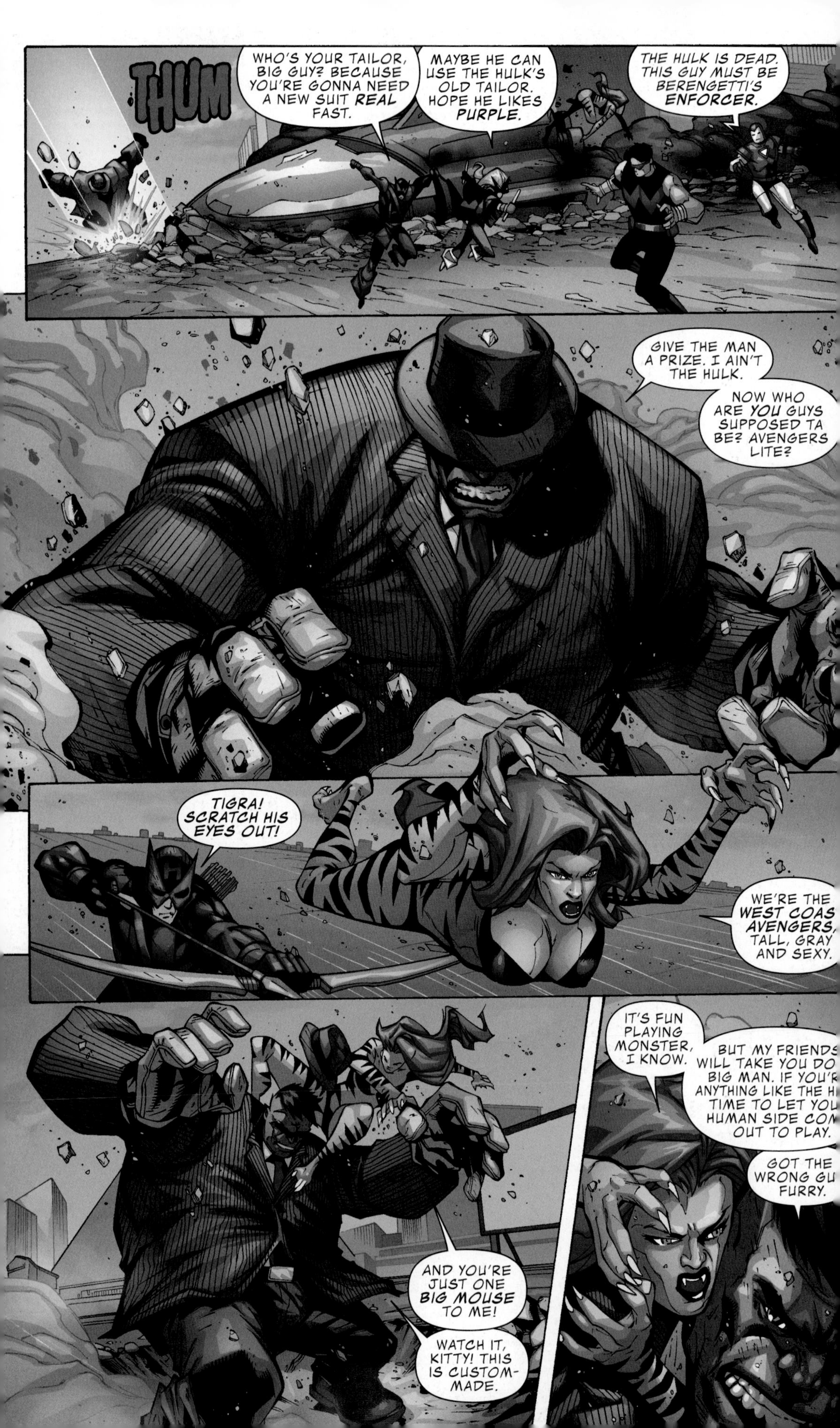
THUM
WHO'S YOUR TAILOR, BIG GUY? BECAUSE YOU'RE GONNA NEED A NEW SUIT REAL FAST.
MAYBE HE CAN USE THE HULK'S OLD TAILOR. HOPE HE LIKES PURPLE.
THE HULK IS DEAD. THIS GUY MUST BE BERENGETTI'S ENFORCER.
GIVE THE MAN A PRIZE. I AIN'T THE HULK.
NOW WHO ARE YOU GUYS SUPPOSED TA BE? AVENGERS LITE?
TIGRA! SCRATCH HIS EYES OUT!
WE'RE THE WEST COAS AVENGERS, TALL, GRAY AND SEXY.
AND YOU'RE JUST ONE BIG MOUSE TO ME!
WATCH IT, KITTY! THIS IS CUSTOM-MADE.
IT'S FUN PLAYING MONSTER, I KNOW.
BUT MY FRIENDS WILL TAKE YOU DO BIG MAN. IF YOU'R ANYTHING LIKE THE H TIME TO LET YOU HUMAN SIDE COM OUT TO PLAY.
GOT THE WRONG GU FURRY.

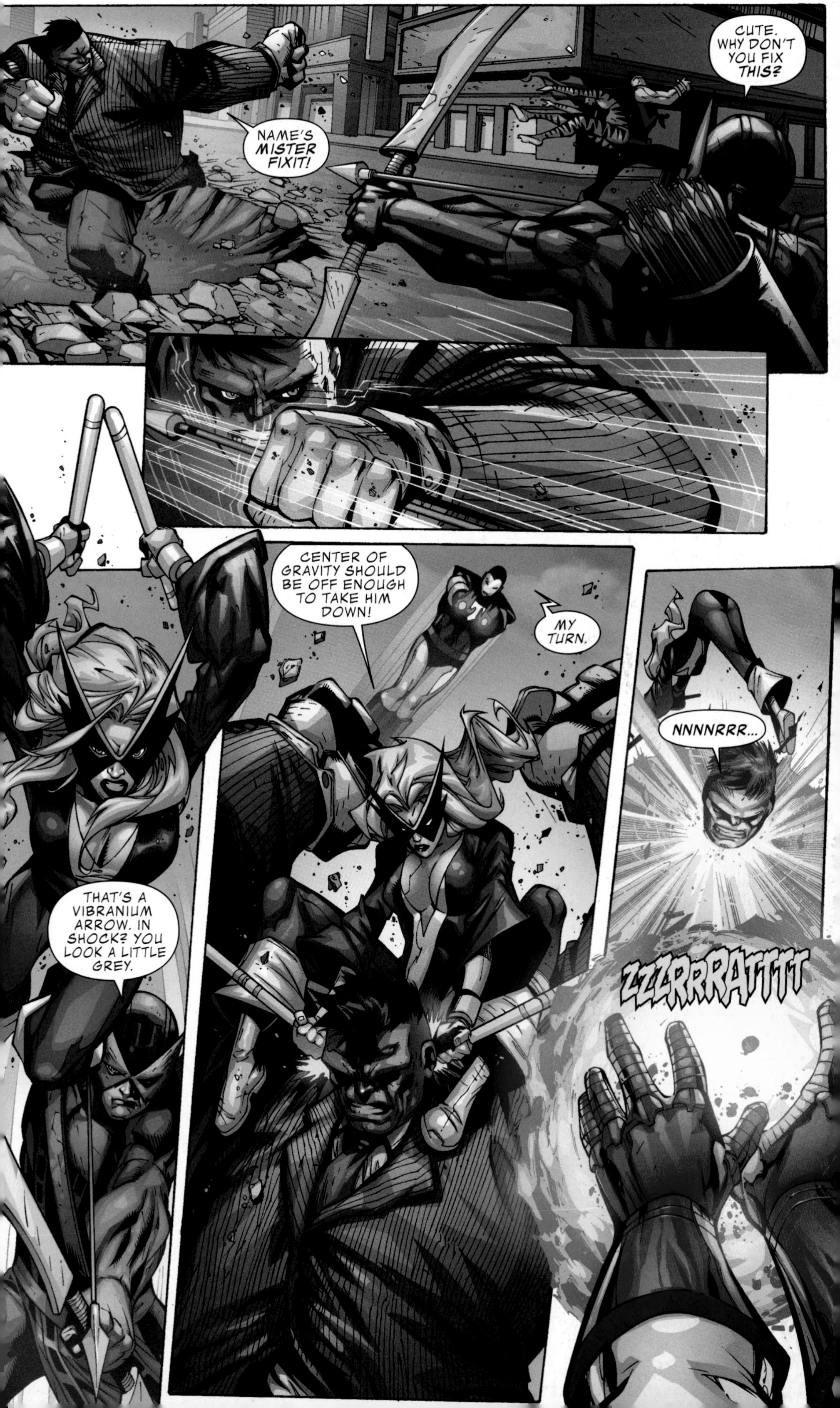
NAME'S MISTER FIXIT!
CUTE. WHY DON'T YOU FIX THIS?
CENTER OF GRAVITY SHOULD BE OFF ENOUGH TO TAKE HIM DOWN!
MY TURN.
THAT'S A VIBRANIUM ARROW. IN SHOCK? YOU LOOK A LITTLE GREY.
NNNNRRR...
ZZZRRRATTTT

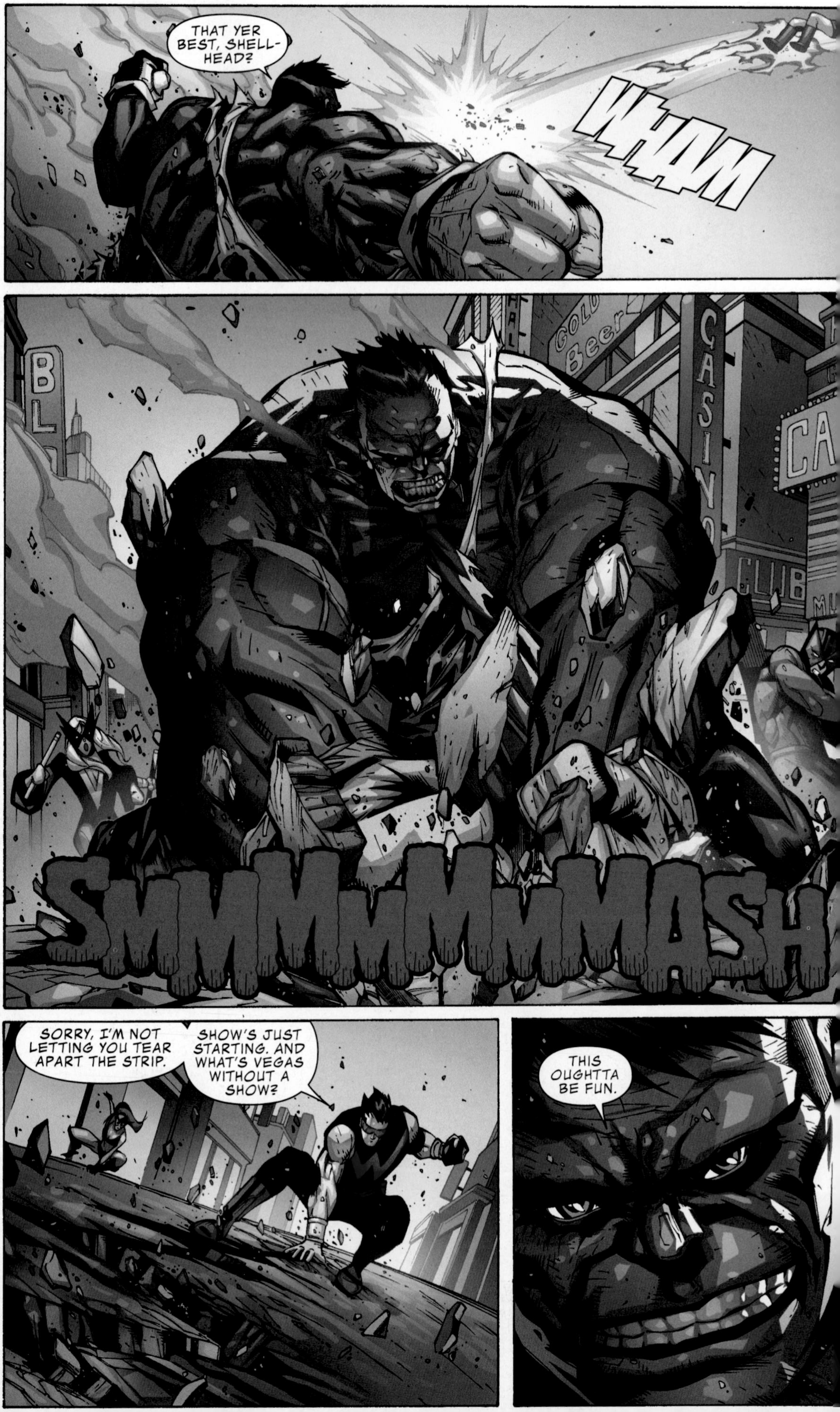
THAT YER BEST, SHELL-HEAD?
WHAM
GOLD Beer
CASINO
CLUB
SMMMMMMASH
SORRY, I'M NOT LETTING YOU TEAR APART THE STRIP.
SHOW'S JUST STARTING. AND WHAT'S VEGAS WITHOUT A SHOW?
THIS OUGHTTA BE FUN.

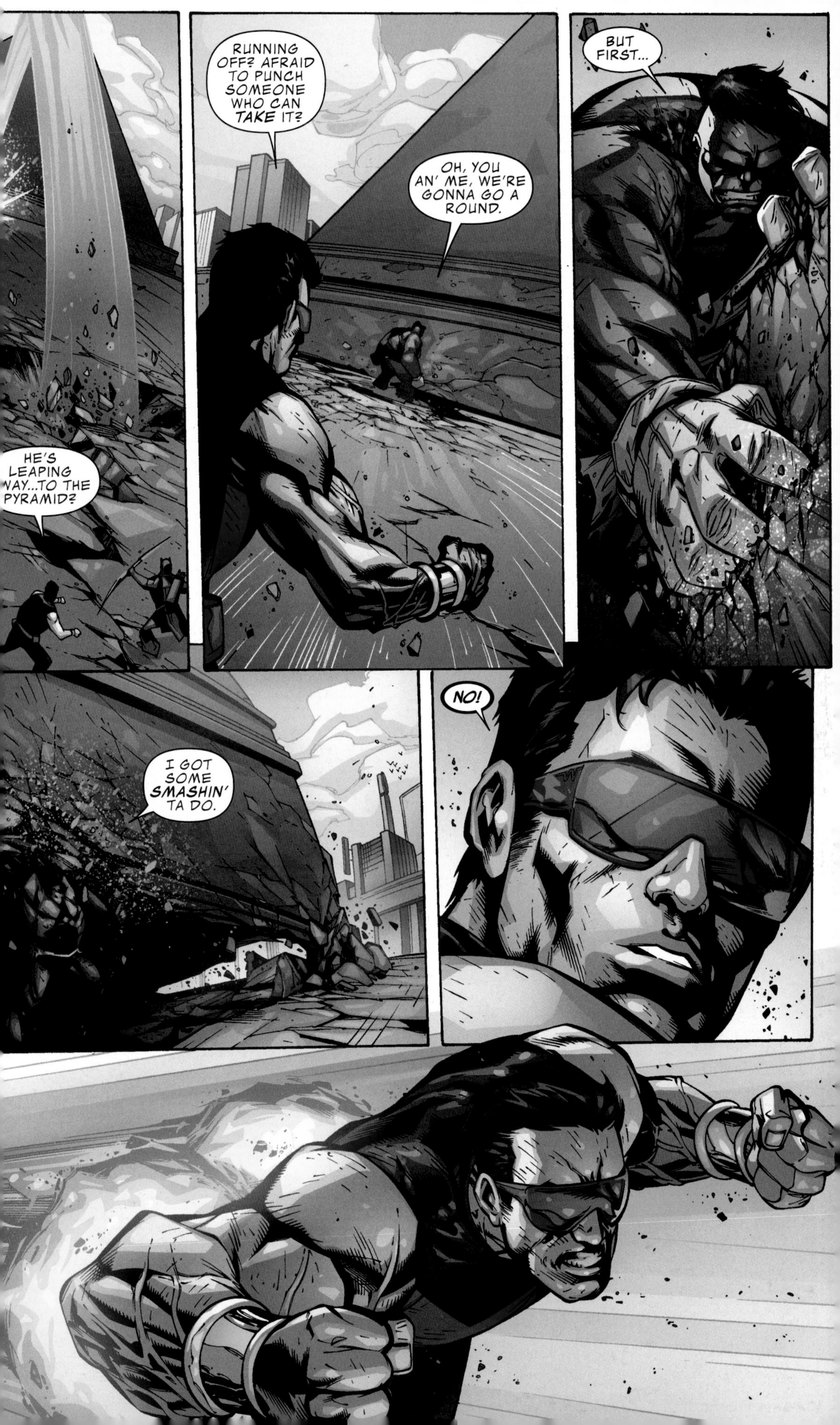

HE'S LEAPING WAY...TO THE PYRAMID?
RUNNING OFF? AFRAID TO PUNCH SOMEONE WHO CAN TAKE IT?
OH, YOU AN' ME, WE'RE GONNA GO A ROUND.
BUT FIRST...
I GOT SOME SMASHIN' TA DO.
NO!

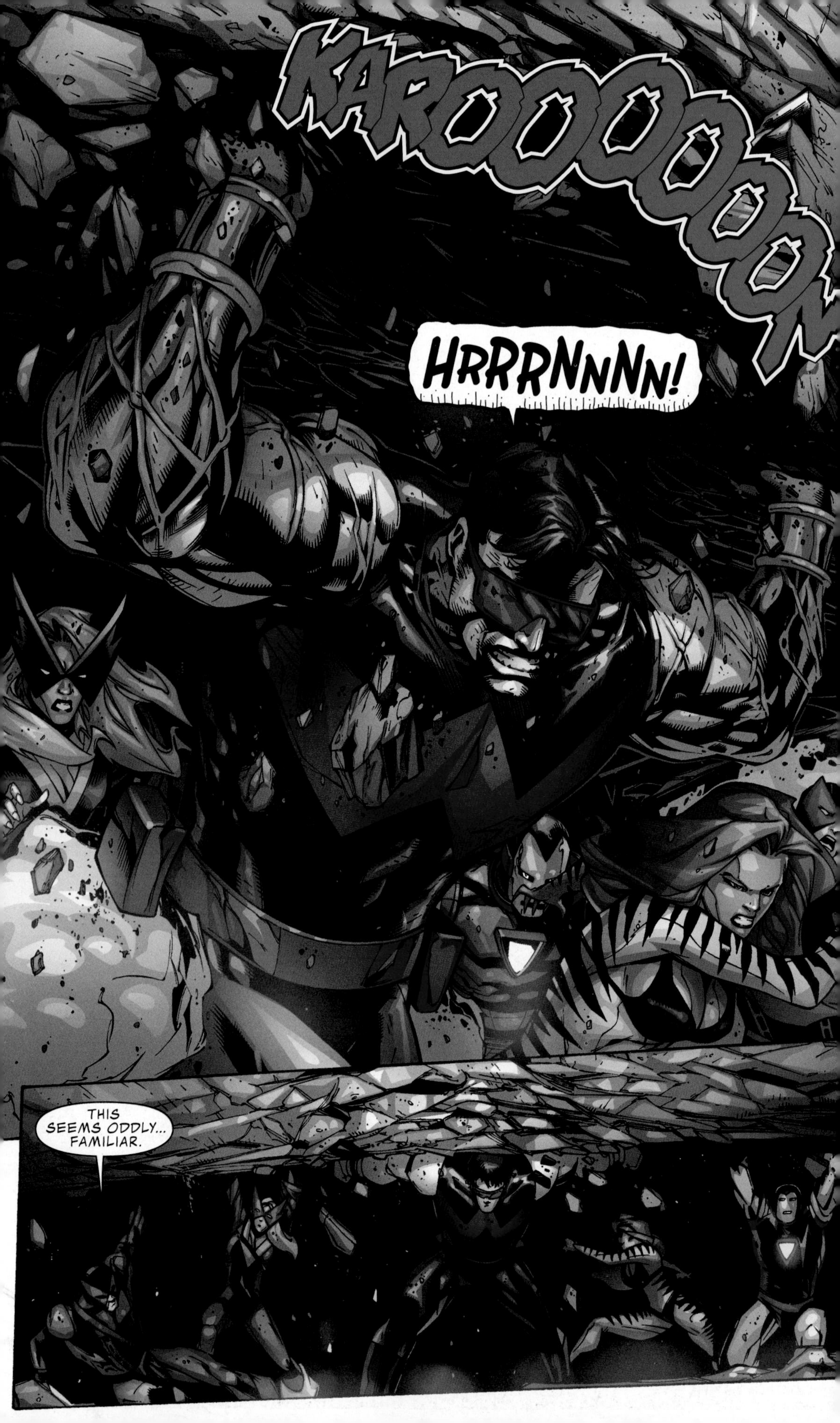
KAROOOOOOM
HRRRNnNN!
THIS SEEMS ODDLY... FAMILIAR.

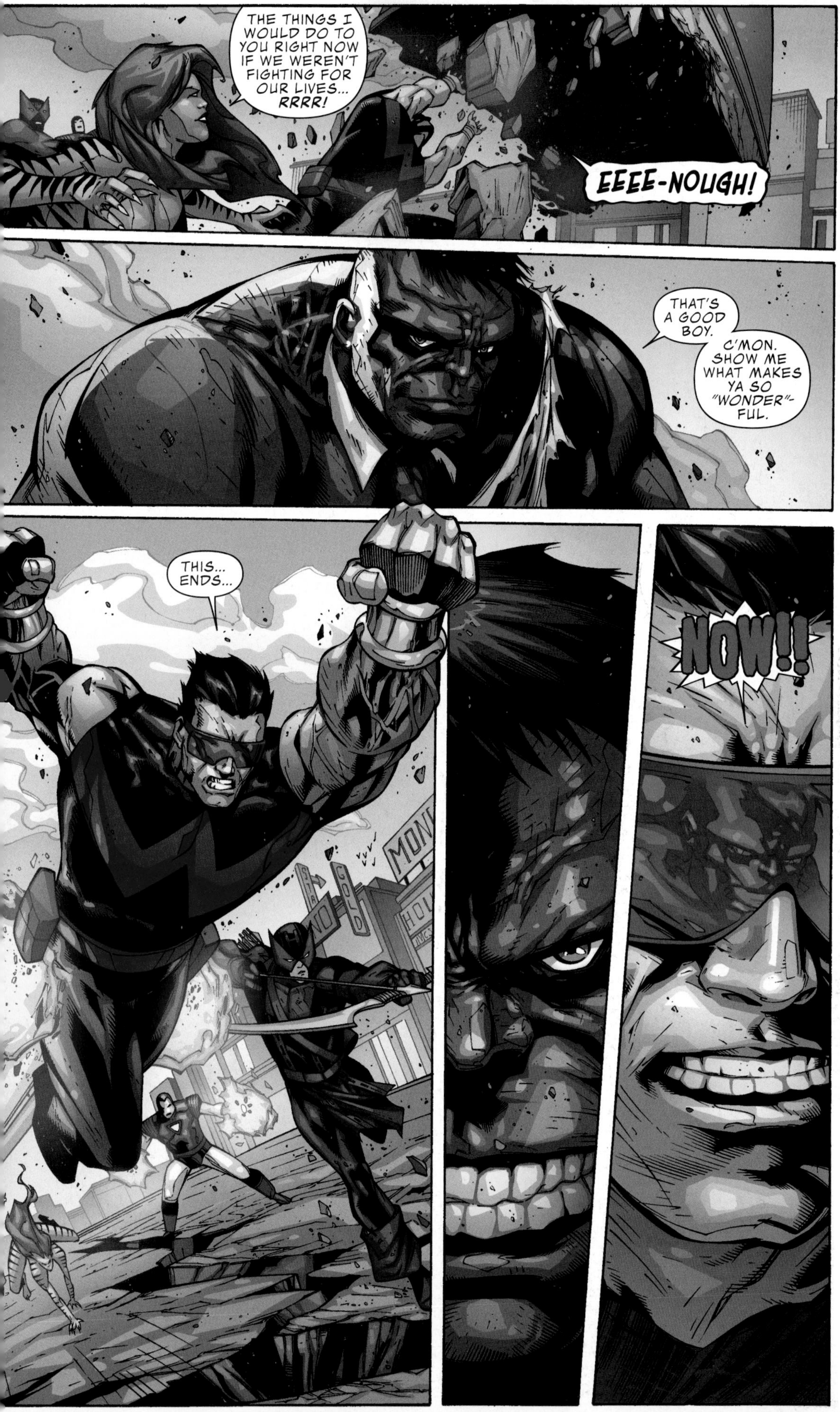
THE THINGS I WOULD DO TO YOU RIGHT NOW IF WE WEREN'T FIGHTING FOR OUR LIVES... RRRR!
EEEE-NOUGH!
THAT'S A GOOD BOY.
C'MON. SHOW ME WHAT MAKES YA SO "WONDER"-FUL.
THIS... ENDS...
NOW!!

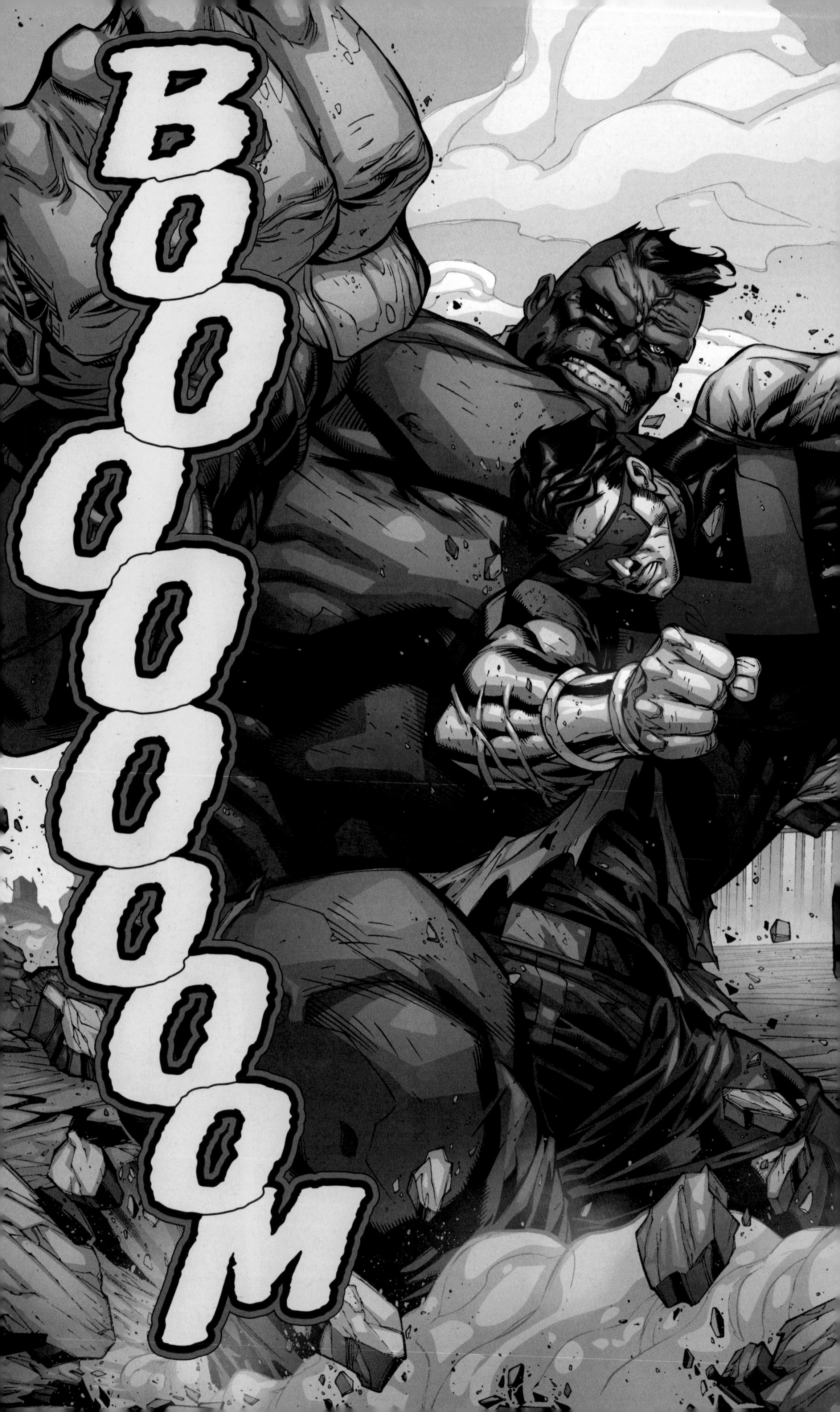
BOOOOOOOM

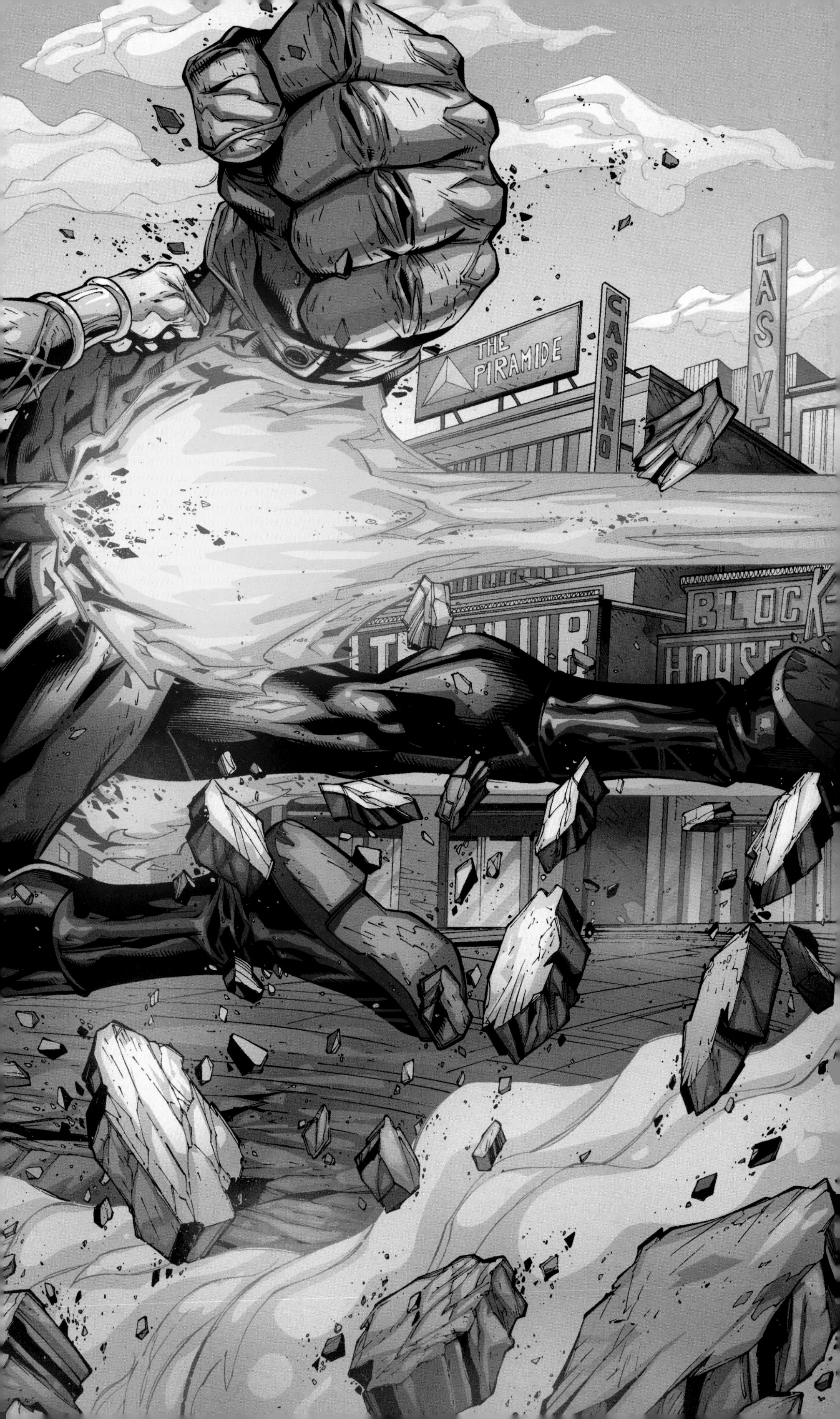
THE PIRAMIDE
CASINO
LAS VE
BLOCK-

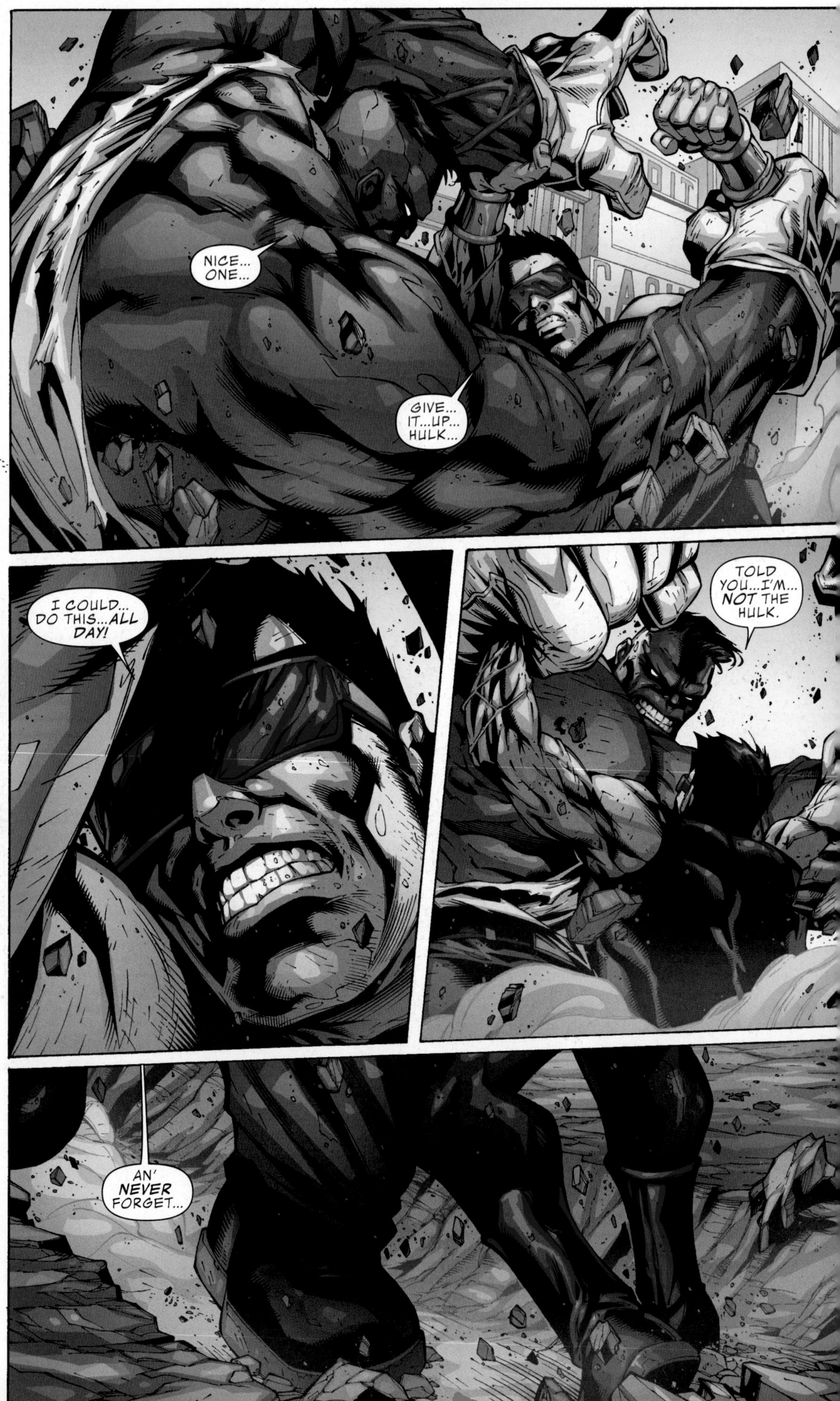
NICE... ONE...
GIVE... IT...UP... HULK...
I COULD... DO THIS...ALL DAY!
TOLD YOU...I'M... NOT THE HULK.
AN' NEVER FORGET...

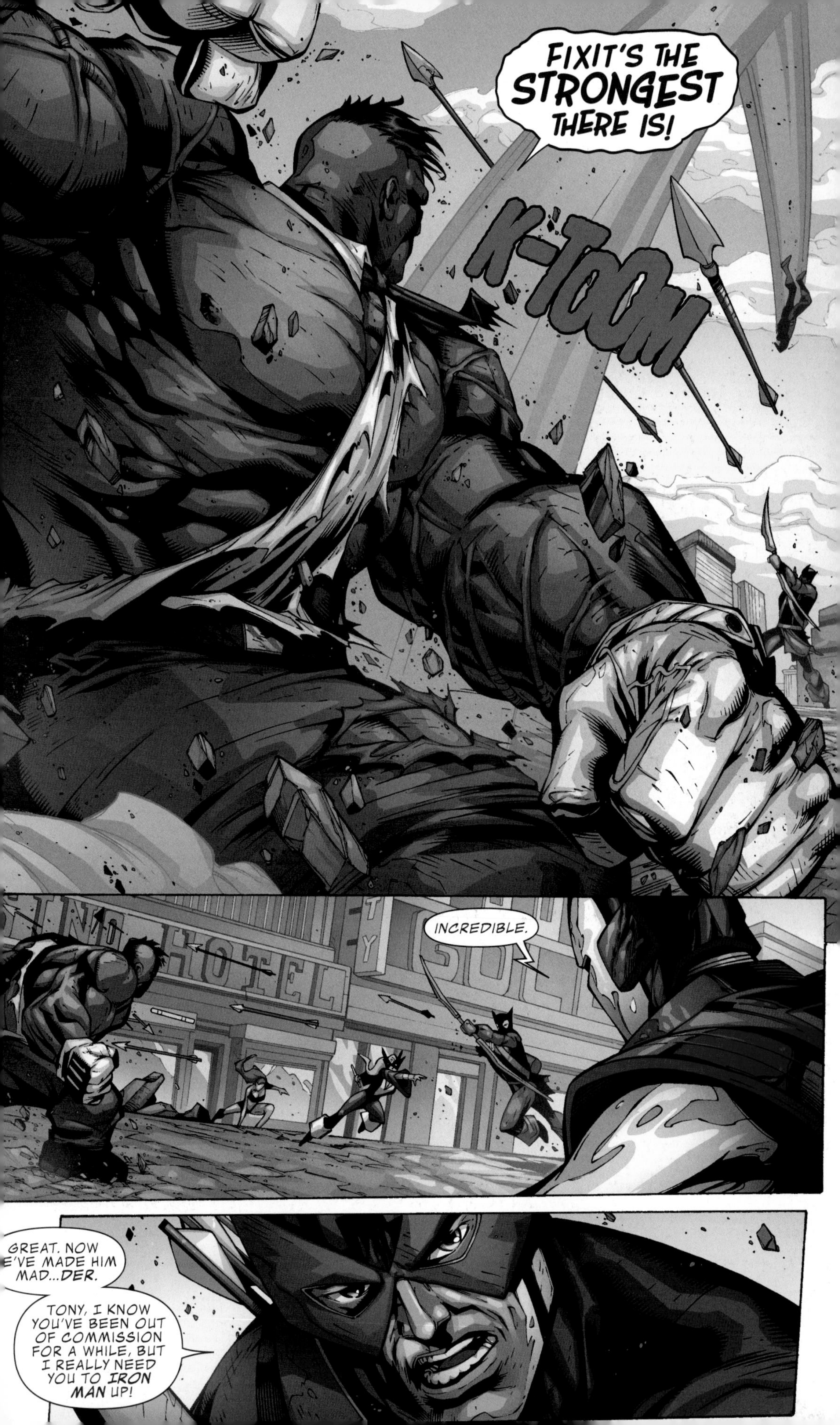
FIXIT'S THE STRONGEST THERE IS!
K-TOOM
INCREDIBLE.
GREAT. NOW E'VE MADE HIM MAD...DER.
TONY, I KNOW YOU'VE BEEN OUT OF COMMISSION FOR A WHILE, BUT I REALLY NEED YOU TO IRON MAN UP!

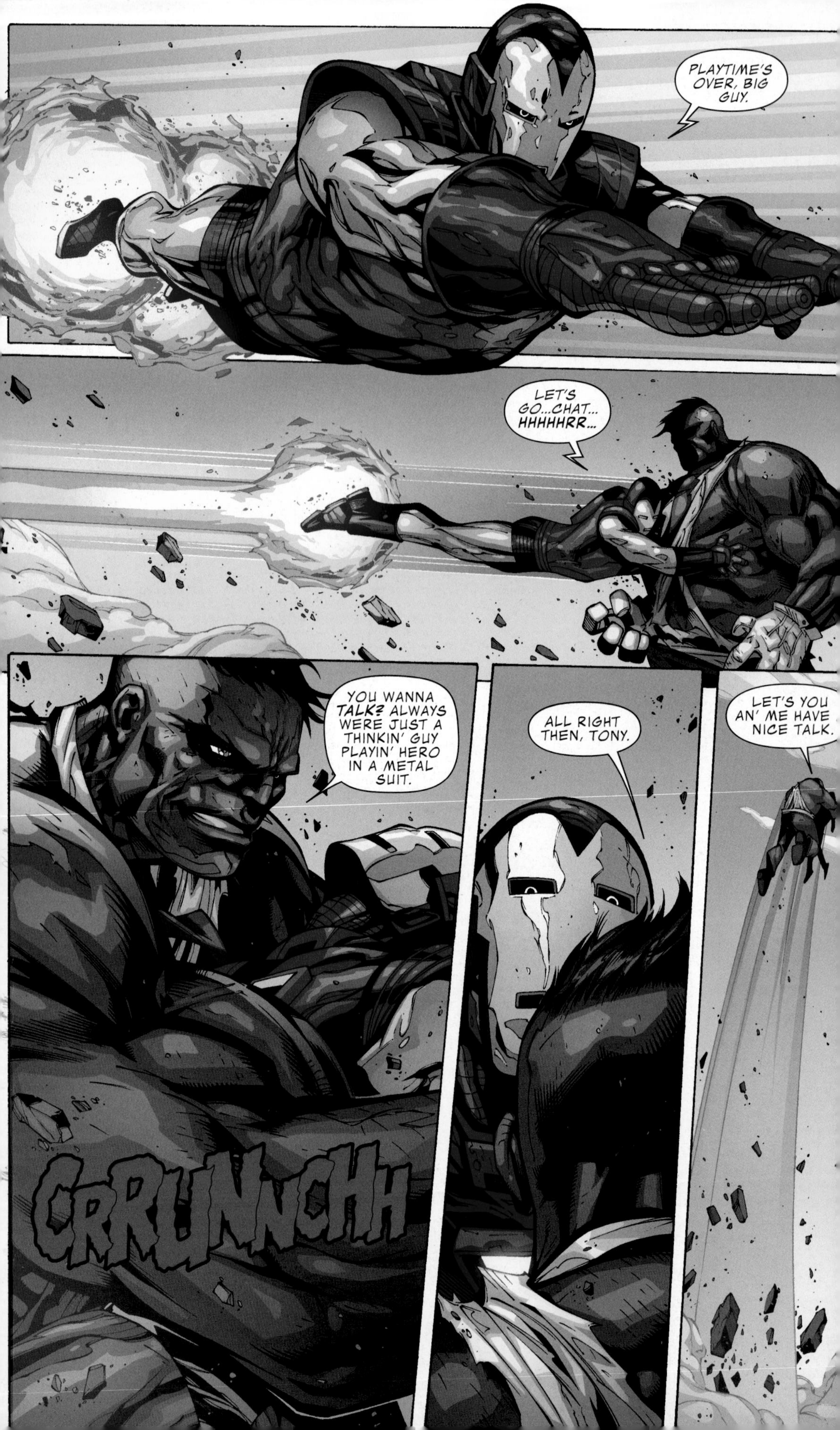
PLAYTIME'S OVER, BIG GUY.
LET'S GO...CHAT... HHHHHRR...
YOU WANNA TALK? ALWAYS WERE JUST A THINKIN' GUY PLAYIN' HERO IN A METAL SUIT.
ALL RIGHT THEN, TONY.
LET'S YOU AN' ME HAVE NICE TALK.
CRRUNNCHH

YA GOT TEN SECONDS.

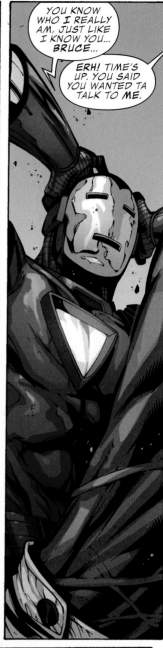

YOU KNOW WHO I REALLY AM, JUST LIKE I KNOW YOU... BRUCE...

ERH! TIME'S UP. YOU SAID YOU WANTED TA TALK TO ME.

THUM

YOU TRULY *ARE* DIFFERENT.

S'WHAT I BEEN TRYIN' TA TELL YA.

LET IT GO, TONY.

HULK...BANNER... THEY DON'T LIVE HERE NO MORE. SO PACK THAT TIN CAN OF YOURS BACK IN A BRIEFCASE AND SPLIT.

SO, I GUESS THE HULK REALLY *DID* DIE IN THAT EXPLOSION A FEW MONTHS BACK.

IN A PLACE LIKE THIS.

IT WOULD APPEAR NEITHER THE HULK *NOR* BRUCE BANNER COULD HAVE SURVIVED THAT.

SOMETHING THAT CLAIMED THOUSANDS OF OTHER LIVES.

FIXIT LIVES HERE NOW.

WE GOT HISTORY, TOO, YOU AN' ME. YO SHOULD KNOW WHAT THIS MEANS, THEN ALL RIGHT?

I'M *HAPPY*. FER ONCE, I GOT THE LIFE I WANT. I'M *ONE GUY*. I DON'T WANNA CHANGE.

AND THE MOB WAR? WE KNOW YOU'RE INVOLVED.

YOU SAY *ENFORCER*... I SAY *PROTECTOR*. I GOT THIS, STARK. NO ONE WHO DON'T *DESERVE IT* WILL GET HURT IN THIS TOWN UNDER MY WATCH.

TRUST ME.

WHOOSH

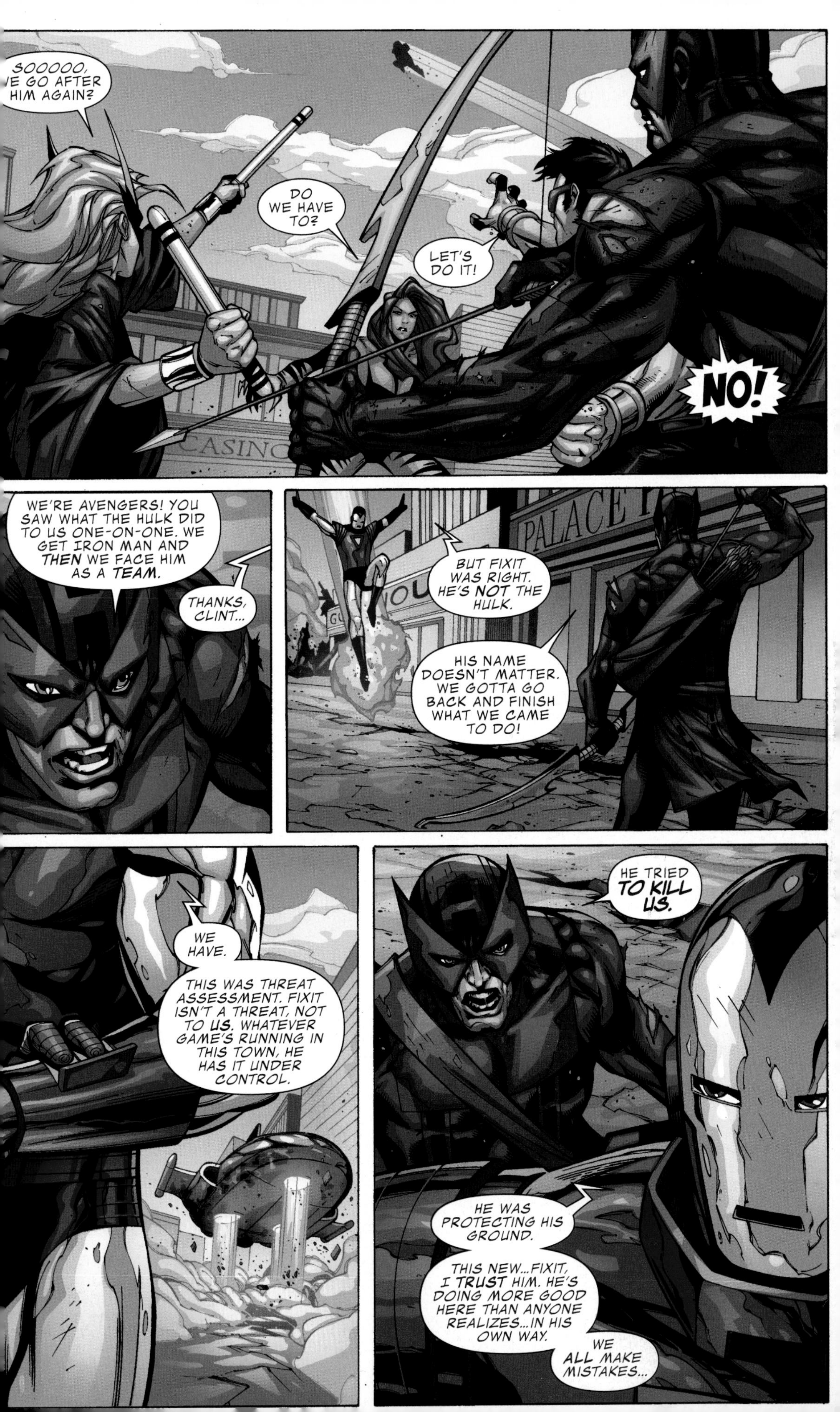
SOOOOO, WE GO AFTER HIM AGAIN?
DO WE HAVE TO?
LET'S DO IT!
NO!
CASINO
WE'RE AVENGERS! YOU SAW WHAT THE HULK DID TO US ONE-ON-ONE. WE GET IRON MAN AND **THEN** WE FACE HIM AS A **TEAM.**
THANKS, CLINT...
PALACE
BUT FIXIT WAS RIGHT. HE'S **NOT** THE HULK.
HIS NAME DOESN'T MATTER. WE GOTTA GO BACK AND FINISH WHAT WE CAME TO DO!
WE HAVE.
THIS WAS THREAT ASSESSMENT. FIXIT ISN'T A THREAT, NOT TO **US.** WHATEVER GAME'S RUNNING IN THIS TOWN, HE HAS IT UNDER CONTROL.
HE TRIED **TO KILL US.**
HE WAS PROTECTING HIS GROUND.
THIS NEW...FIXIT, I **TRUST** HIM. HE'S DOING MORE GOOD HERE THAN ANYONE REALIZES...IN HIS OWN WAY.
WE **ALL** MAKE MISTAKES...

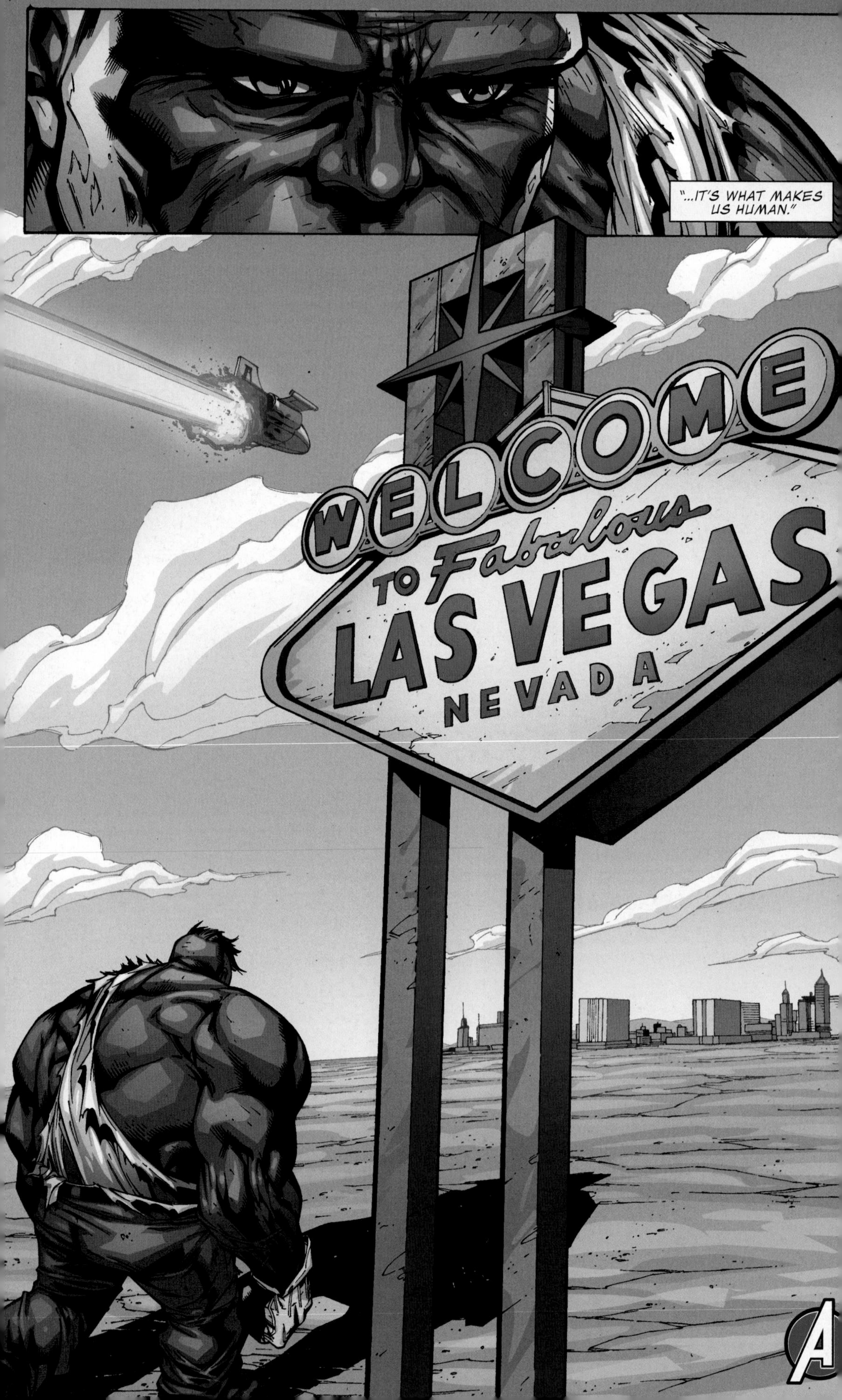
"...IT'S WHAT MAKES US HUMAN."
WELCOME TO Fabulous LAS VEGAS NEVADA

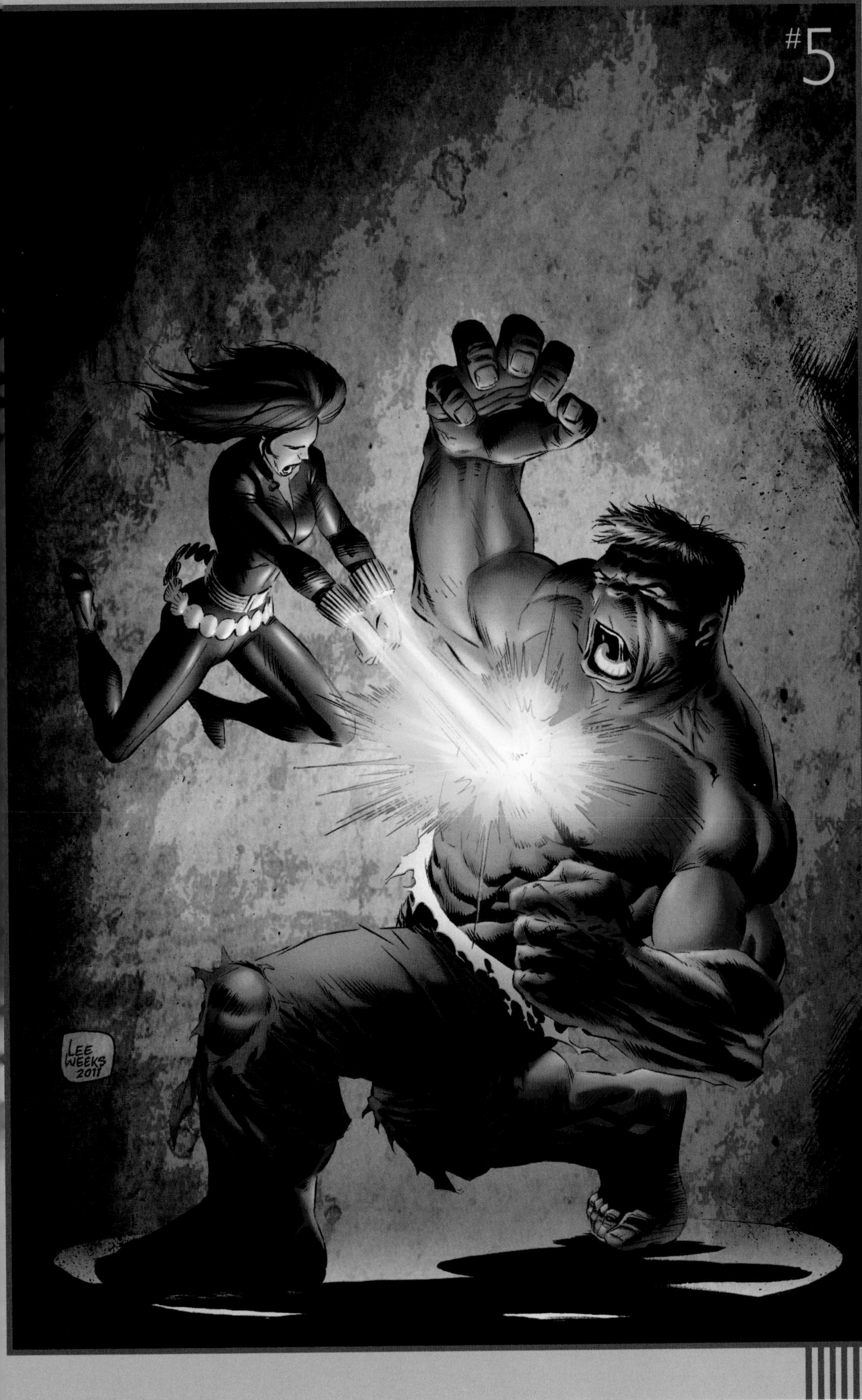
#5
LEE
WEEKS
2011

THIS STORY OCCURS AFTER THE EVENTS OF *CIVIL WAR* AND *WORLD WAR HULK*

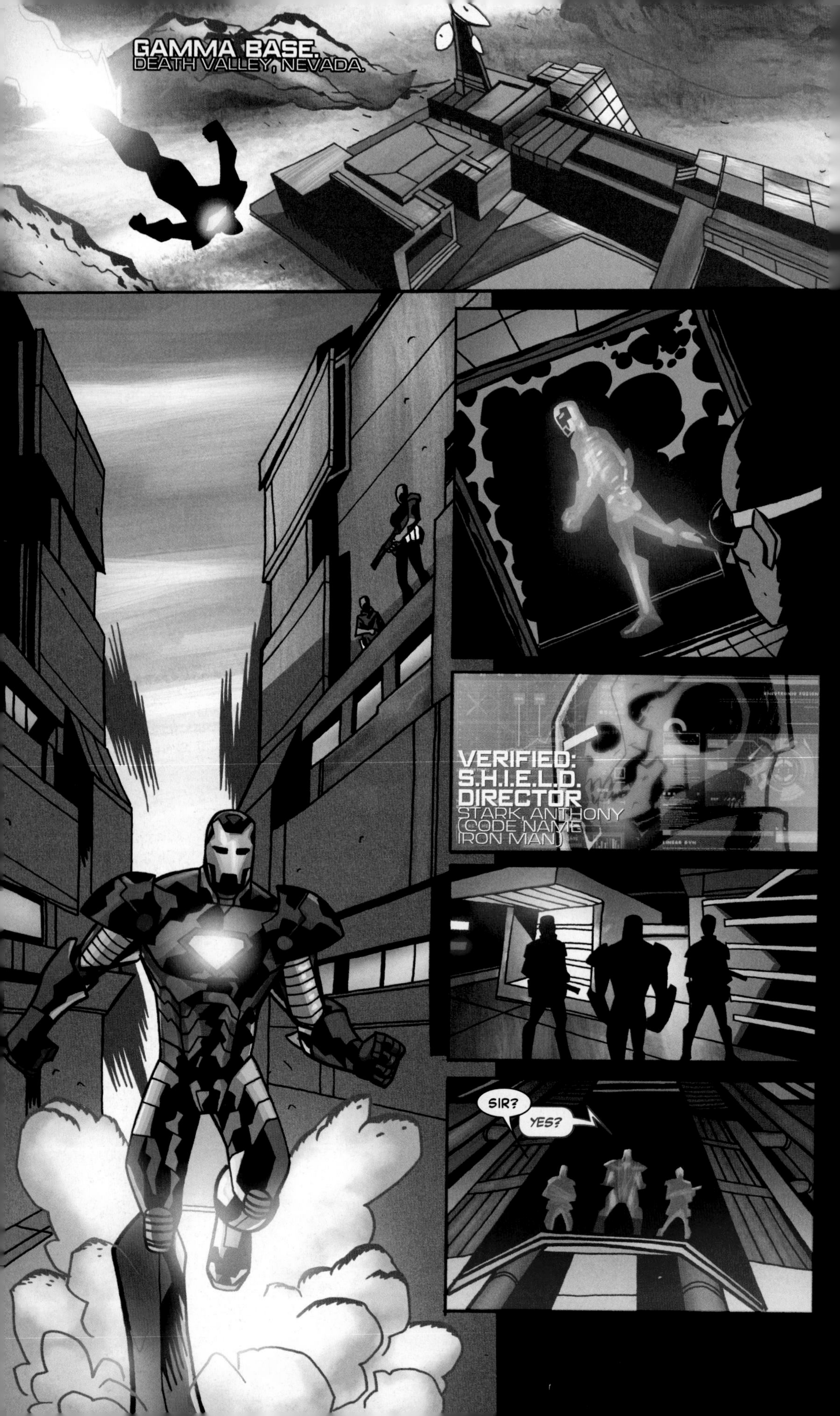
GAMMA BASE.
DEATH VALLEY, NEVADA.
VERIFIED:
S.H.I.E.L.D.
DIRECTOR
STARK, ANTHONY
(CODE NAME
IRON MAN)
SIR?
YES?

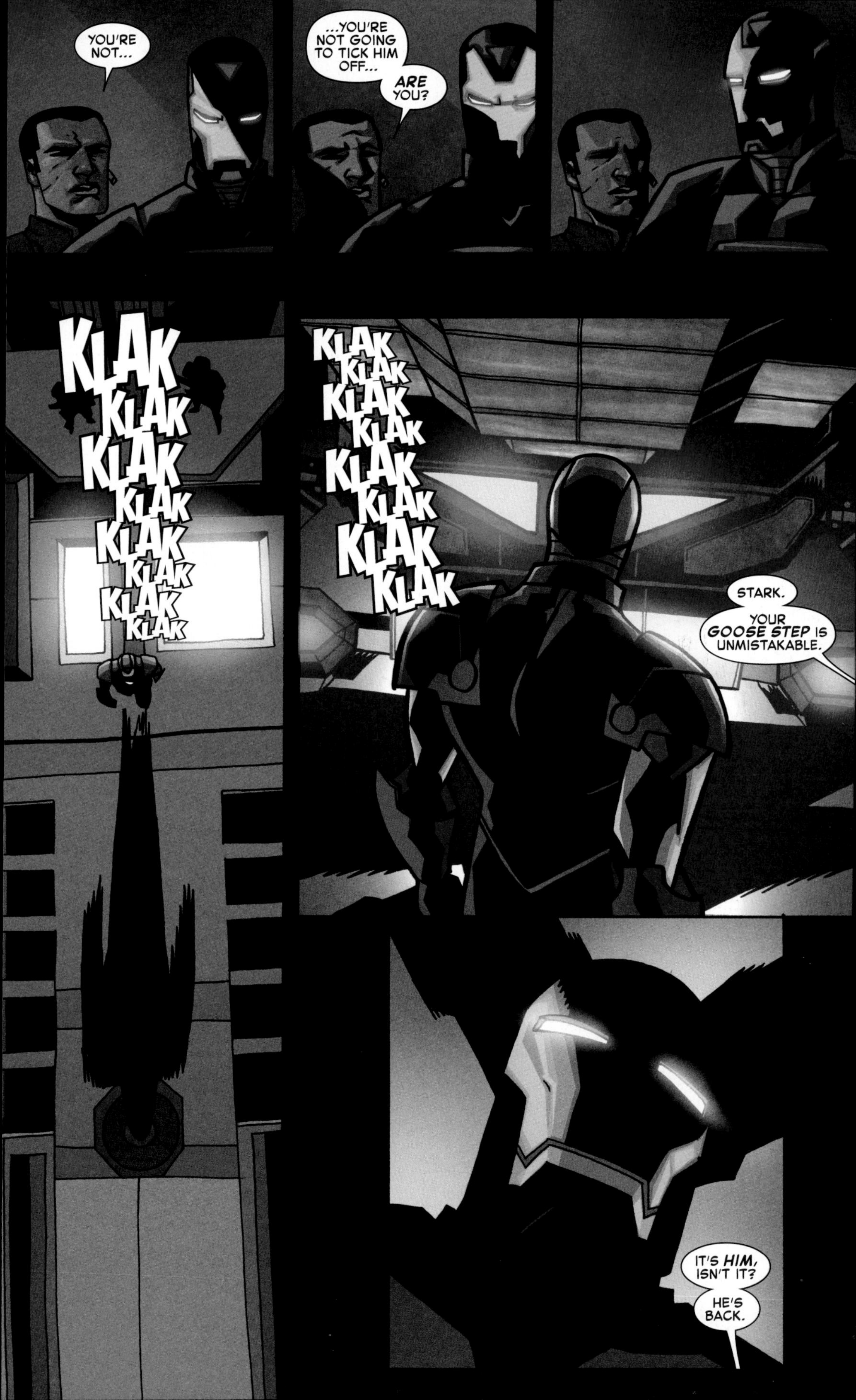
YOU'RE NOT...
...YOU'RE NOT GOING TO TICK HIM OFF...
ARE YOU?
KLAK KLAK KLAK KLAK KLAK KLAK KLAK KLAK
KLAK KLAK KLAK KLAK KLAK KLAK KLAK KLAK
STARK.
YOUR GOOSE STEP IS UNMISTAKABLE.
IT'S HIM, ISN'T IT?
HE'S BACK.

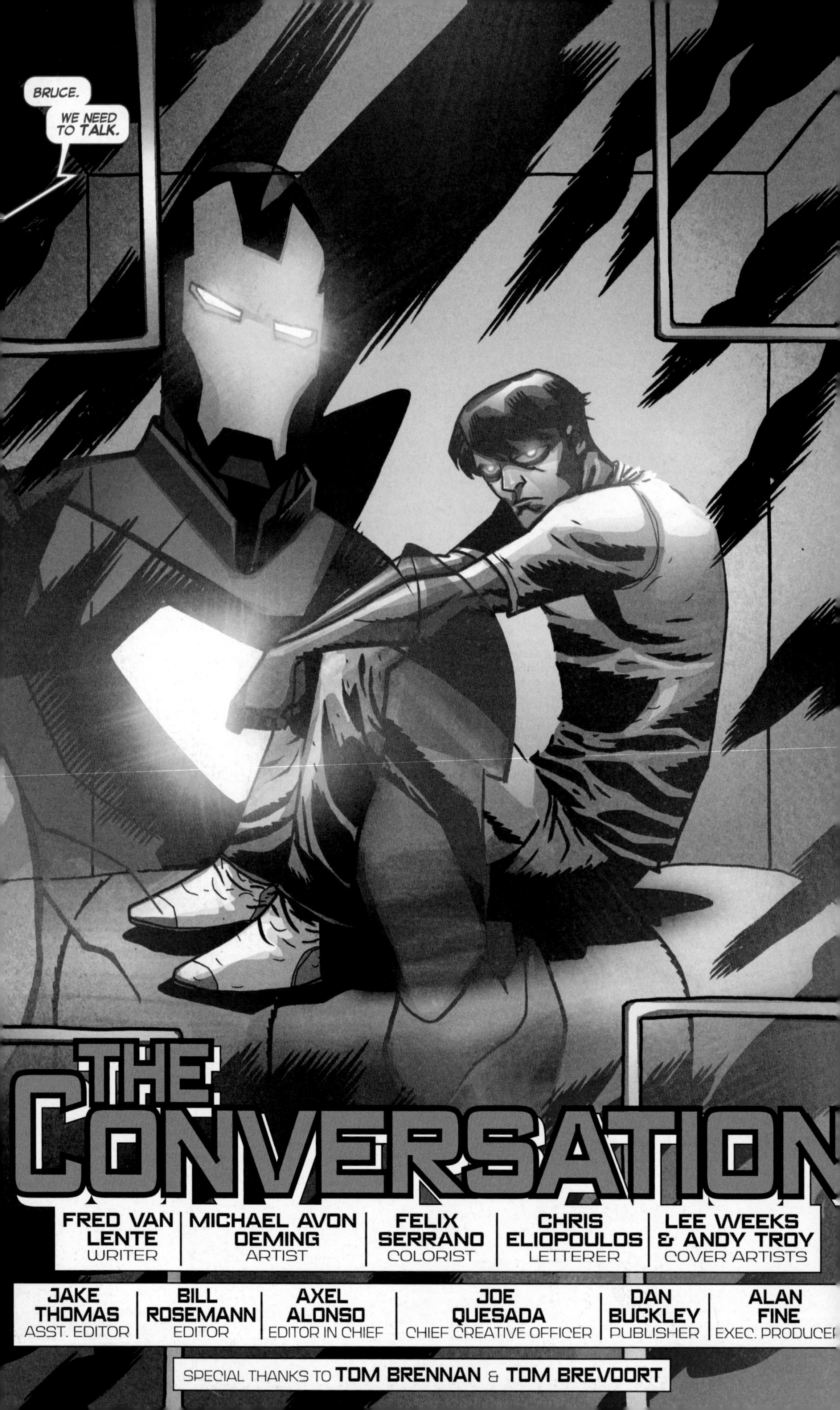
BRUCE.
WE NEED TO TALK.
THE CONVERSATION
FRED VAN LENTE WRITER
MICHAEL AVON OEMING ARTIST
FELIX SERRANO COLORIST
CHRIS ELIOPOULOS LETTERER
LEE WEEKS & ANDY TROY COVER ARTISTS
JAKE THOMAS ASST. EDITOR
BILL ROSEMANN EDITOR
AXEL ALONSO EDITOR IN CHIEF
JOE QUESADA CHIEF CREATIVE OFFICER
DAN BUCKLEY PUBLISHER
ALAN FINE EXEC. PRODUCER
SPECIAL THANKS TO TOM BRENNAN & TOM BREVOORT

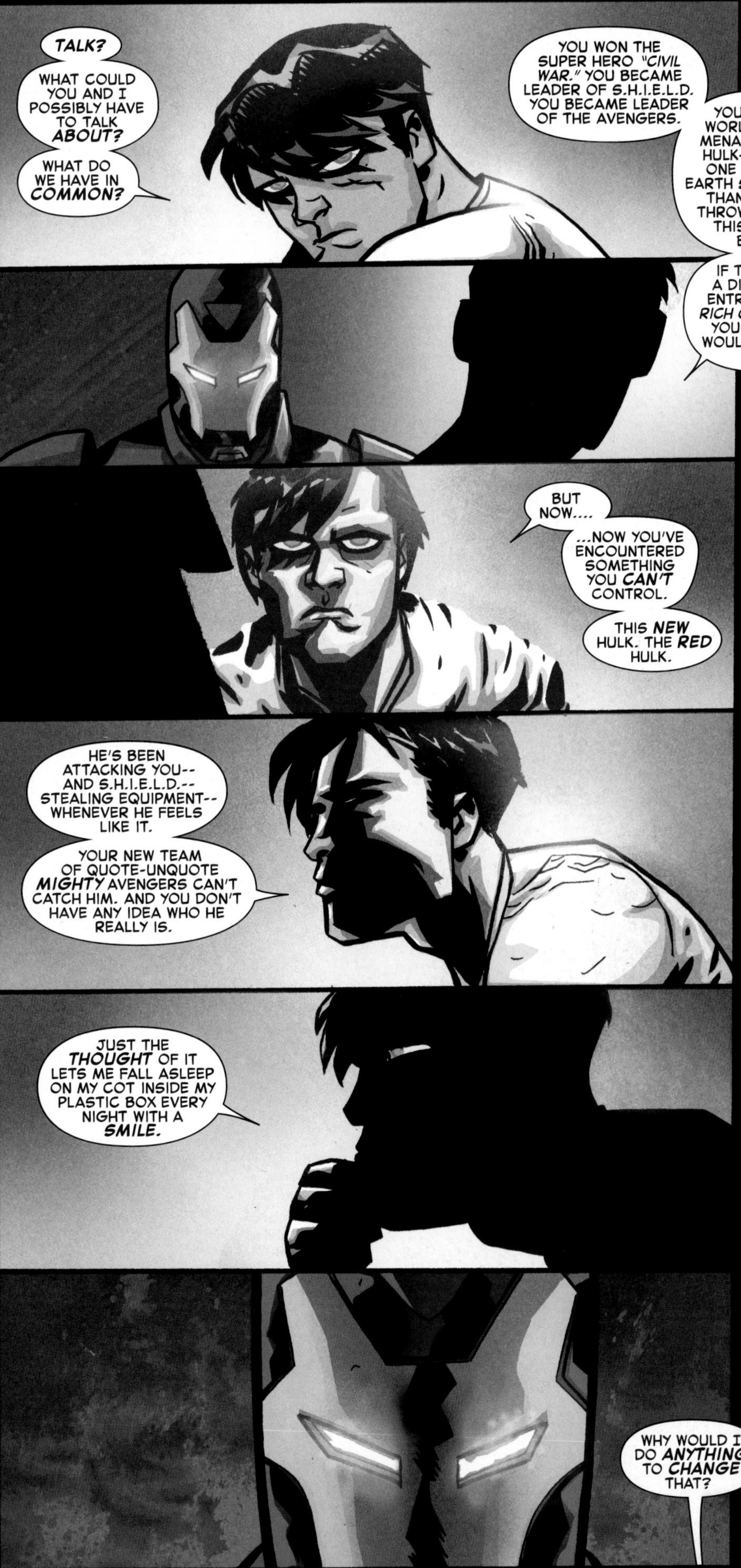
TALK?
WHAT COULD YOU AND I POSSIBLY HAVE TO TALK ABOUT?
WHAT DO WE HAVE IN COMMON?
YOU WON THE SUPER HERO "CIVIL WAR." YOU BECAME LEADER OF S.H.I.E.L.D. YOU BECAME LEADER OF THE AVENGERS.
YOU RID THE WORLD OF THE MENACE OF THE HULK--AND THE ONE BEING ON EARTH STRONGER THAN YOU--BY THROWING ME IN THIS GAMMA BASE.
IF THERE WAS A DICTIONARY ENTRY FOR "THE RICH GET RICHER," YOUR PICTURE WOULD BE NEXT TO IT.
BUT NOW....
...NOW YOU'VE ENCOUNTERED SOMETHING YOU CAN'T CONTROL.
THIS NEW HULK. THE RED HULK.
HE'S BEEN ATTACKING YOU--AND S.H.I.E.L.D.--STEALING EQUIPMENT--WHENEVER HE FEELS LIKE IT.
YOUR NEW TEAM OF QUOTE-UNQUOTE MIGHTY AVENGERS CAN'T CATCH HIM. AND YOU DON'T HAVE ANY IDEA WHO HE REALLY IS.
JUST THE THOUGHT OF IT LETS ME FALL ASLEEP ON MY COT INSIDE MY PLASTIC BOX EVERY NIGHT WITH A SMILE.
WHY WOULD I DO ANYTHING TO CHANGE THAT?

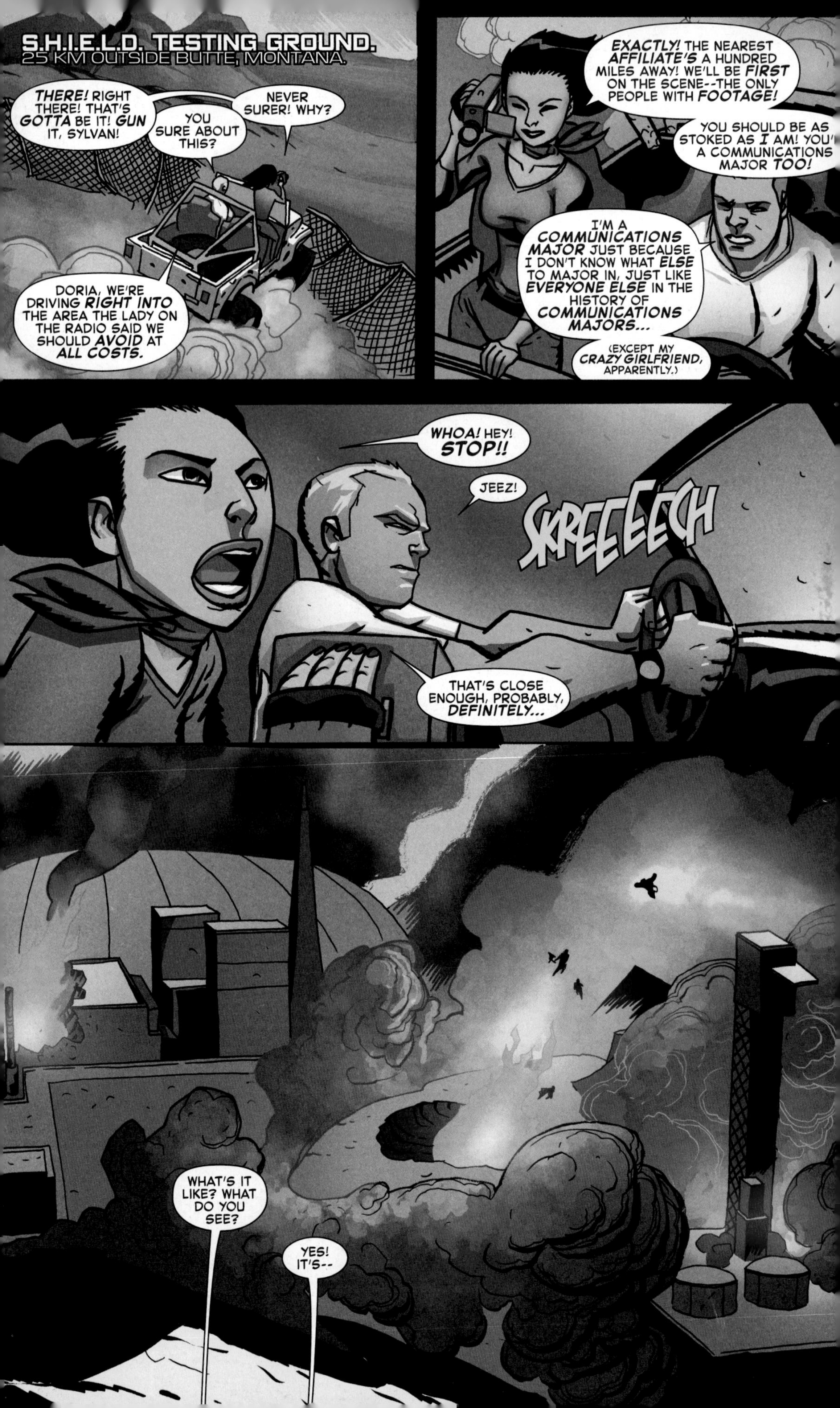
S.H.I.E.L.D. TESTING GROUND.
25 KM OUTSIDE BUTTE, MONTANA.
THERE! RIGHT THERE! THAT'S GOTTA BE IT! GUN IT, SYLVAN!
YOU SURE ABOUT THIS?
NEVER SURER! WHY?
DORIA, WE'RE DRIVING RIGHT INTO THE AREA THE LADY ON THE RADIO SAID WE SHOULD AVOID AT ALL COSTS.
EXACTLY! THE NEAREST AFFILIATE'S A HUNDRED MILES AWAY! WE'LL BE FIRST ON THE SCENE--THE ONLY PEOPLE WITH FOOTAGE!
YOU SHOULD BE AS STOKED AS I AM! YOU' A COMMUNICATIONS MAJOR TOO!
I'M A COMMUNICATIONS MAJOR JUST BECAUSE I DON'T KNOW WHAT ELSE TO MAJOR IN, JUST LIKE EVERYONE ELSE IN THE HISTORY OF COMMUNICATIONS MAJORS...
(EXCEPT MY CRAZY GIRLFRIEND, APPARENTLY.)
WHOA! HEY! STOP!!
JEEZ!
SKREEEEECH
THAT'S CLOSE ENOUGH, PROBABLY, DEFINITELY...
WHAT'S IT LIKE? WHAT DO YOU SEE?
YES! IT'S--

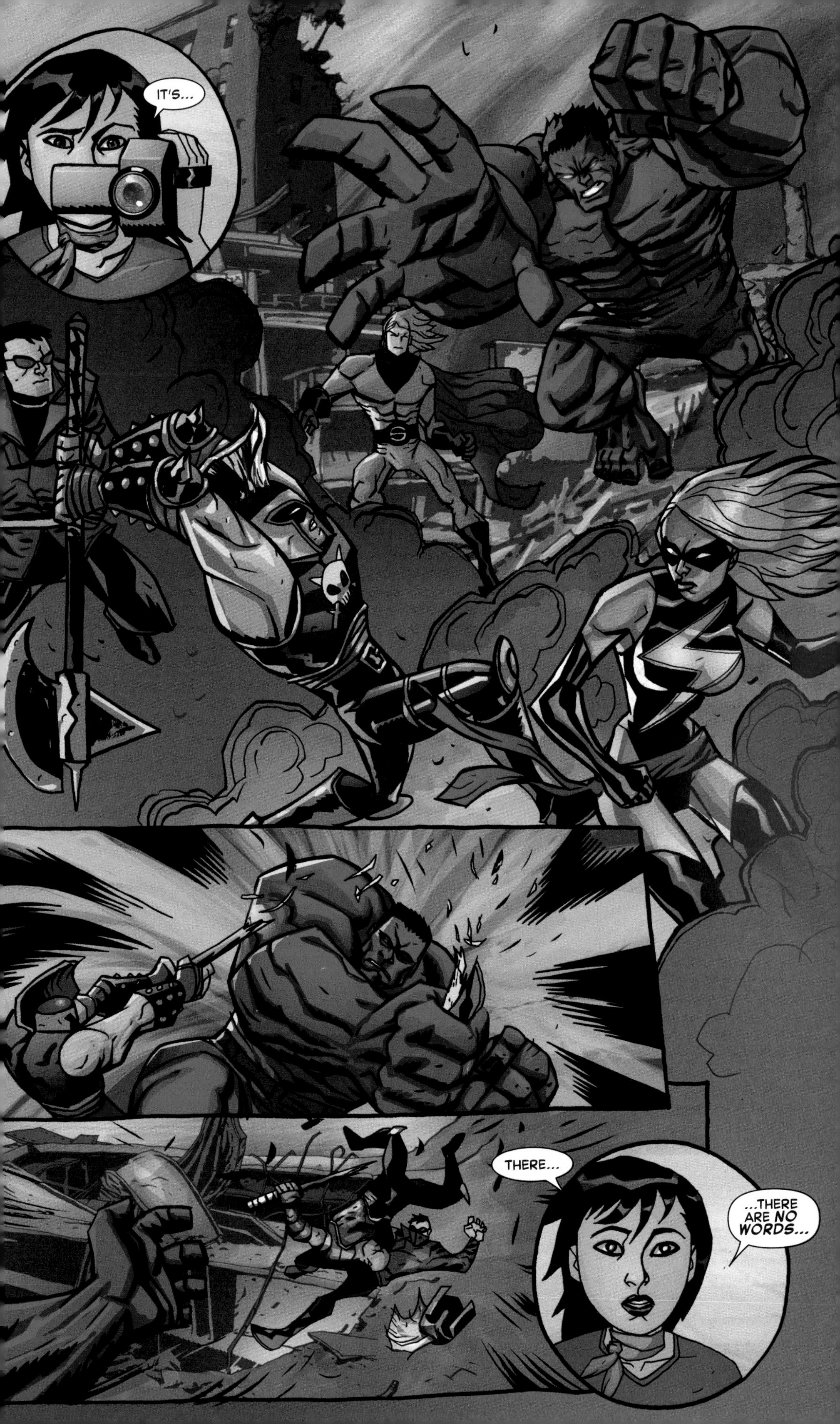
IT'S...
THERE...
...THERE ARE NO WORDS...

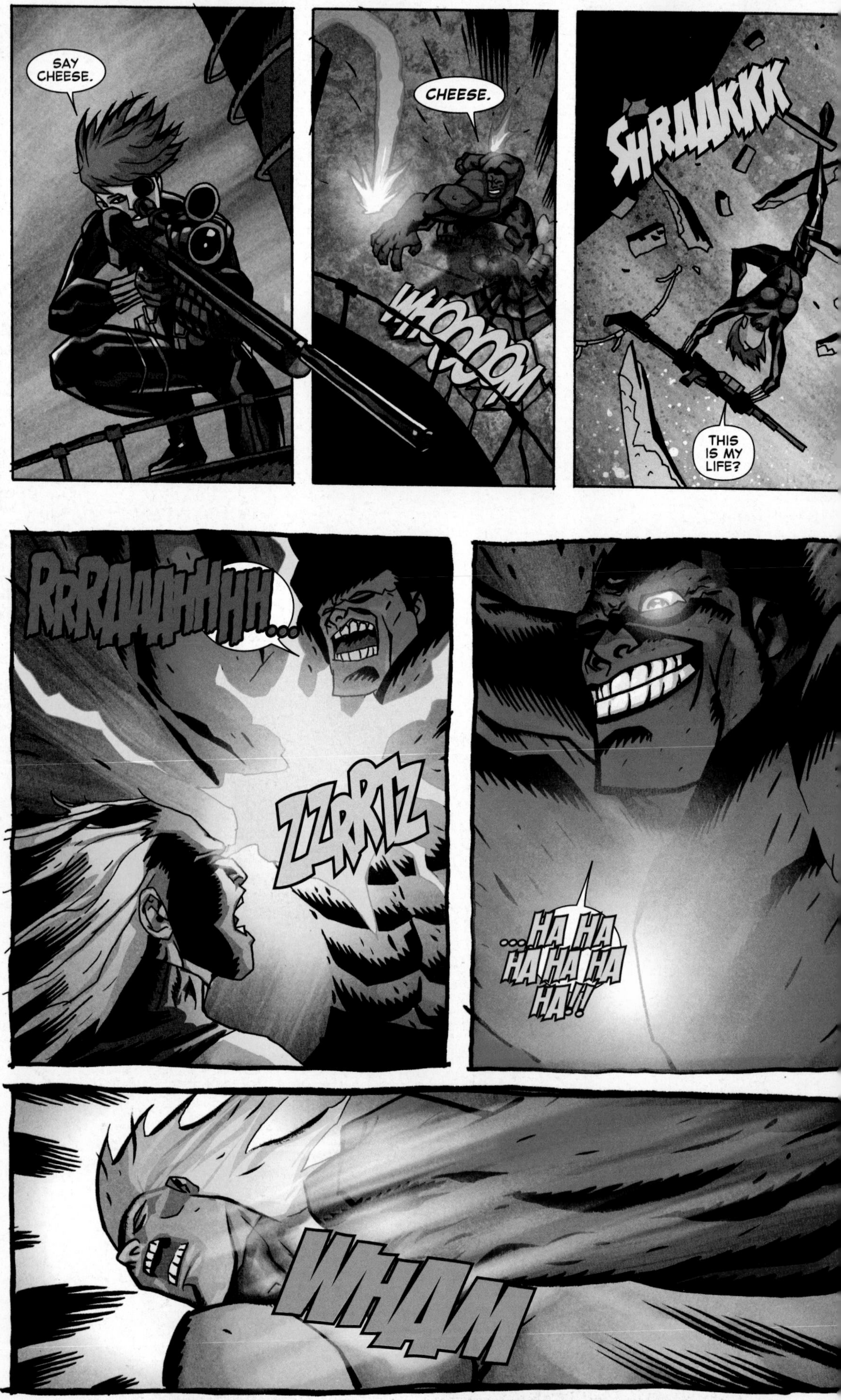
SAY CHEESE.
CHEESE.
WHOOOOOM
SHRAAKKK
THIS IS MY LIFE?
RRRAAAHHHH...
ZZRRRTZ
...HA HA HA HA HA HA!!
WHAM

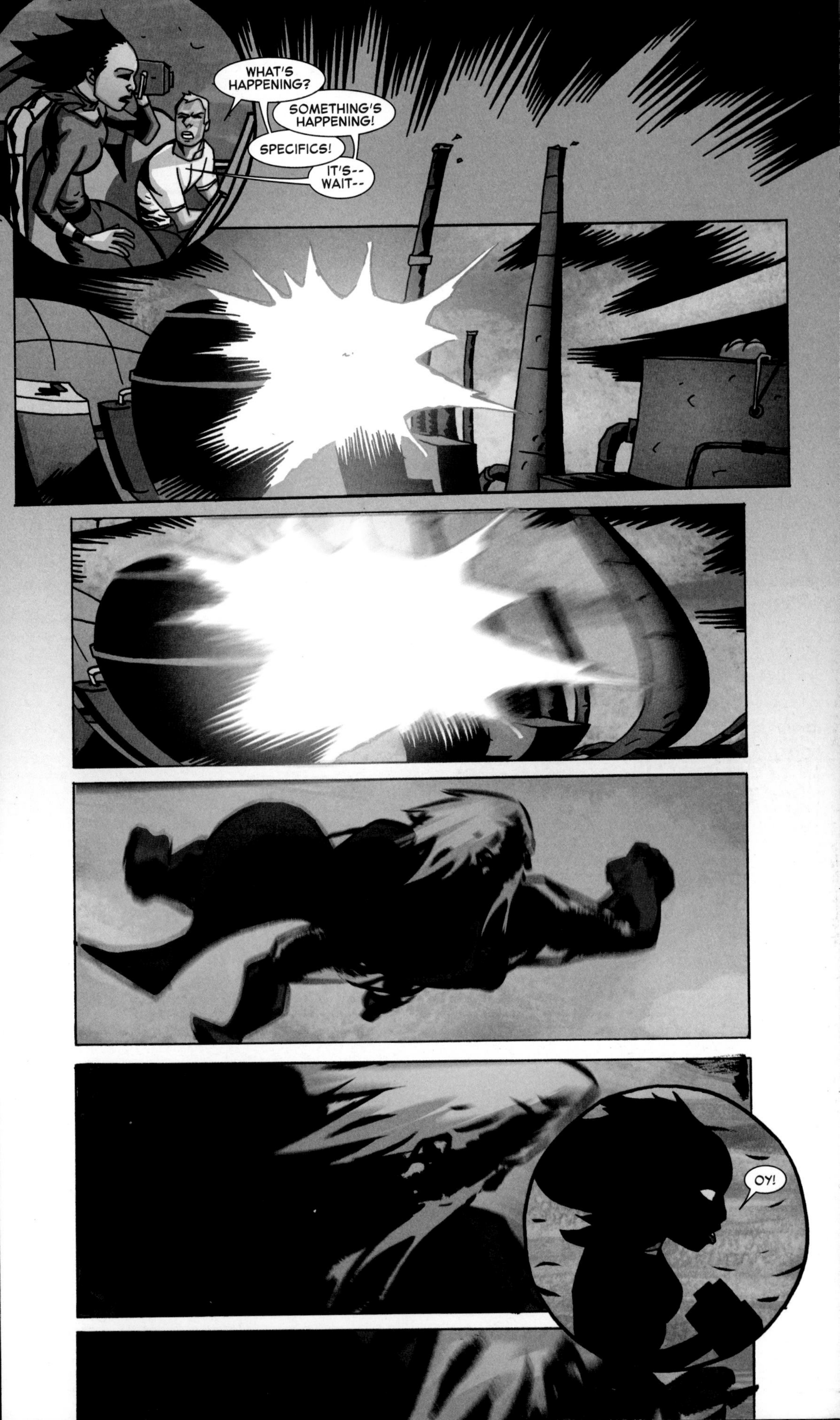
WHAT'S HAPPENING?
SOMETHING'S HAPPENING!
SPECIFICS!
IT'S-- WAIT--
OY!

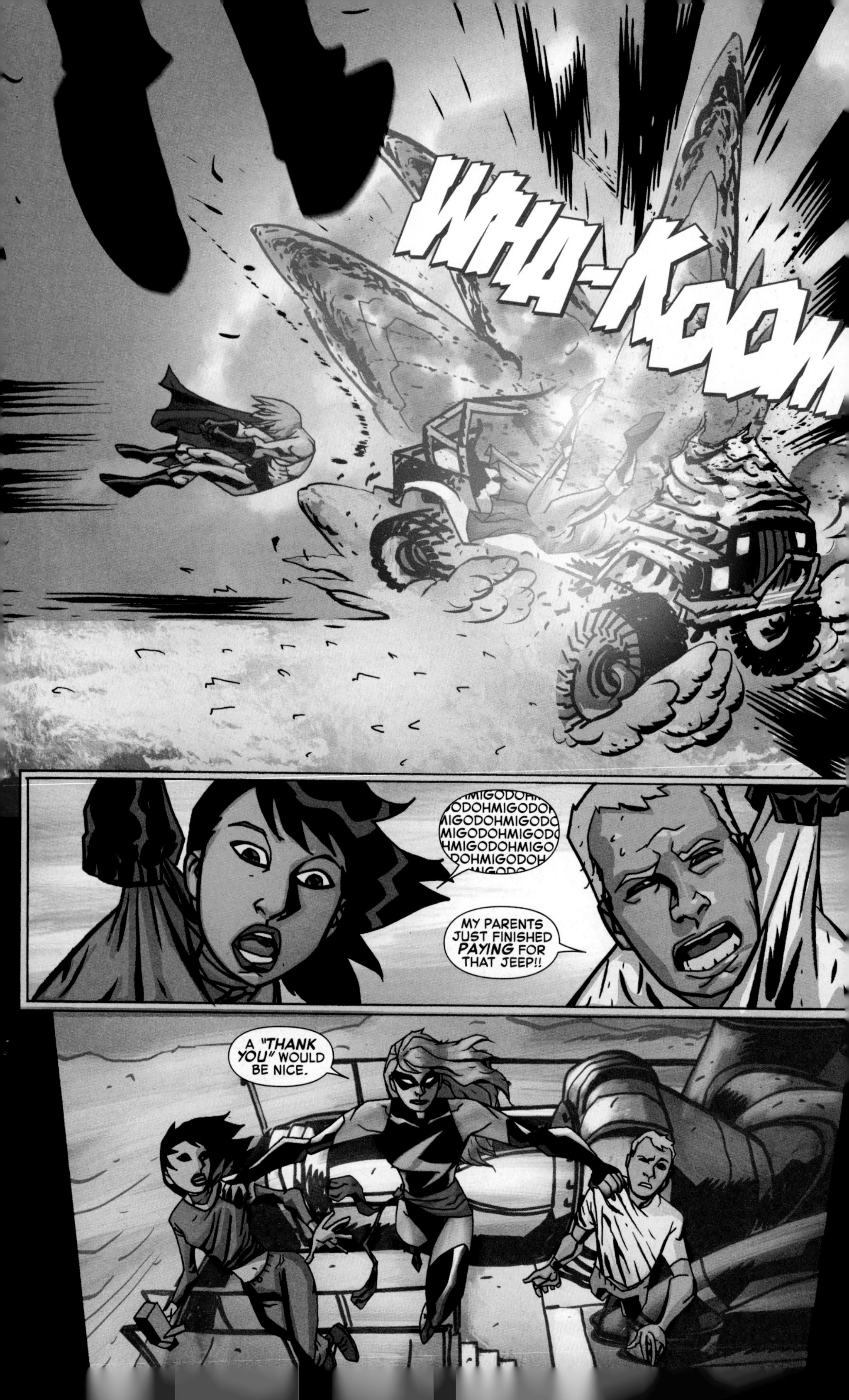
WHA-KOOM
MIGODOH
ODOHMIGODO
IGODOHMIGODO
MIGODOHMIGODO
HMIGODOHMIGO
OHMIGODOH
MY PARENTS JUST FINISHED *PAYING* FOR THAT JEEP!!
A "*THANK YOU*" WOULD BE NICE.

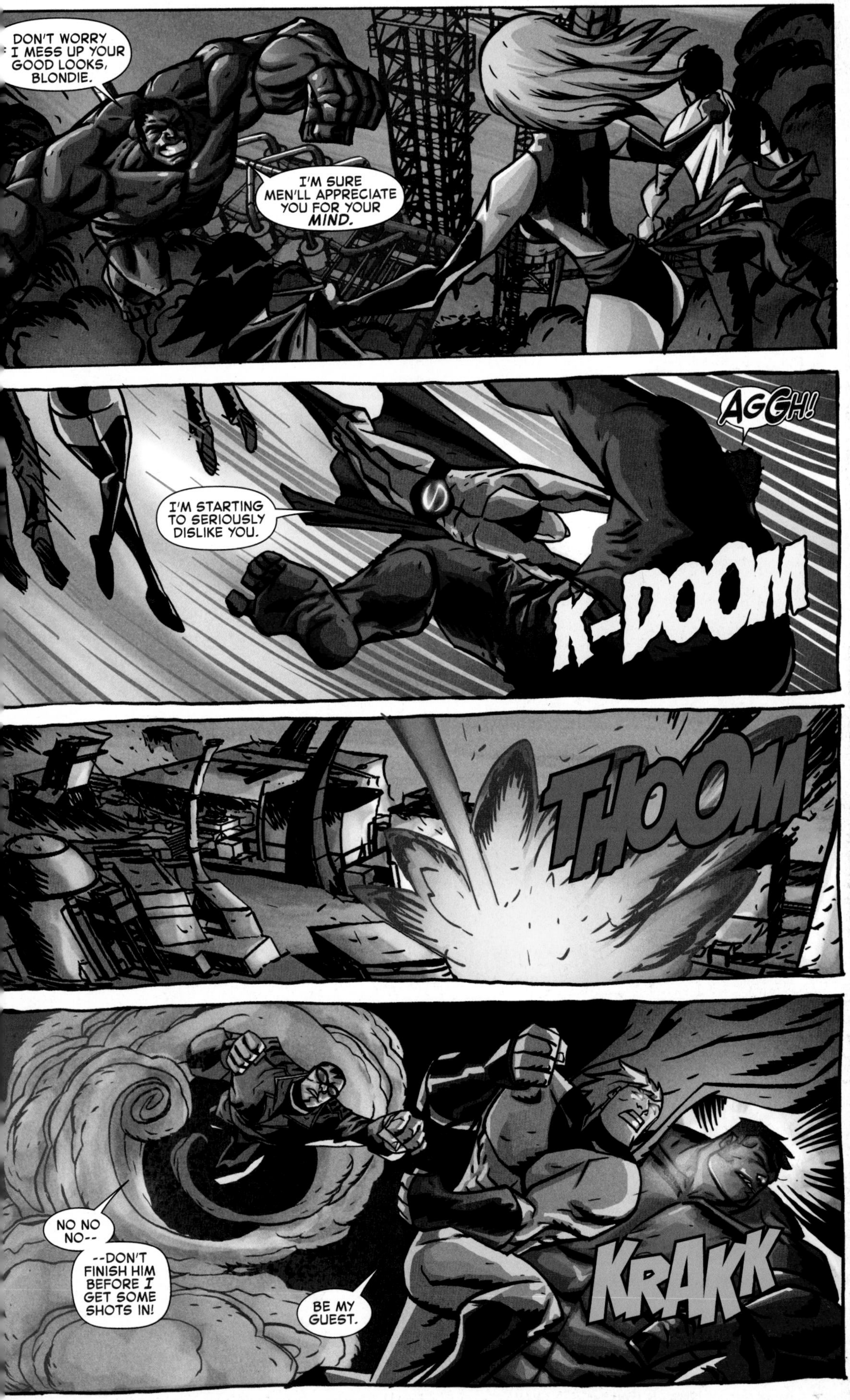
DON'T WORRY I MESS UP YOUR GOOD LOOKS, BLONDIE.
I'M SURE MEN'LL APPRECIATE YOU FOR YOUR MIND.
AGGH!
I'M STARTING TO SERIOUSLY DISLIKE YOU.
K-DOOM
THOOM
NO NO NO--
--DON'T FINISH HIM BEFORE I GET SOME SHOTS IN!
BE MY GUEST.
KRAKK

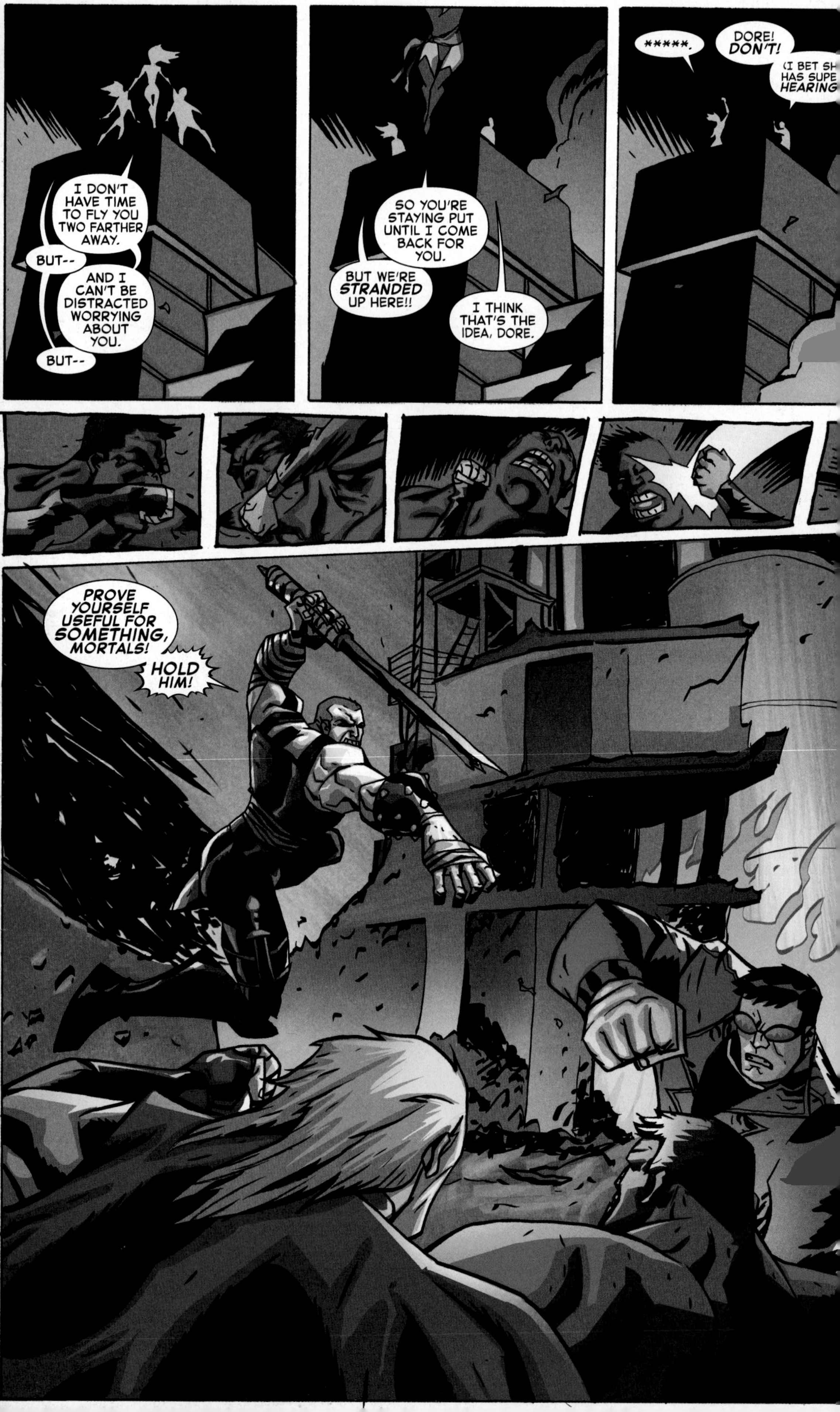
I DON'T HAVE TIME TO FLY YOU TWO FARTHER AWAY.
BUT--
AND I CAN'T BE DISTRACTED WORRYING ABOUT YOU.
BUT--
SO YOU'RE STAYING PUT UNTIL I COME BACK FOR YOU.
BUT WE'RE *STRANDED* UP HERE!!
I THINK THAT'S THE IDEA, DORE.
*****.
DORE! *DON'T!*
(I BET SH HAS SUPE *HEARING*
PROVE YOURSELF USEFUL FOR SOMETHING, MORTALS!
HOLD HIM!

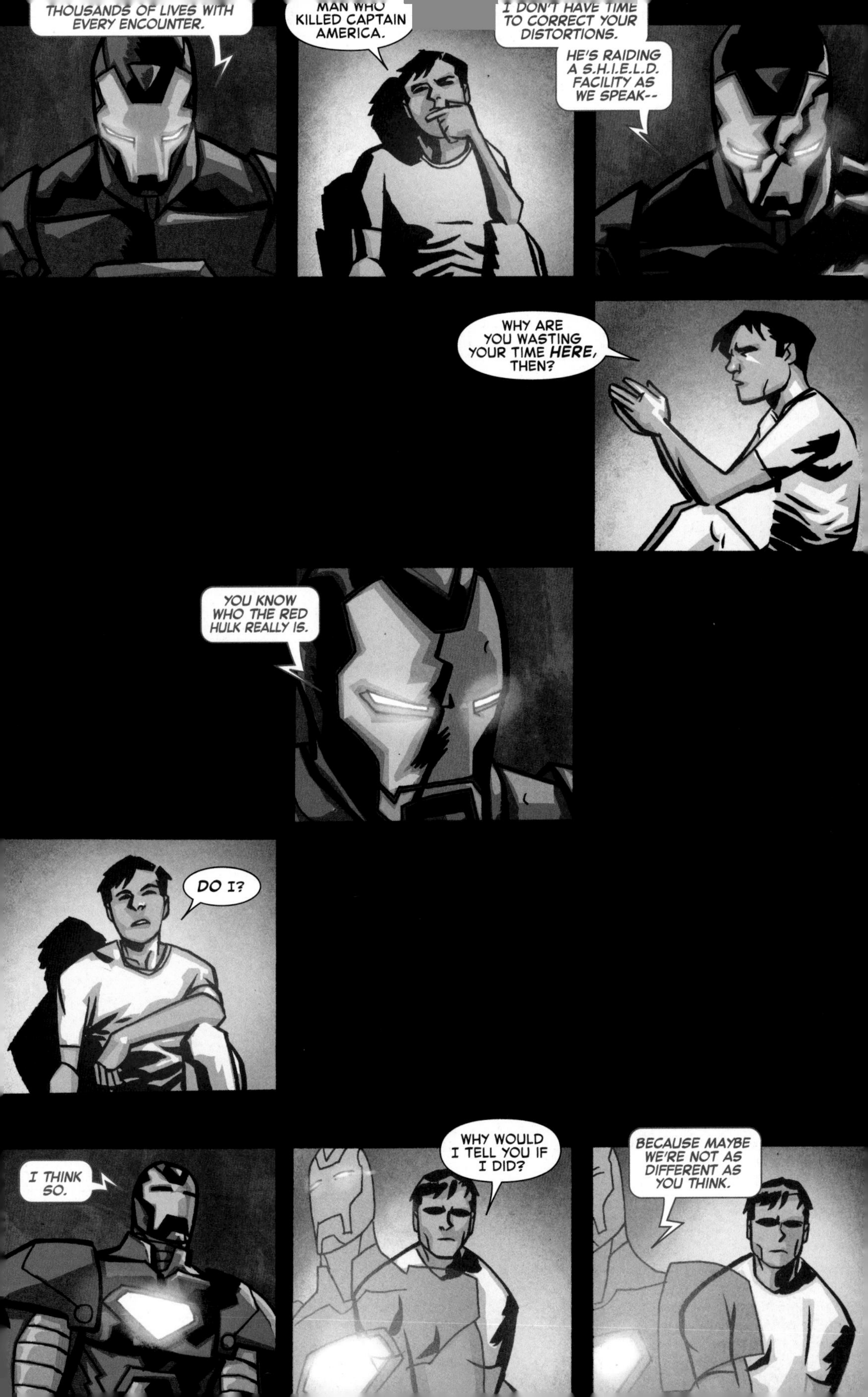
THOUSANDS OF LIVES WITH EVERY ENCOUNTER.
MAN WHO KILLED CAPTAIN AMERICA.
I DON'T HAVE TIME TO CORRECT YOUR DISTORTIONS.
HE'S RAIDING A S.H.I.E.L.D. FACILITY AS WE SPEAK--
WHY ARE YOU WASTING YOUR TIME HERE, THEN?
YOU KNOW WHO THE RED HULK REALLY IS.
DO I?
I THINK SO.
WHY WOULD I TELL YOU IF I DID?
BECAUSE MAYBE WE'RE NOT AS DIFFERENT AS YOU THINK.

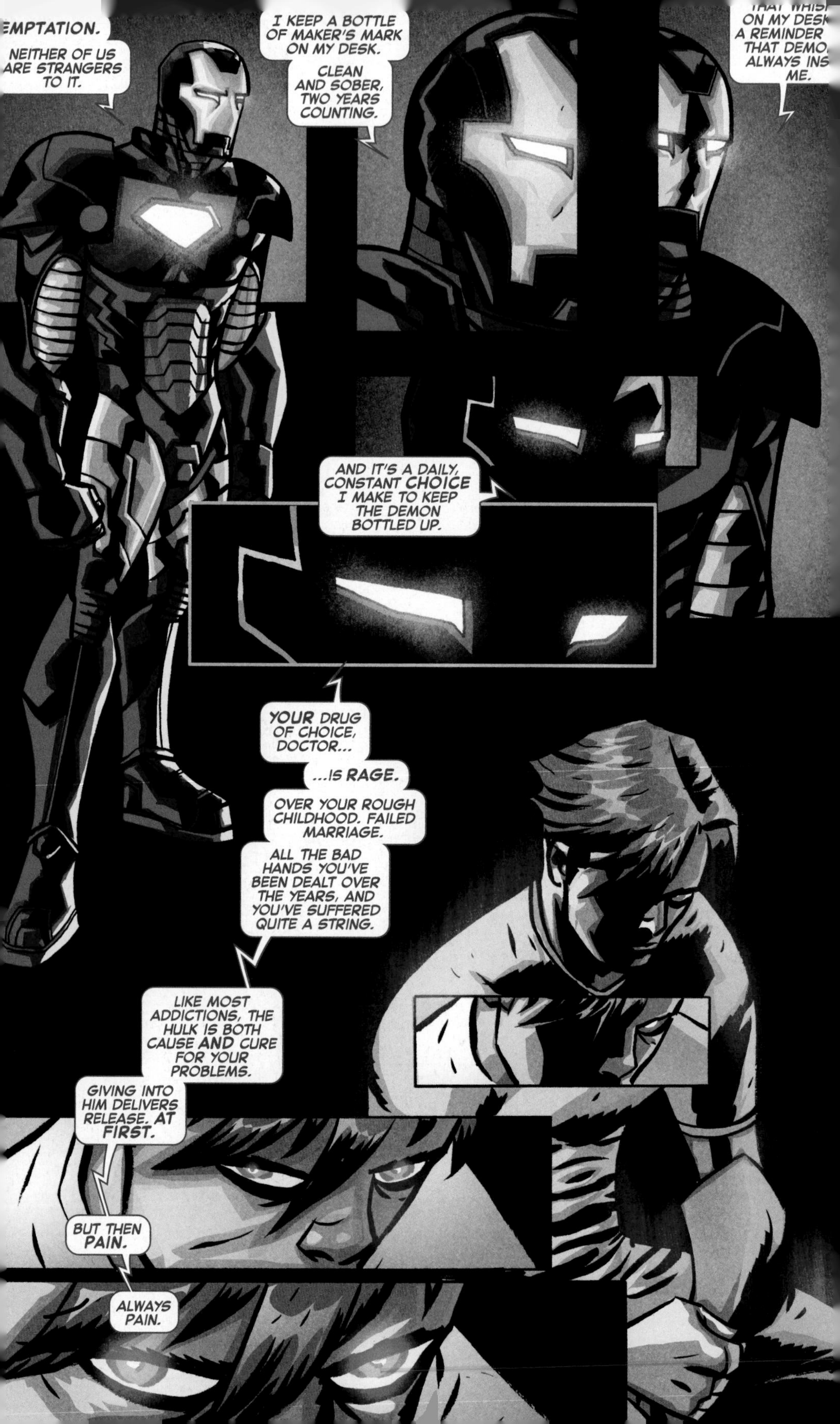
EMPTATION.
NEITHER OF US ARE STRANGERS TO IT.
I KEEP A BOTTLE OF MAKER'S MARK ON MY DESK.
CLEAN AND SOBER, TWO YEARS COUNTING.
THAT WHIS ON MY DESK A REMINDER THAT DEMO ALWAYS INS ME.
AND IT'S A DAILY, CONSTANT CHOICE I MAKE TO KEEP THE DEMON BOTTLED UP.
YOUR DRUG OF CHOICE, DOCTOR...
...IS RAGE.
OVER YOUR ROUGH CHILDHOOD. FAILED MARRIAGE.
ALL THE BAD HANDS YOU'VE BEEN DEALT OVER THE YEARS, AND YOU'VE SUFFERED QUITE A STRING.
LIKE MOST ADDICTIONS, THE HULK IS BOTH CAUSE AND CURE FOR YOUR PROBLEMS.
GIVING INTO HIM DELIVERS RELEASE. AT FIRST.
BUT THEN PAIN.
ALWAYS PAIN.

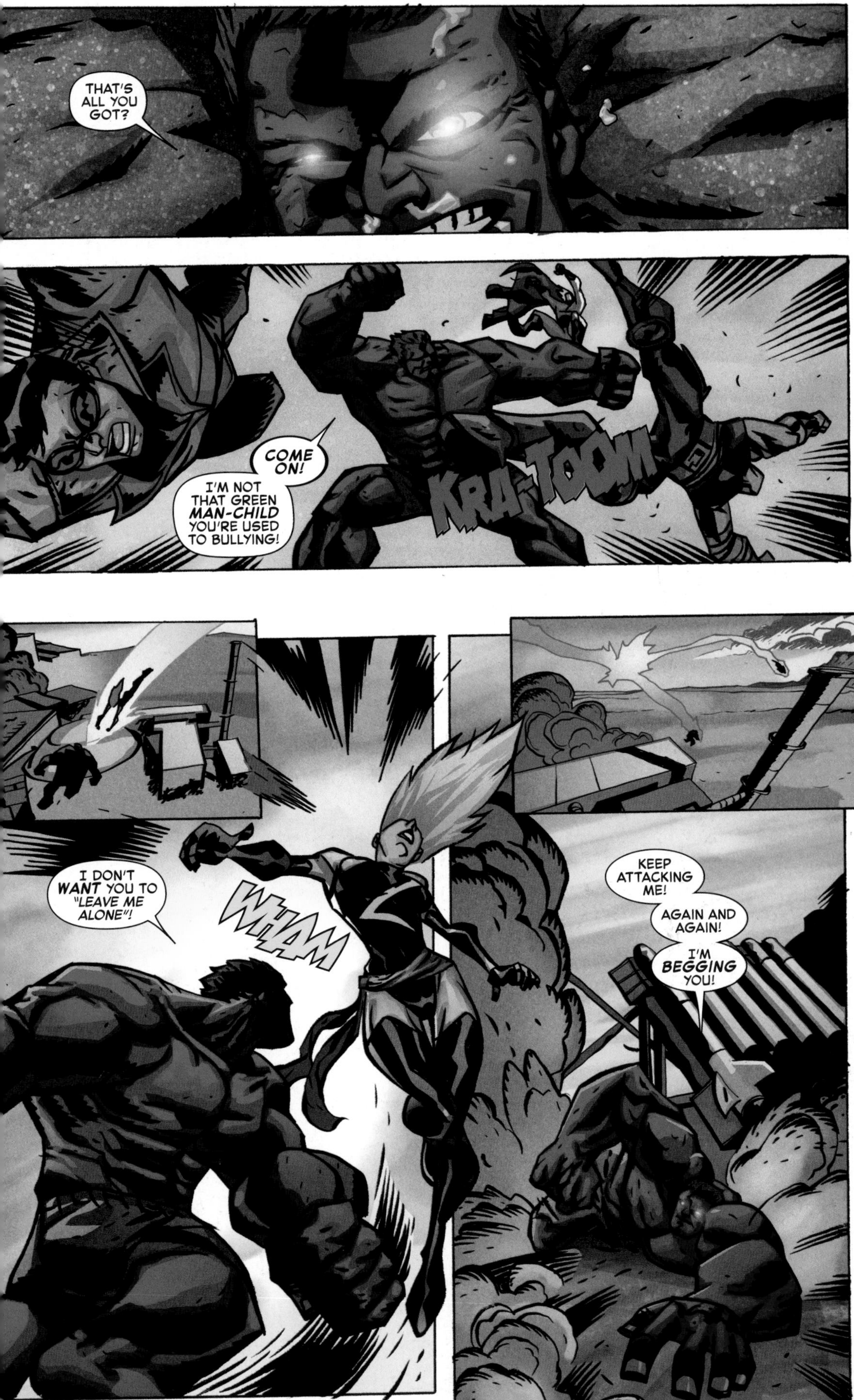

THAT'S ALL YOU GOT?
COME ON!
I'M NOT THAT GREEN MAN-CHILD YOU'RE USED TO BULLYING!
KRA-TOOM
I DON'T WANT YOU TO "LEAVE ME ALONE"!
WHAM
KEEP ATTACKING ME!
AGAIN AND AGAIN!
I'M BEGGING YOU!

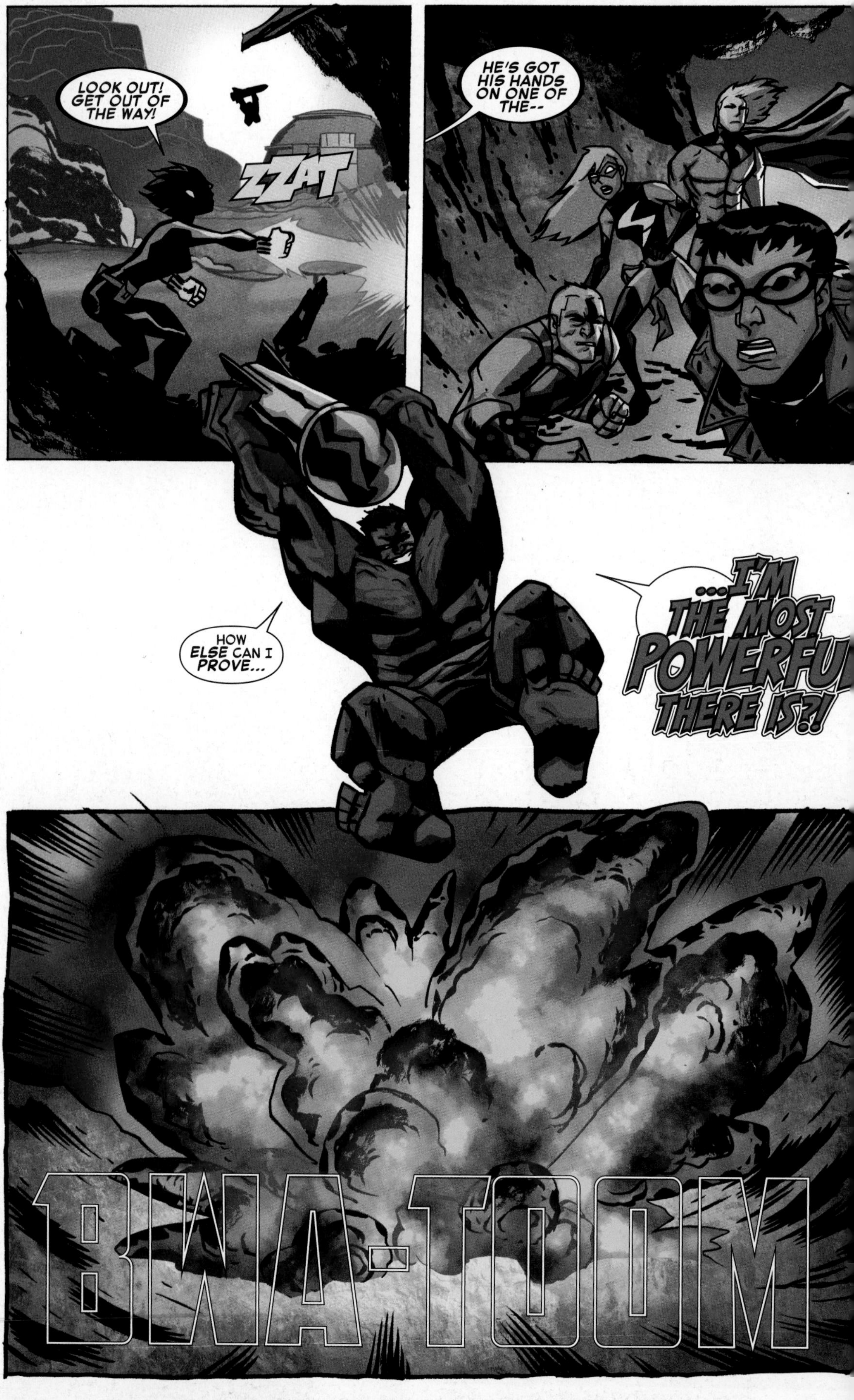
LOOK OUT! GET OUT OF THE WAY!
ZZAT
HE'S GOT HIS HANDS ON ONE OF THE--
HOW ELSE CAN I PROVE...
...I'M THE MOST POWERFUL THERE IS?!
BWA-TOOM

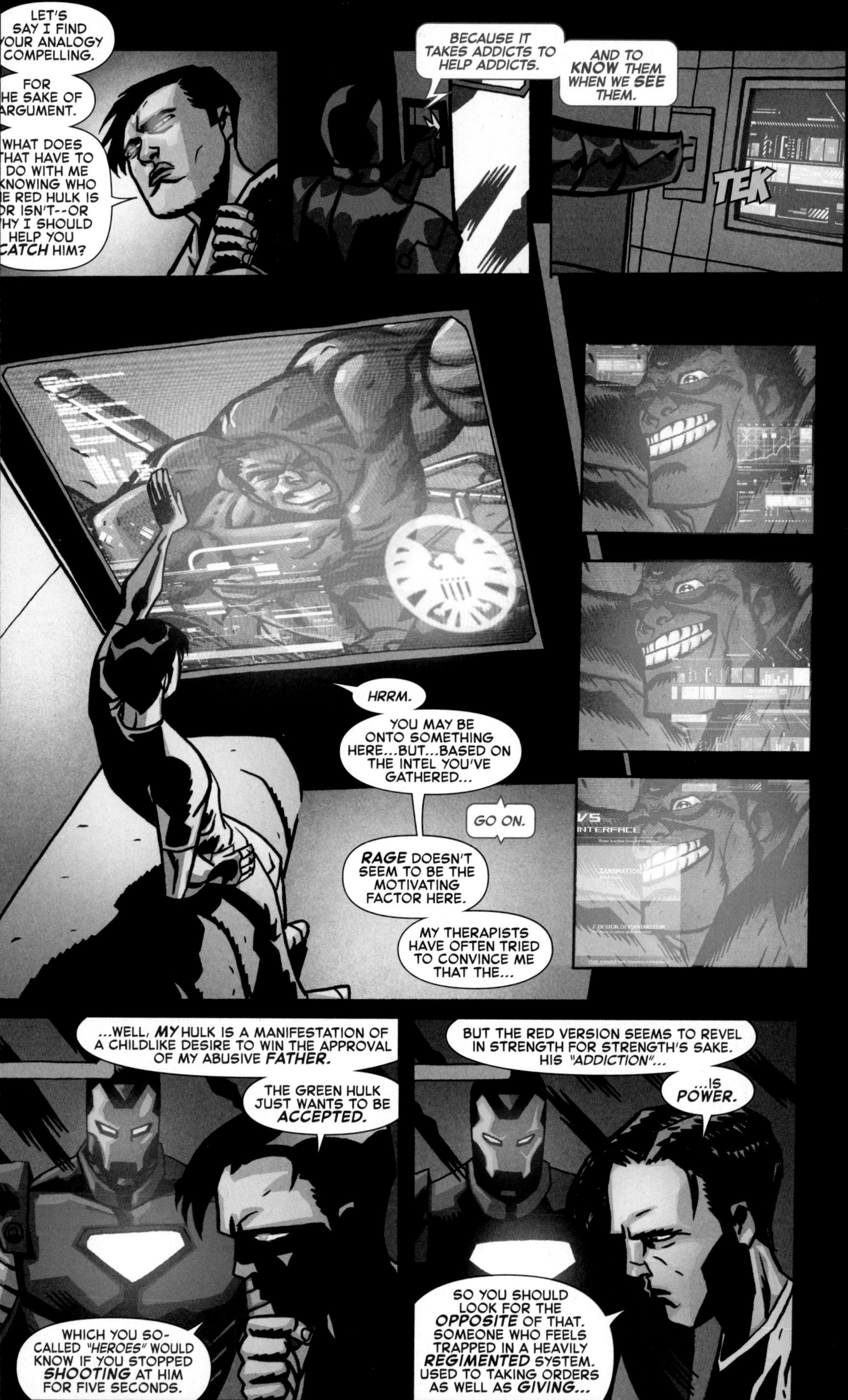
LET'S SAY I FIND YOUR ANALOGY COMPELLING.
FOR THE SAKE OF ARGUMENT.
WHAT DOES THAT HAVE TO DO WITH ME KNOWING WHO THE RED HULK IS OR ISN'T--OR WHY I SHOULD HELP YOU CATCH HIM?
BECAUSE IT TAKES ADDICTS TO HELP ADDICTS.
AND TO KNOW THEM WHEN WE SEE THEM.
TEK
HRRM.
YOU MAY BE ONTO SOMETHING HERE...BUT...BASED ON THE INTEL YOU'VE GATHERED...
GO ON.
RAGE DOESN'T SEEM TO BE THE MOTIVATING FACTOR HERE.
MY THERAPISTS HAVE OFTEN TRIED TO CONVINCE ME THAT THE...
...WELL, MY HULK IS A MANIFESTATION OF A CHILDLIKE DESIRE TO WIN THE APPROVAL OF MY ABUSIVE FATHER.
THE GREEN HULK JUST WANTS TO BE ACCEPTED.
WHICH YOU SO-CALLED "HEROES" WOULD KNOW IF YOU STOPPED SHOOTING AT HIM FOR FIVE SECONDS.
BUT THE RED VERSION SEEMS TO REVEL IN STRENGTH FOR STRENGTH'S SAKE. HIS "ADDICTION"...
...IS POWER.
SO YOU SHOULD LOOK FOR THE OPPOSITE OF THAT. SOMEONE WHO FEELS TRAPPED IN A HEAVILY REGIMENTED SYSTEM. USED TO TAKING ORDERS AS WELL AS GIVING...

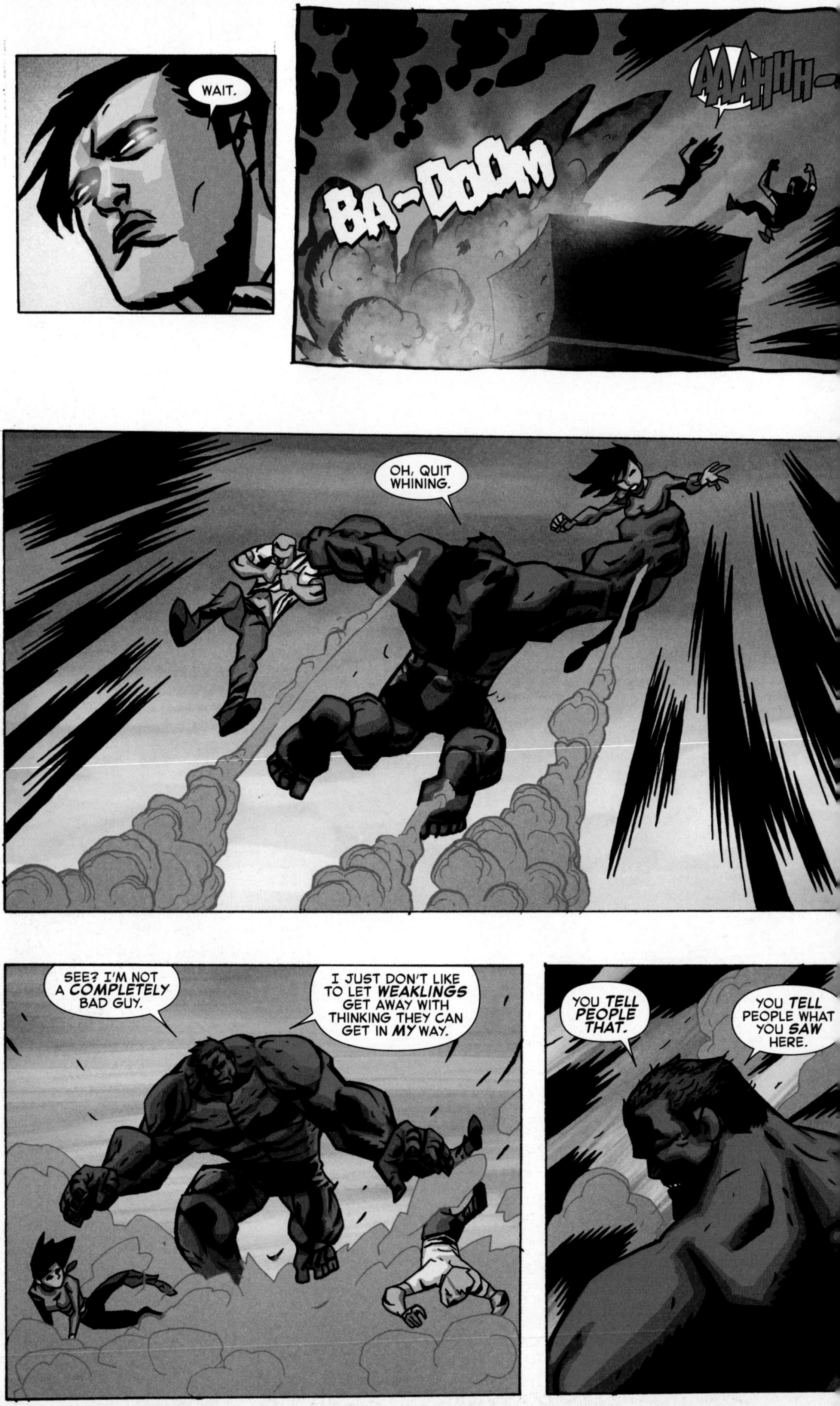
WAIT.
AAAHHH-
BA-DOOM
OH, QUIT WHINING.
SEE? I'M NOT A COMPLETELY BAD GUY.
I JUST DON'T LIKE TO LET WEAKLINGS GET AWAY WITH THINKING THEY CAN GET IN MY WAY.
YOU TELL PEOPLE THAT.
YOU TELL PEOPLE WHAT YOU SAW HERE.

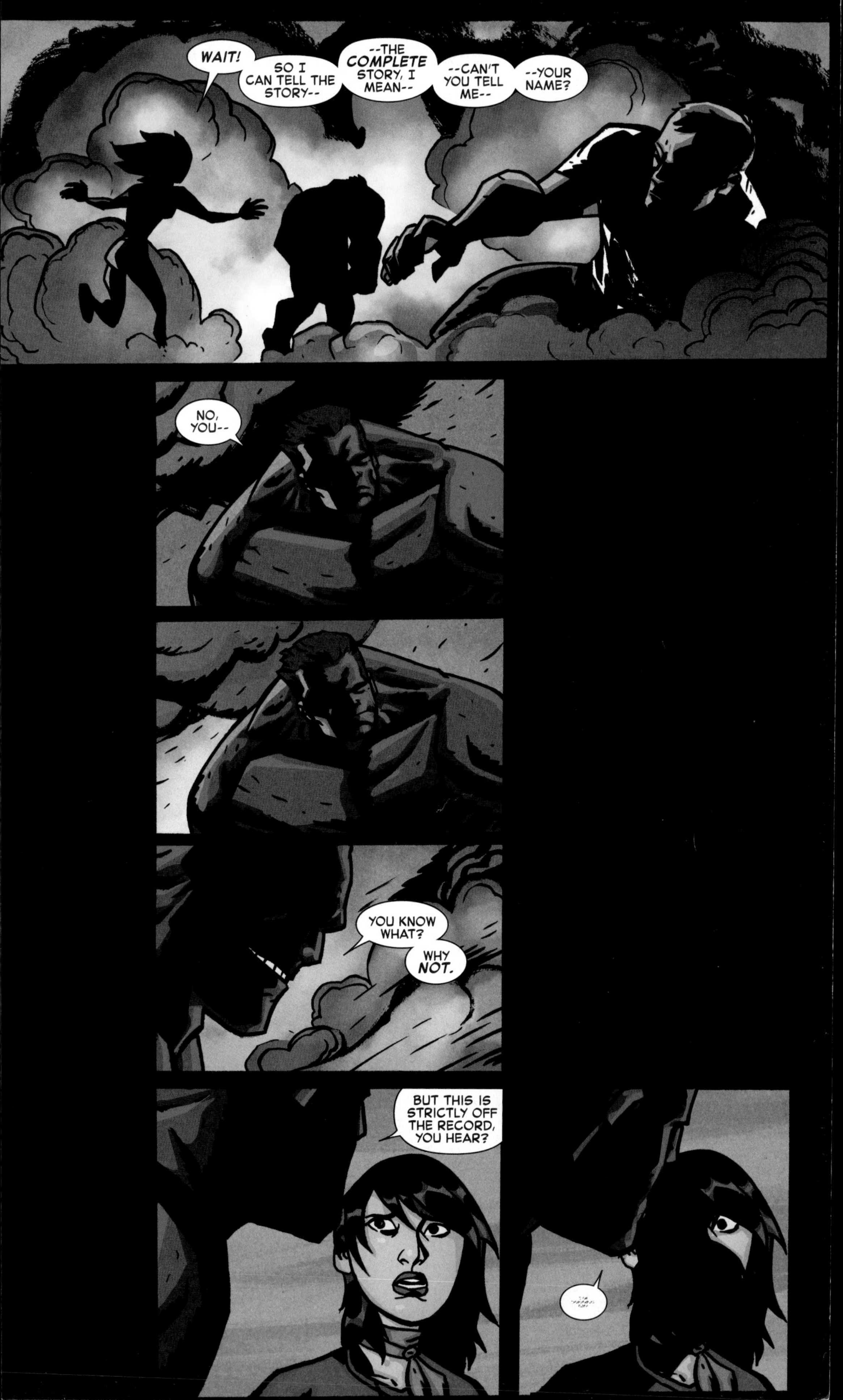
WAIT!
SO I CAN TELL THE STORY--
--THE COMPLETE STORY, I MEAN--
--CAN'T YOU TELL ME--
--YOUR NAME?
NO, YOU--
YOU KNOW WHAT?
WHY NOT.
BUT THIS IS STRICTLY OFF THE RECORD, YOU HEAR?

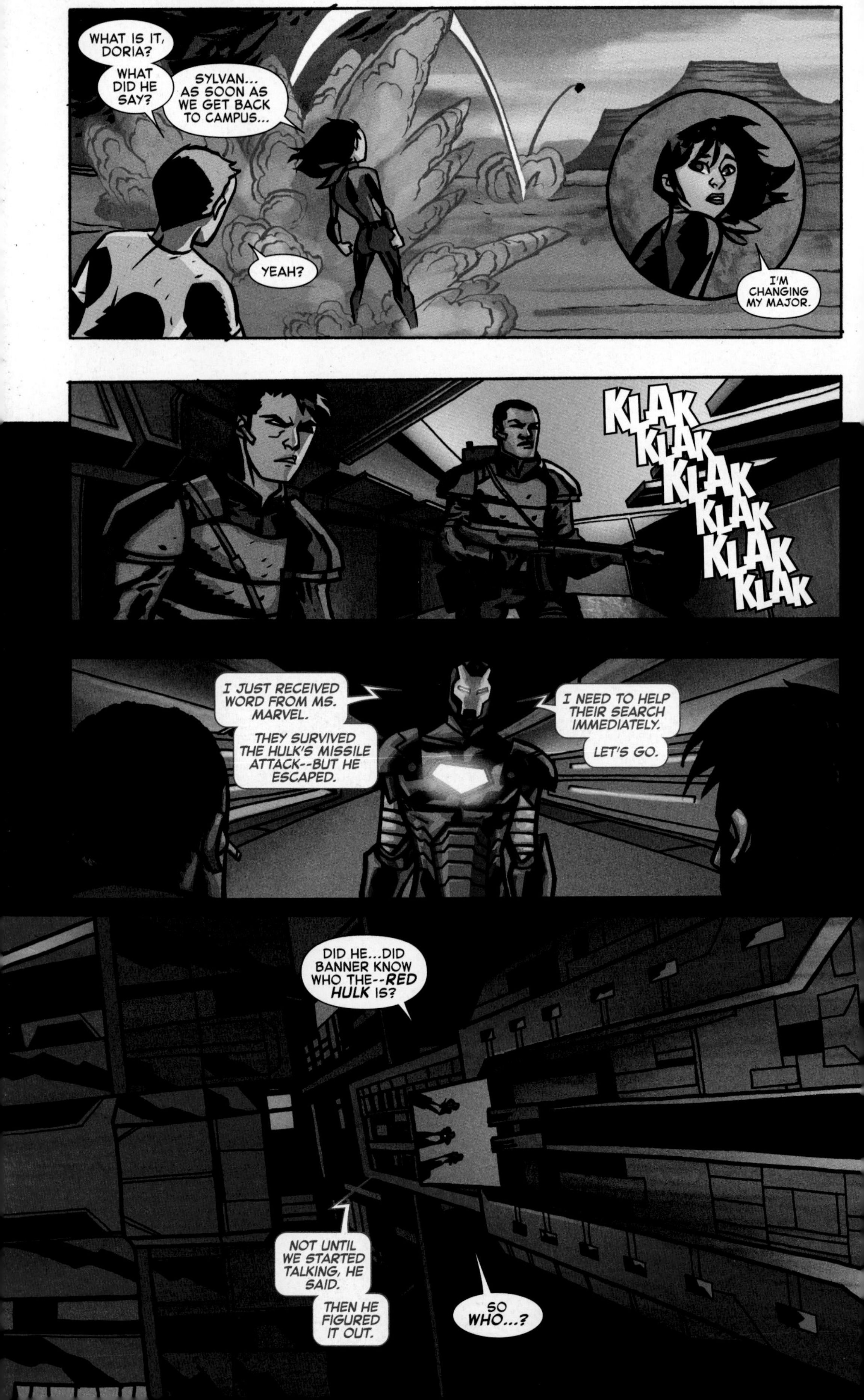
WHAT IS IT, DORIA?
WHAT DID HE SAY?
SYLVAN... AS SOON AS WE GET BACK TO CAMPUS...
YEAH?
I'M CHANGING MY MAJOR.
KLAK KLAK KLAK KLAK KLAK KLAK
I JUST RECEIVED WORD FROM MS. MARVEL.
THEY SURVIVED THE HULK'S MISSILE ATTACK--BUT HE ESCAPED.
I NEED TO HELP THEIR SEARCH IMMEDIATELY.
LET'S GO.
DID HE...DID BANNER KNOW WHO THE--RED HULK IS?
NOT UNTIL WE STARTED TALKING, HE SAID.
THEN HE FIGURED IT OUT.
SO WHO...?

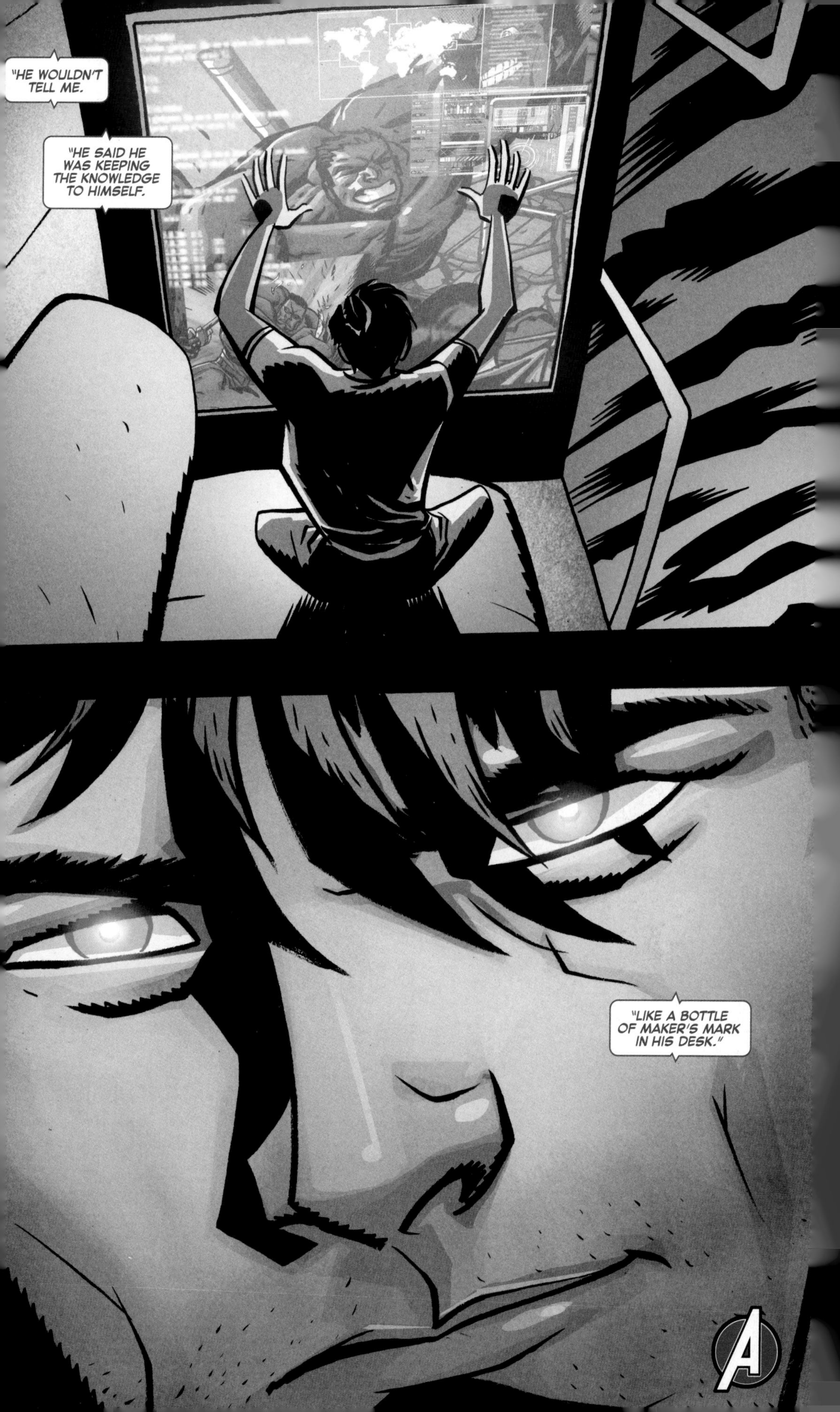
"HE WOULDN'T TELL ME.
"HE SAID HE WAS KEEPING THE KNOWLEDGE TO HIMSELF.
"LIKE A BOTTLE OF MAKER'S MARK IN HIS DESK."

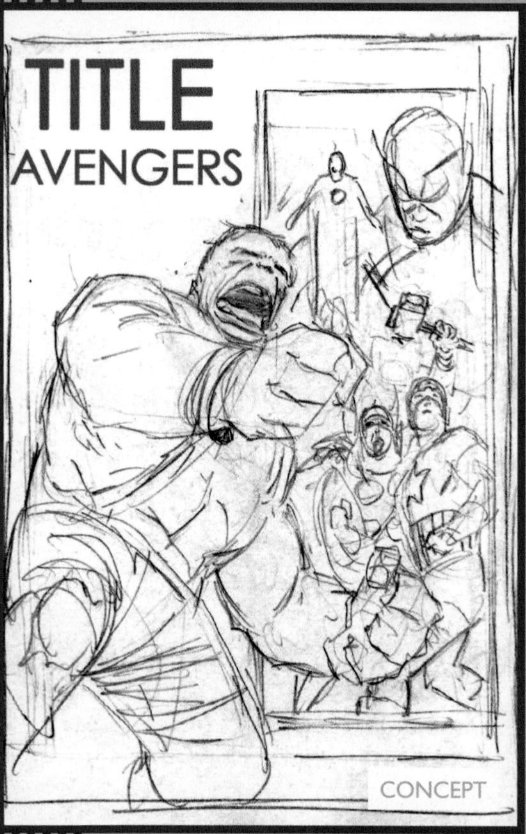
TITLE
AVENGERS
CONCEPT

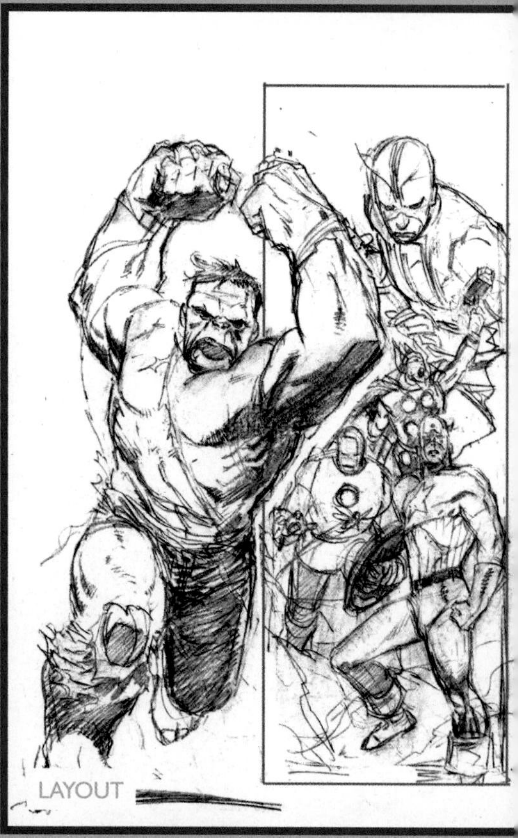
LAYOUT

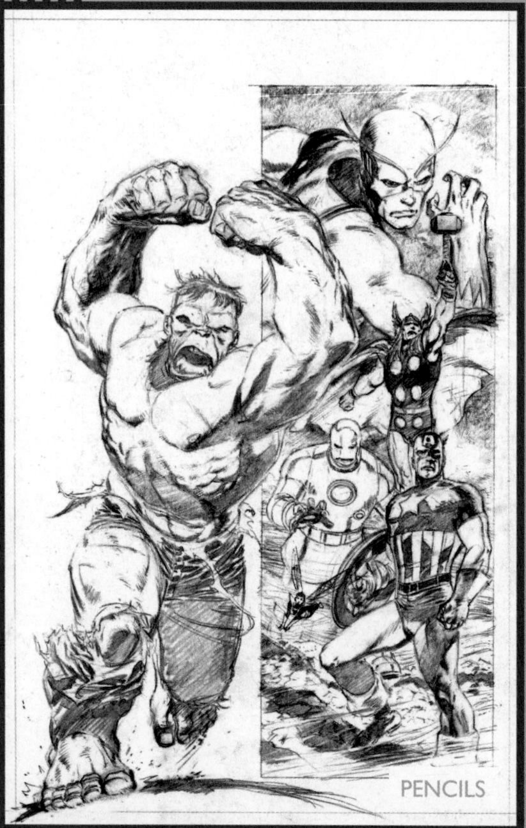
PENCILS

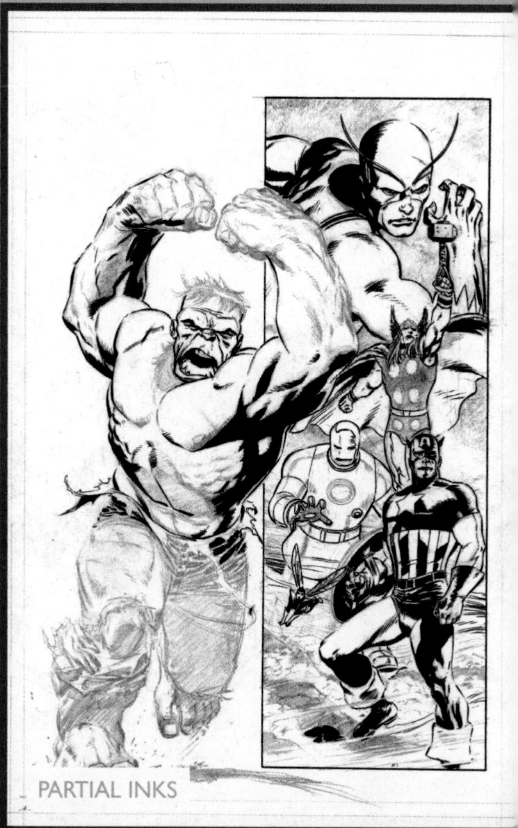
PARTIAL INKS

ISSUE #1 COVER PROCESS BY LEE WEEKS

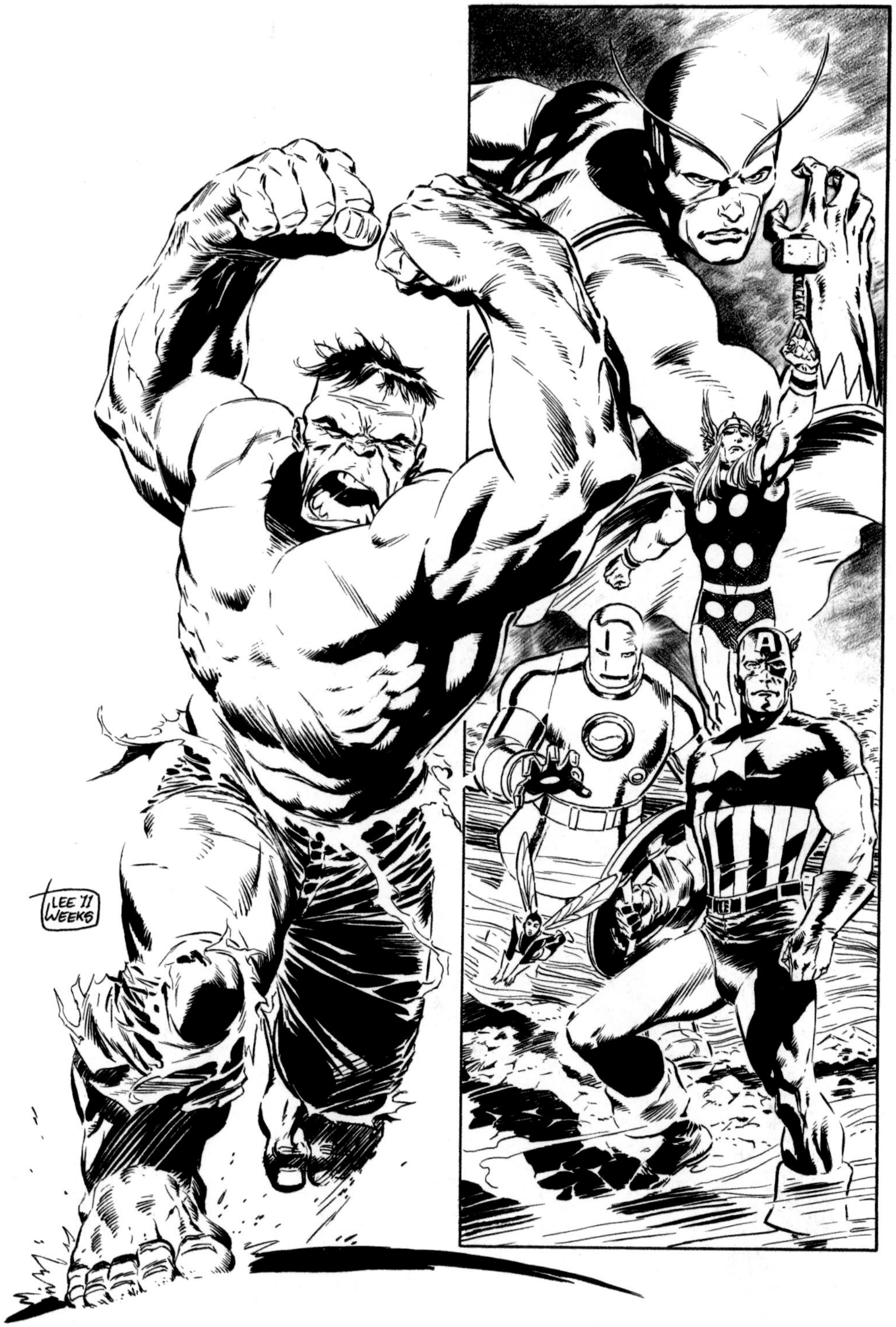
LEE '11
WEEKS

FINAL INKS

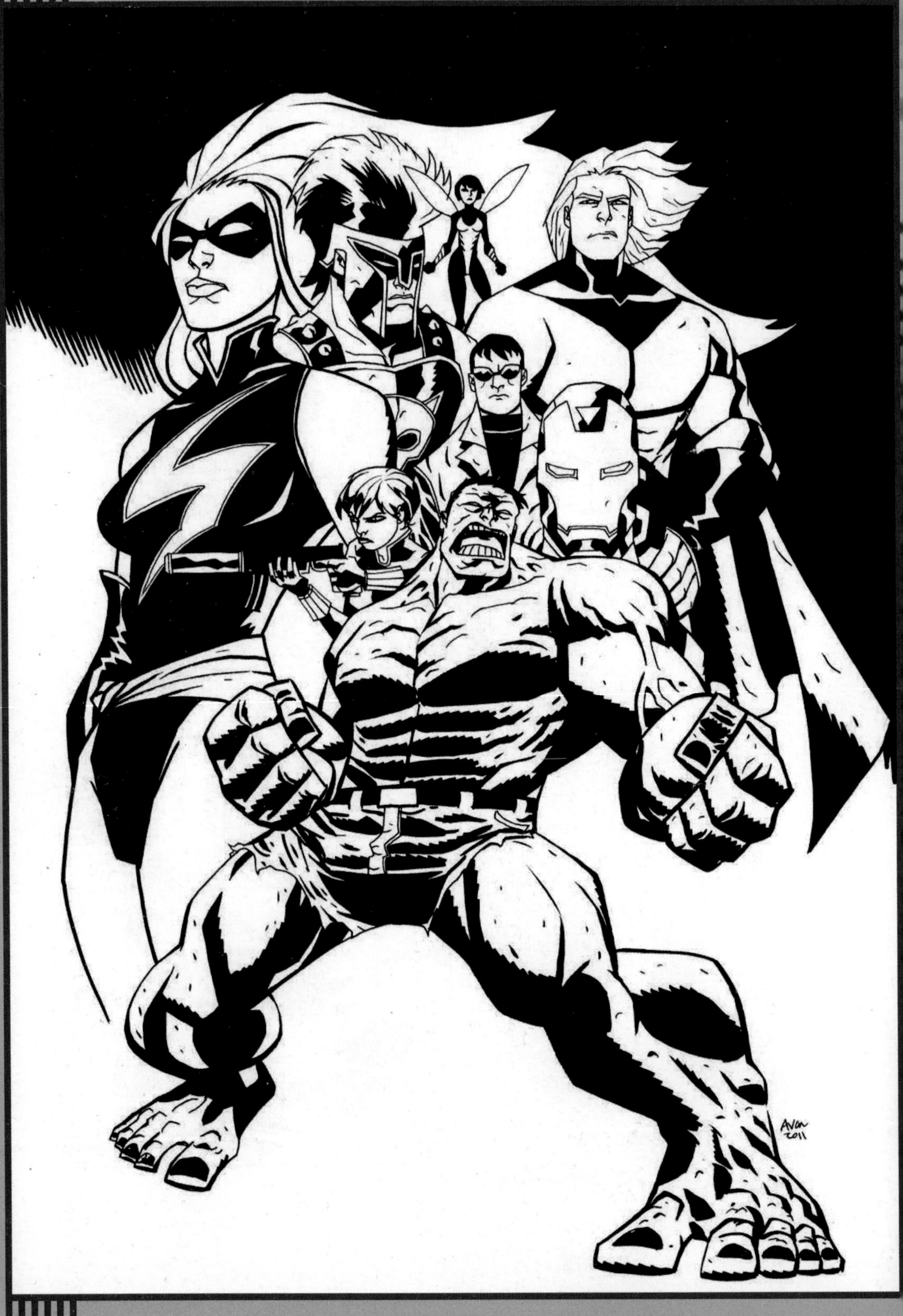
AVON
2011

CHARACTER STUDY BY MICHAEL AVON OEMING